Dollar Adjustment: How Far? Against What?

INSTITUTE FOR INTERNATIONAL ECONOMICS

Dollar Adjustment: How Far? Against What?

C. Fred Bergsten and John Williamson, editors

Washington, DC
November 2004

C. Fred Bergsten has been director of the Institute for International Economics since its creation in 1981. He was also chairman of the Competitiveness Policy Council, which was created by Congress, throughout its existence from 1991 to 1995 and chairman of the APEC Eminent Persons Group throughout its existence from 1993 to 1995. He was assistant secretary for international affairs of the US Treasury (1977–81), assistant for international economic affairs to the National Security Council (1969–71), and a senior fellow at the Brookings Institution (1972–76), the Carnegie Endowment for International Peace (1981), and the Council on Foreign Relations (1967–68). He is the author, coauthor, or editor of numerous books on a wide range of international economic issues, including *No More Bashing: Building a New Japan-United States Economic Relationship* (2001), *Whither APEC? The Progress to Date and Agenda for the Future* (1997), *Global Economic Leadership and the Group of Seven* (1996), *The Dilemmas of the Dollar* (second edition, 1996), *Reconcilable Differences? United States-Japan Economic Conflict* (1993), and *Pacific Dynamism and the International Economic System* (1993).

John Williamson, senior fellow at the Institute for International Economics since 1981, was project director for the UN High-Level Panel on Financing for Development (the Zedillo Report) in 2001; on leave as chief economist for South Asia at the World Bank during 1996–99; economics professor at Pontificia Universidade Católica do Rio de Janeiro (1978–81), University of Warwick (1970–77), Massachusetts Institute of Technology (1967, 1980), University of York (1963–68), and Princeton University (1962–63); adviser to the International Monetary Fund (1972–74); and economic consultant to the UK Treasury (1968–70). He is author, coauthor, editor, or coeditor of numerous studies on international monetary and developing-world debt issues, including *Dollar Overvaluation and the World Economy* (2003), *Delivering on Debt Relief: From IMF Gold to a New Aid Architecture* (2002), and *Exchange Rate Regimes for Emerging Markets: Reviving the Intermediate Option* (2000).

INSTITUTE FOR INTERNATIONAL ECONOMICS
1750 Massachusetts Avenue, NW
Washington, DC 20036-1903
(202) 328-9000 FAX: (202) 659-3225
www.iie.com

C. Fred Bergsten, *Director*
Valerie Norville, *Director of Publications and Web Development*
Edward Tureen, *Director of Marketing*

Typesetting by Circle Graphics
Printing by Kirby Lithographic Company, Inc.

Printed in the United States of America

06 05 04   5 4 3 2 1

Library of Congress Cataloging-in-Publication Data

Dollar adjustment : how far? against what? / C. Fred Bergsten, John Williamson, editors.
    p. cm. — (Special report ; 17)
    Based on a conference held in Washington, D.C. on May 25, 2004.
    Includes bibliographical references and index.
    ISBN 0-88132-378-0
    1. Dollar, American—Congresses.
2. Foreign exchange—Congresses. 3. United States—Foreign economic relations—Congresses. I. Bergsten, C. Fred, 1941- II. Williamson, John, 1937- III. Institute for International Economics (U.S.) IV. Special reports (Institute for International Economics (U.S.); 17.

HG540.D646 2004
332.4'56'0973—dc22   2004054941

Contents

Preface

The Institute has published a number of studies that have voiced concern about the harm that the "strong dollar" has done to the US economy. These concerns have been based on the research that we have done, and published extensively, on the concept and measurement of the fundamental equilibrium exchange rate (FEER) and the consequences of allowing exchange rates to deviate far from their FEERs. This prior work is highly relevant to the current volume, which reports on a conference held in May 2004 to update the Institute's earlier analysis of the magnitude and consequences of the dollar overvaluation that, with official blessing, peaked in the early years of the current century.

The papers presented to that earlier conference in September 2002 were published in early 2003 as *Dollar Overvaluation and the World Economy*, edited—like the present volume—by John Williamson and myself. As in that preceding volume, leading researchers from around the world were asked to write papers to present estimates of the extent to which the dollar is overvalued (after the decline that already occurred in 2002 and 2003). There is much discussion of the specific currencies that need to appreciate as the counterparts to any new dollar depreciation, with a particular focus on the Chinese renminbi, the Japanese yen, and others in East Asia. Papers in the volume also examine the impact that a major dollar depreciation could be expected to have on each of the principal regions of the world economy. In addition, the conference included two papers presenting new research on whether intervention in the foreign exchange markets could be used to influence currency values. All this is summarized in the editors' overview chapter.

The Institute for International Economics is a private, nonprofit institution for the study and discussion of international economic policy. Its purpose is to analyze important issues in that area and to develop and communicate practical new approaches for dealing with them. The Institute is completely nonpartisan.

The Institute is funded importantly by philanthropic foundations. Major institutional grants are now being received from the William M. Keck, Jr. Foundation and the Starr Foundation. A number of other foundations and private corporations contribute to the highly diversified financial resources of the Institute. About 18 percent of the Institute's resources in our latest fiscal year were provided by contributors outside the United States, including about 8 percent from Japan. Major support for this study came from Jaqui Safra, the Automotive Trade Policy Council, and the National Association of Manufacturers.

The Board of Directors bears overall responsibilities for the Institute and gives general guidance and approval to its research program, including the identification of topics that are likely to become important over the medium run (one to three years), and which should be addressed by the Institute. The director, working closely with the staff and outside Advisory Committee, is responsible for the development of particular projects and makes the final decision to publish an individual study.

The Institute hopes that its studies and other activities will contribute to building a stronger foundation for international economic policy around the world. We invite readers of these publications to let us know how they think we can best accomplish this objective.

C. FRED BERGSTEN
Director
November 2004

OVERVIEW

1

Overview: Designing a Dollar Policy

C. FRED BERGSTEN and JOHN WILLIAMSON

The primary goal of the Institute's conference on dollar adjustment, held in Washington on May 25, 2004, was to assess the progress that has been made in correcting the sizable misalignments of key national currencies that had developed in the late 1990s and early 2000s. It also sought to aid understanding of the needed adjustment process and contribute to its promotion. To further these objectives, the conference drew on a number of recent analyses from around the world.

Developments since 2002

This conference was a sequel to an earlier conference held at the Institute on September 24, 2002, which had tried to estimate the magnitude and explore the implications of the dollar overvaluation that had developed in the preceding years (see Bergsten and Williamson 2003).

At that time, the dollar had declined by a trade-weighted average of about 5 percent from its peak in early 2002, after rising by an average of 35 to 50 percent from its lows in 1995 (table 1.1). One result of that prolonged dollar appreciation (together with faster growth in the United State than in its main trading partners) was a sharp rise of the US current account deficit to about $550 billion, or 5 percent of GDP. Indeed, the deficit hit a record level in April 2004, as was announced just before the update conference. Catherine L. Mann (2004) projects a renewed and progressive

C. Fred Bergsten is the director of the Institute for International Economics. John Williamson is a senior fellow at the Institute for International Economics.

Table 1.1   Movements in the dollar exchange rate, 1995–2004

	Federal Reserve broad (nominal)	Federal Reserve broad[a] (real)	Dollar-euro[b]	Yen-dollar
1995 low	89.0 May 8, 1995	84.7 July 1995	1.35 July 28, 1995	81.1 April 19, 1995
1995–2002 high	130.1 February 27, 2002	113.6 February 2002	0.83 October 26, 2000	147.1 August 11, 1998
2002 low	122.4 July 22, 2002	108.5 July 2002	0.86 January 31, 2002	115.7 July 16, 2002
Value at time of 2002 conference	127.1 September 24, 2002	110.6 September 2002	0.98 September 24, 2002	123.4 September 24, 2004
2004 low	111.6 January 9, 2004	98.5 January 2004	1.29 January 9, 2004	103.7 April 1, 2004
Value at time of 2004 conference	116.8 May 25, 2004	102.9 May 2004	1.21 May 25, 2004	112.2 May 25, 2004
Appreciation (1995 low to 1995–2002 high, percent)	46.1	34.2	62.7	81.5
Depreciation (1995–2002 high to 2004 low, percent)	14.2	13.4	35.6	29.5
Appreciation (2004 low to 2004 conference, percent)	4.7	5.5	6.1	8.2

a. Data were available only on a monthly basis.
b. This is the 1995–99 synthetic euro exchange rate, based on the weighted average of initial euro area member states.

Sources: IMF, *International Financial Statistics;* Federal Reserve Board; Pacific Exchange Rate Service.

increase in the deficit in the absence of further major changes in relative growth rates and/or exchange rates.

The earlier conference addressed four central issues. First, there was unanimous agreement among the participants that further depreciation of the dollar was needed to achieve a sustainable relationship among national currencies and current account positions. The participants also observed that there were two important advantages in achieving this realignment promptly. One was the presence of considerable slack in the US economy, which meant that the dollar could decline without much (if any) adverse impact on US inflation and interest rates. The other was the superiority of US economic performance relative to other industrial countries, which reduced the risk of capital flight from the United States and thus of a disorderly dollar depreciation that could lead to a "hard landing" for the US and world economies.

Second, there was considerable disagreement among the participants on the magnitude of the further decline needed in the dollar. Estimates ranged between 10 and 25 percent, centering on 20 percent. These differences, in turn, mainly reflected varying views on the sustainable level of the US current account deficit, which ranged between 2 and 4 percent of US GDP.

The third issue was the distribution of the further dollar depreciation among counterpart currencies. There was widespread agreement among the participants that the adjustment needed to range considerably beyond Europe and Japan, against whose currencies most of the depreciation until then had occurred. In fact, there was considerable debate over the proper direction of future movements of the yen, with some arguing for renewed depreciation in light of the fragility of the Japanese economy and others strongly criticizing Japan's sizable interventions to limit further appreciation of its currency.

The corollary of these views was that additional countries needed to become important participants in the global adjustment effort. Though there was some mention of Canada and, less convincingly, Mexico as potential candidates, the main focus was on Asia, particularly on China. Many participants argued that China needed to abandon its fixed exchange rate against the dollar in light of its sizable surpluses and rapid accumulation of foreign exchange reserves. Moreover, China's failure to move against the dollar had deterred many of the other Asian countries, which see China as one of their main competitors, from letting their currencies appreciate against it as well. Hence a large part of the world economy and trading system—and a major component of the counterpart external surpluses to the US deficit—had not participated in the adjustment process.

The fourth issue was how to promote the needed further adjustment among the key currencies and current account imbalances. No participant advocated a deliberate slowdown in US economic growth. Everyone supported an acceleration of growth in the surplus countries, though no one argued that this would suffice to restore equilibrium. Some argued that further appreciation of those countries' currencies would spur the reforms they needed to achieve faster expansion.

There was considerable discussion, and much disagreement, on whether sterilized intervention in the currency markets represented an additional policy instrument to influence exchange rates. The only widespread agreement was that countries should avoid intervening in ways that prevent market forces from pushing rates in equilibrating directions. In particular, concern was expressed about the aggressive intervention in the currency markets that a number of these countries, especially Japan and China, had used to block appreciation of their currencies.

The dollar resumed its decline about a month after the 2002 conference. As table 1.1 shows, by early 2004 it had come down by a trade-weighted average of about 15 percent on the Federal Reserve's broad real exchange rate index.[1] During the same period, it fell by 33 percent against the euro and by 23 percent against the yen. The decline had been gradual, orderly, and consistent with a strong recovery of both the US and world economies. Presumably as a result of the dollar's decline, the US current account deficit stopped growing in the middle of 2003 and remained relatively stable for the succeeding months, despite a sharp pickup in US economic growth that would otherwise have been expected to produce a further increase in the imbalances. As was noted above, however, signs of a renewed increase in the deficit emerged just before the May 2004 conference, and at least some projections indicate that a large, progressive increase is likely in future.

From early 2004 on, the dollar's decline stalled out and, to some extent, was reversed. As of May 25, the date of the conference, the dollar had appreciated by about 4.5 to 5 percent on the Fed's broad indices after hitting its most recent low in early January. Hence the net decline of the dollar, from its high point in early 2002, was now only about 10 percent. As at the earlier conference, a key point in the latest discussion was that the dollar's decline had to some extent been reversed during the preceding months.

This change in the markets had begun to raise the question of whether the dollar's decline was over, or might even have started to be reversed on a lasting basis. The US economy was growing strongly, and interest rates were expected to move up during the next couple of years. Conversely, the current account deficit had not begun to decline and may even be increasing again. Moreover, much more policy attention had been paid to the impact of the external deficit on employment since the previous conference, particularly as the "jobless recovery" continued through 2003. In the six weeks

---

1. The table does not include the IMF's real effective exchange rate index, which shows a larger decline, because it is understood that IMF staff have become concerned that the weighting system in this index has become outdated (especially for the dollar). The subject is currently under study.

following the conference, there was a renewed though modest decline in the dollar.

On the policy front, there had been much focus on the intervention question during 2003 and 2004. Secretary of the Treasury John Snow went to Asia in September 2003 to talk explicitly about the issue in Tokyo and Beijing. President George W. Bush reportedly raised it with Premier Wen Jiabao on his visit to the United States in December 2003. The Group of Seven (G-7) issued three communiqués, starting in Dubai in September 2003, that addressed the need for greater flexibility of exchange rates by countries whose rates do not now flex. There has been continuing pressure from Congress, most recently on May 19, 2004, at a hearing of the Senate Banking Committee. What was said at the Institute's earlier conference about reducing the amount of intervention clearly had no effect: China's intervention in 2003 exceeded the total amount of its GDP increase in that year, and Japan's intervention in the first quarter of 2004 was sufficiently large to more than finance the entirety of the US budget deficit or the US current account deficit in that period.

Against this background, the second conference convened in May 2004 to update the discussion of 20 months earlier and to again discuss some of the same questions: Does the dollar need to resume its decline in order to achieve a sustainable current account position for the United States and the world? If so, by how much? Against which currencies? And how should that be achieved—particularly if market pressures head in the other direction? What course of action could lead to a renewed decline of the dollar if that were desired?

How Large a Dollar Decline?

The first step in deciding how much of a dollar decline is needed is to address the question: What does a decline need to achieve? The larger the improvement that is sought in the US current account balance, the larger the dollar's decline will need to be. If one sees no danger in a progressively increasing US current account deficit, which according to the projections of Mann (2004) is likely to exceed 10 percent of GDP by 2010 on present trends, then no decline in the dollar is needed. Conversely, if one thinks it necessary to avoid any current account deficit or to convert the deficit into a surplus, then a very substantial dollar depreciation—or else a drastic recession in the United States not matched in the rest of the world—will be needed. Because no one at the conference declared a wish to see the United States pushed into recession to cure the deficit,[2] the

---

2. Indeed, some people argued that a US recession would in practice lead to severe recessions elsewhere rather than to an improvement in the US current account.

needed dollar depreciation is linked to the size of the desired improvement in the US current account.

The first paper given at the conference, by John Williamson (which appears in this volume as chapter 2), asserts that a reasonable target would be to halve the current account deficit during the next three years or so. No rigorous justification for an objective of exactly this size is offered, but he argues that deficits of the present size result in an explosive growth of the US ratio of foreign debt[3] to GDP, whereas a deficit of half that size would be consistent with stabilization of this ratio at a value of around 40 percent (see chapter 5).

In Ellen Hughes-Cromwick's comment on Williamson's argument (which appears as a comment to part II of this book), she asks how long a deficit of the present size might be sustainable, and what reason there is for thinking that deficits of the present size are unsustainable. Mann (2003) tried to address those questions in a paper for the Institute's earlier conference, and she ended up with a rather agnostic assessment that although the large share of US assets in global portfolio wealth might suggest pressure for depreciation, the continuing outlook for relatively high returns in the United States might make appreciation more likely. Her new work, however, suggests that the prospective growth of the current account deficit at the present exchange rate, or even with a modest future depreciation of the dollar, is so substantial as to make a drastic depreciation at some stage virtually inevitable (Mann 2004).

Hughes-Cromwick also asked just what deficit might be sustainable—a question to which it is not possible to give a satisfactory answer. Everyone agrees that a permanent increase in the debt/GDP ratio is not conceivable. This does not imply that one can place any definite limit on the duration of deficits of the current size, but it does suggest that, the higher the debt/GDP ratio climbs, the more likely is a forced, abrupt ending. For this reason, many analysts conclude that it makes sense to try to secure a relatively early end to the increase in the debt/GDP ratio.

Michael Mussa's paper (chapter 5) also hypothesizes a reduction of the US current account deficit to around 2 percent of GDP during the next few years, on the grounds that a much higher figure would increase the likelihood of crisis. He analyzes the policy adjustments that would need to be made to accommodate such a change without damaging the world economy. These include a further substantial depreciation of the dollar, on the order of 20 percent. A significantly less extreme view on this issue was offered by Jim O'Neill in his comment on this first session of the conference (appearing in this volume at the end of part II), in which he suggests that

---

3. Actually, the relevant magnitude is not strictly speaking "debt" but the US net international investment position (which includes foreign direct investment and other equity-type assets and liabilities).

a further 10 percent depreciation, similar to what had already occurred, might suffice.[4]

The main challenge at the conference to the contention that it is urgent to cut the US deficit was mounted by Peter Garber, one of the authors of a series of recent Deutsche Bank studies that have described present international monetary arrangements as a revived Bretton Woods system (e.g., see Dooley, Folkerts-Landau, and Garber 2003; Garber's conference contribution appears as a comment in part III). These studies argue that China is following the Japanese model of the 1960s in giving priority to absorbing labor in the production of exports, which requires a highly competitive exchange rate. If the cost of doing that is a large accumulation of low-yielding reserves, it is a price that China (like other Asian countries) is willing to pay; the end result is much preferable to the premature exhaustion of growth that occurred in Latin America, where exchange rates were by and large allowed to respond to market forces. An incidental but highly significant result is that the United States has its current account deficit financed in a stable and reliable way by the reserve accumulation of China and other Asian countries. The process is likely to continue for as long as China has excess labor to absorb, which means at least for the next decade, after which India will take over.

The counterargument (posed by John Williamson in chapter 2) does not deny that China gains enormously by the ability to absorb its surplus labor in the production of exports, but asks what China thinks it gains by locking up the resulting earnings in low-yielding dollar reserves when it has large unmet needs for increased consumption. It could cool its overheating economy in a way that would strengthen rather than undermine its capacity for future growth by some expenditure switching toward foreign-produced goods.

Apart from Garber's objection, the notion that the objective should be to cut the US current account deficit by something like half seemed to be generally accepted at the conference. No one disagreed that this implies a need for substantial further dollar depreciation. The paper that deals primarily with how large that depreciation might need to be is that of Simon Wren-Lewis (chapter 3). He uses a model similar in spirit to the one he previously employed in estimating fundamental equilibrium exchange rates (FEERs) for the Institute (Wren-Lewis and Driver 1998) and in informing the UK Treasury for its assessment of entry to the euro. However, this new model directly estimates equilibrium bilateral values for the main currencies rather than the overvaluation of the dollar on an effective basis, so his results are most appropriately presented along with others in the next section.

---

4. Even this is more than his own Goldman Sachs dynamic equilibrium exchange rate (GSDEER) model is indicating; this model, which attaches much significance in driving exchange rates to the strong productivity performance of the United States, actually estimates that the US dollar is currently somewhat undervalued. But his central estimate of the dollar's equilibrium value at the present time does not correspond to the result given by the GSDEER model.

Another paper considered at the first session of the conference—which did yield inter alia estimates of dollar overvaluation—is that by Agnès Bénassy-Quéré and her colleagues (chapter 4). They use a panel cointegration approach to estimate equilibrium exchange rates for almost all the Group of Twenty (G-20) currencies. These are not FEERs but the real rates to which actual real exchange rates had tended to return during the estimation period of 1980–2001. They assume that the relationship between the equilibrium exchange rate and its underlying determinants (net foreign assets and relative prices, measured by the ratio of the consumer price index to the producer price index as a proxy for the relative price of nontradables) is the same for every country. On this assumption, the dollar was overvalued in 2001 by 14 percent, with only the United Kingdom (16 percent) and Mexico (26 percent) higher, although Argentina (13 percent) was also in the same range (see table 4.2). The significantly undervalued currencies were those of Turkey (11 percent), Canada (15 percent), China and India (both 16 percent), Euroland (17 percent), South Korea (28 percent), Indonesia (31 percent), and South Africa (33 percent). Because the dollar depreciated by about 10 percent up to the date of the conference, this analysis also suggests that it has already had most of the needed adjustment.

The usual fear is that a forced end to the debt buildup caused by a refusal of the rest of the world to finance increases in US indebtedness would lead to an abrupt ("disorderly") decline in the value of the dollar. If this decline were large enough, and especially if it occurred at a time when the US economy was close to full employment, it could ignite severe inflationary pressure in the United States. The Federal Reserve might seek to counter this pressure by raising interest rates, and in any event the market would be sure to push longer-term rates up, which together might push the economy into recession. Conceivably, the higher interest rates would spill over to the rest of the world, although the concern of other countries to limit the appreciation of their currencies might prevent such imitation and thus a general world recession.

Another route from an abrupt dollar decline to world recession is conceivable, however, and could operate even if the United States is not subjected to inflationary pressure leading to higher interest rates. A global recession could occur if other countries simply did not react to dollar depreciation by expanding their domestic demand in response to the shift in demand away from them and toward the United States that would be induced by the depreciation. This is perhaps the most likely channel through which a dollar collapse could induce a world recession.

US inflation and world recession are not the only perils posed by the growth of the US deficit resulting from an overvalued dollar. Another danger is an intensification of protectionist pressures in the United States. If increasing imports and stagnant exports continue to cause large and increasing current account deficits, one will have to expect protectionist actions to be magnified and unimpeded by strong counterpressures by exporters perceiving a threat to their continuing success. The burst of protectionist moves against China during 2003 and 2004 is the latest manifestation of this traditional relationship.

In their paper (chapter 6), Martin Baily and Robert Lawrence set out to estimate the contribution of the increase in the trade deficit to the recent loss of jobs in the United States. They use two methods to make this estimate and argue that the true figure will lie between a low estimate of 250,000 jobs lost and a high of 600,000. They thus conclude that only a moderate fraction of the total of about 2 million jobs lost during the period 2001–03 was trade related (and even this arose principally because of export weakness rather than a surge in imports). They also examine the data on offshoring, and they conclude that this was responsible for an even smaller proportion of job losses. These findings suggest that increased protection is not a rational response to large trade deficits, but it is not clear that they also provide assurance that it is an unlikely response.

Which Currencies Should Appreciate Against the Dollar?

Knowing that the dollar needs to depreciate more is only the starting point. It has very different implications for the counterpart countries whether a given dollar depreciation is accomplished by appreciation of the euro or the Asian currencies. The presumption going into the conference was that most of the adjustment vis-à-vis the euro had already taken place, so that the big remaining disequilibrium was in the exchange rates of a number of the Asian currencies. This original hypothesis was confirmed and also quantified in the course of the conference.

Table 3.2 in Wren-Lewis's chapter presents estimates of the dollar exchange rates of the euro, the yen, and the pound that would generate various current account positions. The objective that was hypothesized above was a halving of the US current account deficit, which was 4.6 percent of GDP in 2002. Table 3.4 suggests that this goal would be consistent with the euro being in the range $1.15 to $1.20, the yen between ¥95 and ¥100 to the dollar, and the pound sterling around $1.60. Table 3.7 looks at China and gives an estimate of 6.47 renminbi to the dollar as the exchange rate needed to achieve a balanced current account (versus the current pegged rate of 8.28 renminbi, implying the need for an appreciation of 28 percent). Of course, Wren-Lewis's model would estimate that an even larger appreciation would be needed if the objective were to achieve a current account deficit to balance the capital inflow in China, as Morris Goldstein hypothesizes in his paper (chapter 9).

Bénassy-Quéré and her colleagues also develop estimates of bilateral equilibrium exchange rates. Their estimates depend to some extent on which currency is used as the numeraire, but in the end they use the euro. (For most currencies, this has little effect on the results, though the euro itself was in virtual equilibrium in 2003 using the euro as the numeraire, whereas it was still some 8 percent undervalued if the dollar was used as the numeraire[5]).

Assuming that the equilibrium exchange rate had not changed in real terms since 2001, the estimated misalignments in 2003 ranged downward from a massive 88 percent undervaluation of the Argentine peso, to 44 percent for the Chinese renminbi, 35 percent for the Korean won, 28 percent for the Indian rupee, 27 percent for the South African rand, 23 percent for the Brazilian real, 19 percent for the Japanese yen and the Indonesian rupiah, and 7 percent for the Canadian dollar. The Mexican peso (14 percent), pound sterling (11 percent), Australian dollar (7 percent), and Turkish lira (6 percent) were estimated to be overvalued with respect to the dollar.

Michael Mussa is more hawkish on the size of the needed exchange rate changes than other authors. He suggests that even bilateral rates of $1.35 to $1.45 per euro, $1.90 per pound, $0.85 per Canadian dollar, ¥85 to ¥90 per dollar, and a Chinese appreciation of 15 to 25 percent against the dollar might not be quite sufficient to reach his target of a 30 percent real dollar depreciation from the average of mid-2000 to mid-2002.

The afternoon session was mainly devoted to considering the impact of a major dollar realignment on the principal regions of the world economy. To start with Euroland, the main message of the presentation that Jean Pisani-Ferry made at the conference is that the eurozone believes that its former undervaluation against the dollar has already been eliminated.[6] This is consistent with the results presented by Wren-Lewis and Bénassy-Quéré et al. Pisani-Ferry also made the point that in the past, exchange rate adjustment has tended to be helpful to the United States in its conjunctural policy, with the dollar strengthening when the economy was strong in the late 1990s. Much the same has been true in Japan, where the depreciation of the yen has helped mitigate deflationary pressures in some recent years. But the opposite has been true for Euroland, where the fluctuations of the floating dollar-euro rate have tended to amplify rather than mitigate the cycle. A simulation on the NIGEM model that froze G-3 exchange rates at their 1995 levels confirmed that this would have amplified cyclical fluctuations in the United States and Japan but moderated them in Europe. However, a change in the dollar-euro rate has an asymmetrical impact on the different economies that constitute Euroland, which should in principle be addressed by asymmetrical responses of fiscal policy, which were evident to a limited extent in France but not elsewhere. Hence any further

---

5. They explain this by noting that in their multilateral calculations the amount of euro undervaluation in 2001 is less than the amount of dollar overvaluation. Hence, neglecting euro undervaluation in effective terms (i.e., taking the euro as the numeraire) leads to less euro undervaluation against the dollar than when the dollar's effective overvaluation is neglected.

6. Unfortunately, there is no written version of his presentation included in this volume.

changes in the dollar-euro rate would be likely to create further difficulties within Europe and would further test the institutions of monetary union.

Paul Masson's paper on Canada (chapter 7) was included because the previous conference had suggested that the Canadian dollar was one of the additional currencies that would need to appreciate against the US dollar. Canada is the United States' single largest trading partner, so an appreciation of the Canadian dollar is potentially important in achieving the depreciation of the US dollar. Moreover, though Canada has historically had large current account deficits, in recent years it has moved into a substantial current account surplus (2 to 3 percent of GDP), suggesting that it might also have the balance of payments space to accommodate a sizable appreciation.

Masson points out that the Canadian dollar had already experienced a sharp appreciation of about 22 percent in the course of 2003. This is even larger than the euro's 20 percent appreciation, though still not as large as the moves in the Australian and New Zealand dollars. But after peaking in January 2004, the Canadian dollar had depreciated again by about 9 percent by the time of the conference.[7] Masson presents forecasts that assume the Canadian dollar will stabilize at a rate of 75 US cents per Canadian dollar, intermediate between its peak in January (almost 79 US cents) and its value at the time of the conference (about 72 US cents). On that assumption, his model suggests that Canada is likely to experience relatively subdued growth and inflation in both 2004 and 2005, largely reflecting the lagged effects of the 2003 appreciation. A further 10 percent appreciation[8] would lead to distinctly sluggish growth, which could be offset only to a modest extent by a 1 percent cut in the Canadian interest rate. Masson obviously thinks it is good that this development is (in his view) highly improbable. (He did not see Mussa's suggestion that the Canadian dollar needs to appreciate to 85 US cents.)

Takatoshi Ito contributed a paper about Japan and the yen (chapter 8). Models that ask what would be necessary for Japan to reduce its current account surplus to reasonable levels have tended for years to suggest that the yen needs to appreciate to under ¥100 per dollar, and as noted above this was true of both Wren-Lewis's model (between ¥90 and ¥100) and that of Bénassy-Quéré and her colleagues (which showed a bilateral undervaluation of 19 percent in 2003, when the yen rate averaged ¥116). The big question, which arose at the earlier conference, has for a long time been whether such an appreciation would be appropriate for a country mired in an intractable recession.

---

7. Canada is a relatively easy country to analyze, because its trade is so overwhelmingly dominated by the United States that one does not need to bother unduly with the usual distinctions between bilateral and effective exchange rates.

8. The model assumed that this appreciation would be caused by an exogenous portfolio shift.

Ito expresses optimism that the long period of recession in Japan is now coming to an end and that the prospects for growth are much better than they have been for a while, although he cautions that price deflation is not yet securely over. He also notes a sharp yen appreciation as among the downside risks that could bring the expansion to an abrupt halt. He discusses the large interventions between early 2003 and March 2004 and suggests that these were probably motivated by exactly such a fear. Foreign criticism of these interventions led to their withdrawal for a couple of weeks in September 2003 and may also have been instrumental in the cessation of intervention in March 2004, although he argues that this was primarily a consequence of the authorities deciding that they could afford to stop intervening because the market pressure for yen appreciation had vanished. He does not suggest that the Japanese authorities would as yet be prepared to acquiesce happily in an appreciation as large as that implied by the models of Wren-Lewis or Bénassy-Quéré and colleagues, although he does make the point that the long period of deflation in Japan means that a yen below 100 to the dollar is no longer as strong in real terms as formerly.

Ito acknowledges that the rapid growth in trade with China and other Asian countries means that the dollar exchange rate is less crucial for Japan than in former times and that the effective exchange rate has correspondingly gained in policy salience. The same is true of many of the other Asian economies, which is one reason why the fixed renminbi-dollar exchange rate attracted so much attention at the conference.

Goldstein's paper is based on his work with Nicholas Lardy addressing the issue of the renminbi directly. He outlines two approaches to calculating whether the renminbi is misaligned. The first is the "underlying balance approach," which involves comparing normal capital flows with the underlying (adjusting for cyclical and temporary factors) current account surplus. This suggests that China needs to engineer a current account adjustment of about 4 percent of GDP, which an elasticities-based model suggests would require a real appreciation of 20 to 30 percent.

Goldstein's second approach starts from the size of the world disequilibrium and the hypothesis that correcting this would require a dollar depreciation on the order of 25 percent from the time when the dollar hit its peak. He argues that China has aggravated the problem until now by riding the dollar down, whereas it is in at least as strong a position to contribute positively as any other country. Thus both of Goldstein's estimates of the Chinese undervaluation are somewhat less than those of Wren-Lewis and of Bénassy-Quéré and her colleagues.

According to standard analysis (although not according to the ultra-Keynesian analysis of Garber and his colleagues at Deutsche Bank, which assumes no constraints), such a revaluation of the renminbi would be in China's interest as much as that of the rest of the world. This is not a "dilemma" case, in which an exchange rate change that would push the country toward external equilibrium would worsen its position with regard to "internal balance."

On the contrary, the Chinese economy has been overheating. Some Chinese observers talk of the inflation this is inducing as part of the adjustment process, for if left to run its course it will induce a real appreciation just like a nominal appreciation would. However, official Chinese policy has sought to end the overheating and thus cut short the inflation, which is what most of the conference participants regard as a sensible way to conduct macroeconomic policy. We believe that revaluing the renminbi would be a much better policy than the mandated credit restraint that has actually been used to combat this overheating, not only because it would use market incentives rather than require their suppression to be effective, but also because it would combat overheating by enlarging supply by increasing import availability as well as curtailing (export) demand.

Goldstein also argues that the large speculative capital inflow being attracted by the renminbi's undervaluation is particularly dangerous to China because it is feeding the rapid credit growth that is almost sure to be generating a new wave of bad loans by the commercial banks. Others added that its refusal to revalue is dangerous to China because it is likely to generate protectionist reactions, as we have already seen extensively in the United States (for apparel, television sets, furniture, etc.). In the worst case, this could stop the Chinese export expansion in its tracks. Even short of this, it could undermine the ability of the Chinese leadership to use the country's integration with the world trading system to promote its agenda of policy reform.

Still another point noted by Goldstein is that the renminbi exchange rate is seen as crucial by many other Asian economies, such as Hong Kong, Indonesia, South Korea, Malaysia, the Philippines, Singapore, Taiwan, Thailand, and even India and Japan—all important competitors of (as well as suppliers to) China. Because of this relationship with China, they are reluctant to allow their currencies to appreciate ahead of the renminbi. Even excluding Japan, Williamson's table 2.1 shows that about a half of the current account adjustment of Asia would be absorbed by China under his scenario.[9] Goldstein (2003) estimated that if there was a 20 percent revaluation of the renminbi and a 10 percent revaluation of the other Asian currencies (excluding Japan's), the US deficit might be cut by about $50 billion.

In the light of these facts, it really is not very relevant to say that no conceivable change in China's multilateral balance can be expected to offset more than a small proportion of the needed improvement in the US current account: It does not need to. If China is the critical blockage preventing a general adjustment of Asian exchange rates and the bulk of additional adjustment needs to be against Asia, then the fixed renminbi-dollar rate is *the* big obstacle to a successful adjustment.

Table 1.2 assembles relevant data for each of the main Asian economies. The first two columns give two alternative measures of the size of each

---

9. Including Japan, the proportion falls to less than 20 percent.

Table 1.2 Economic data for main Asian economies, 2000–04

Country	Period	GDP (billions of dollars, market rates)[a]	Merchandise exports, shares of world total (reexports included)[b] (percent)	Total weight in Federal Reserve broad exchange rate index[c] (percent)	Current account balance (percent of GDP)[a]	Current account balance (billions of dollars)[a]	Total reserves, minus gold/total imports[d] (percent)	Bilateral appreciation in nominal exchange rate from dollar high in January 2002 to May 25, 2004[e] (percent)	Change in IMF REER value from January 2002 to March 2004 (most recent data)[f] (percent)
China	2000	1080.8	3.9	7.8	1.9	20.5	64.5		
	2001	1175.8	4.3	8.7	1.5	17.4	76.3		
	2002	1266.1	5.0	9.8	2.8	35.4	85.3	0.0	−11.5
	2003	1409.9	5.9	9.8	2.1	29.6	87.5		
	2004(p)	1583.2	n.a.	9.8	1.6	25.0	n.a.		
Hong Kong	2000	165.4	3.1	2.4	4.3	7.1	45.1		
	2001	162.8	3.1	2.4	6.1	9.9	49.1		
	2002	161.5	3.1	2.0	8.5	13.7	48.1	0.1	n.a.
	2003	158.6	3.0	2.0	11.0	17.4	46.2		
	2004(p)	163.4	n.a.	2.0	10.3	16.9	n.a.		
India	2000	460.8	0.7	0.9	−1.1	−5.1	53.0		
	2001	473.8	0.7	1.0	−0.2	−0.8	62.3		
	2002	492.6	0.8	1.1	1.0	4.8	85.2	6.6	n.a.
	2003	575.3	0.7	1.1	0.5	3.0	110.7		
	2004(p)	635.6	n.a.	1.1	0.2	1.3	n.a.		
Indonesia	2000	150.2	1.0	1.0	5.3	8.0	59.0		
	2001	143.2	0.9	1.0	4.8	6.9	58.5		
	2002	173.4	0.9	1.0	4.5	7.8	64.3	11.6	n.a.
	2003	208.3	0.8	1.0	3.9	8.0	n.a.		
	2004(p)	228.8	n.a.	1.0	2.9	6.7	n.a.		
Japan	2000	4748.7	7.4	12.8	2.5	119.6	71.7		
	2001	4163.1	6.5	11.6	2.1	87.8	86.6		
	2002	3973.4	6.4	11.1	2.8	112.7	103.9	16.6	1.3
	2003	4301.8	6.3	11.1	3.2	136.4	134.6		
	2004(p)	4612.0	n.a.	11.1	3.1	144.0	n.a.		

	Year							
South Korea	2000	511.7	2.7	4.2	2.4	12.2	49.7	
	2001	481.9	2.4	3.7	1.7	8.0	59.2	
	2002	546.9	2.5	3.9	1.0	5.4	64.8	
	2003	605.4	2.6	3.9	2.0	12.3	71.4	11.4
	2004(p)	656.0	n.a.	3.9	1.5	9.5	n.a.	n.a.
Malaysia	2000	90.2	1.5	2.3	9.4	8.5	30.0	
	2001	88.0	1.4	2.1	8.3	7.3	33.7	
	2002	94.9	1.4	2.3	7.6	7.2	35.6	
	2003	103.2	1.3	2.3	11.1	11.4	45.7	0.0
	2004(p)	110.2	n.a.	2.3	10.9	12.0	n.a.	−16.0
Philippines	2000	74.8	0.6	1.2	8.4	6.3	30.1	
	2001	71.0	0.5	1.1	1.9	1.3	33.5	
	2002	76.8	0.6	1.2	5.5	4.2	31.7	
	2003	79.2	0.5	1.2	2.1	1.7	30.8	−8.2
	2004(p)	82.7	n.a.	1.2	1.6	1.3	n.a.	−18.3
Singapore	2000	92.6	2.1	2.4	14.3	13.2	49.7	
	2001	86.0	2.0	2.2	18.7	16.1	52.8	
	2002	88.3	1.8	2.2	21.4	18.9	57.1	
	2003	91.3	1.9	2.2	30.9	28.2	61.7	7.4
	2004(p)	99.5	n.a.	2.2	28.0	27.9	n.a.	−6.5
Taiwan	2000	309.4	2.3	3.7	2.9	8.9	64.4	
	2001	281.2	2.0	3.1	6.4	17.9	93.4	
	2002	281.9	2.1	3.0	9.1	25.6	118.5	
	2003	286.0	2.0	3.0	10.0	28.6	135.3	4.6
	2004(p)	309.0	n.a.	3.0	7.3	22.5	n.a.	n.a.
Thailand	2000	122.7	1.1	1.5	7.6	9.3	41.4	
	2001	115.5	1.1	1.5	5.4	6.2	42.5	
	2002	126.9	1.1	1.4	5.5	7.0	46.8	
	2003	143.2	1.1	1.4	5.6	8.0	43.8	7.6
	2004(p)	162.3	n.a.	1.4	4.4	7.1	n.a.	n.a.

n.a. = not available; (p) = projection; REER = real effective exchange rate

a. Data from International Monetary Fund *World Economic Outlook* database, April 2004.
b. Data from World Trade Organization Total Merchandise Database.
c. Data from the Federal Reserve.
d. Data from the World Trade Organization; IMF, *International Financial Statistics*, July 2004; Central Bank of China.
e. Data from the Pacific Exchange Rate Service.
f. Data from the International Monetary Fund, *International Financial Statistics*, July 2004.

economy: (1) its GDP (converted at market exchange rates) and (2) its visible exports as a percentage of the global total. The third column shows the percentage of the Federal Reserve index of the dollar's broad (i.e., effective) exchange rate accounted for by each economy. The fourth and fifth columns show each economy's average current account balance since the new millennium started (1) as a percentage of its GDP and (2) in dollars. The sixth column shows each economy's year-end level of reserves deflated (as is conventional) by its level of imports. The last two columns show two measures of the change in each economy's exchange rate from the dollar's peak in January 2002 until the date of the 2004 conference: (1) the nominal bilateral exchange rate against the dollar and, where available, (2) the real effective rate.

The table confirms that these economies account for a sizable part of the world economy and also of the dollar's effective exchange rate. All have current account surpluses, and most have reserves well above the conventional safety level of 25 to 35 percent. With the possible exception of the Philippines, they have ample scope to accept a deterioration in their current account balances. Yet, while only the Philippines has depreciated in nominal terms against the dollar since the dollar's peak, several others have held their bilateral dollar rates constant. Except for Japan, most of those that have accepted appreciation in their dollar rates have kept these modest (at best, just reaching double digits). The result is that all these economies except Japan for which we have data on changes in real effective exchange rates have depreciated in real effective terms, and even Japan's appreciation is negligible on this measure.

It is not an accident that changes in effective exchange rates are systematically less than those in dollar rates. This is something that would remain true in the event of a concerted Asian move to revalue against the dollar. Because these economies now trade so much with one another, a concerted revaluation by all of them against the dollar would result in much smaller appreciations in their effective exchange rates, precisely because it would not involve their losing competitiveness vis-à-vis each other. If the dollar's adjustment is not to fall far short of what is needed, the world needs such a concerted revaluation of the Asian currencies. Yet one can understand why each of these economies, including China, is anxious to avoid or limit a unilateral appreciation. This would result in their losing competitiveness vis-à-vis all their peers, and it could thus be unacceptably costly.

Concerted revaluations do not happen by themselves. Someone has to take the lead, as the G-7 did in organizing the Plaza Accord. It would be ridiculous for the G-7 to think of taking the lead on this issue, however, for only one of the relevant countries is a member. The G-20 would be better, because five of the relevant countries (China, India, Indonesia, Japan, and South Korea) are members. But that still leaves out many of the countries that would need to be persuaded to participate. So the G-7 and G-20 should simply issue a call to arms, yielding the actual work of organizing a concerted revaluation to the institution that is supposed to be responsible for overseeing the international adjustment process: the International Monetary Fund.

Unfortunately, this major IMF responsibility has been shamefully neglected for many years, and all too often the Fund acts as though balance of payments policies and exchange rates are none of its business. In our view, the IMF's main objective in the coming months should be to secure a concerted appreciation of the East Asian currencies so as to facilitate the needed adjustment of the US balance of payments without imposing an intolerable burden on any one country. If the IMF continues to ignore this need, then even its natural friends will begin to wonder whether it is worth maintaining the institution.

The Instruments of Adjustment

The standard theory of balance of payments determination points to two major systematic sets of influences on a country's current account outcome. One is the relative strength of demand at home and in the country's trading partners. The other is the exchange rate (this of course means the real effective exchange rate, i.e., the nominal exchange rate adjusted for relative inflation at home and abroad, and the weighted average of the real exchange rates against all the country's trading partners).

Several of the conference papers, especially those of Mussa and Williamson, emphasize that achieving adjustment without pushing the world economy into recession will require both restraint in the growth of domestic demand in the United States and more rapid growth in domestic demand in the rest of the world. Demand restraint in the United States will be needed to make available the real resources to reduce the current account deficit. If the Federal Reserve gets no help from the fiscal authorities in restraining demand as output approaches full employment, then it will have to raise interest rates more than would have been necessary with a more responsible fiscal policy. That may curb the weakening of the dollar and therefore thwart the adjustment process; that is one of the disadvantages of conducting macroeconomic policy with one hand tied behind the authorities' back (which is what a refusal to raise taxes or cut spending when the time comes amounts to). But because the exchange rate has a life of its own rather than being simply a reflection of monetary policy, it is still possible that adjustment will occur even if all the burden of restraining demand in the United States falls on monetary policy.

If a diversion of demand to the United States is induced by a weaker dollar and the US authorities (doubtless aided by the market in pushing up interest rates) provide the space to satisfy this by restraining internal American demand, then maintaining world output growth will require faster growth in demand in the rest of the world. Perhaps the main reason for wanting to see an orderly fall of the dollar rather than an abrupt decline is to make it easier for other countries to undertake the demand expansion that will be essential if adjustment is to take place in a context of global prosperity rather than world recession. It is historically inaccurate to argue that all countries other than the United States have had to run large export surpluses to grow rapidly. In fact, there are instances (e.g., most of the East Asian emerging-market economies prior to the Asian crisis) of countries having used the market confidence inspired by rapid export expansion to borrow and finance current account deficits caused by an even more rapid growth in imports. That is the sort of virtuous circle that countries other than the United States will need to achieve in the next few years if the adjustment process is to succeed.

The other imperative for effecting the current account adjustment that the United States needs is to secure exchange rate changes roughly along the lines explored above: a further significant dollar depreciation (the magnitude of which we discuss again later), reflecting primarily the appreciation of the Asian currencies. If the United States were to restrain demand and other countries were to stimulate it (as described earlier) without a weaker dollar, the consequence would be a weak economy in the United States and the return of inflationary pressures in the rest of the world. This scenario would benefit no one. In other words, the two changes need to be phased in jointly.

That presents a problem, inasmuch as the exchange rate is no longer a policy variable, as it was under the Bretton Woods system. This issue also was debated in the Institute's 2002 conference: Is sterilized intervention a policy tool that can be used to influence the exchange rate (as it was assumed to be at the time of the Plaza Accord and in other G-7 intervention episodes)? Two very interesting papers in this volume cast new light on this issue.

In one of these papers (chapter 11), Marcel Fratzscher argues that the authorities really have two intervention instruments. Along with the purchase and sale of foreign exchange that has figured in the literature, they also have what he calls "oral intervention" (perhaps more familiarly known as "jawboning"). It seems rather commonsensical to hypothesize that if one believes that traditional intervention works by informing the market of the beliefs of the central bank about the equilibrium exchange rate (as a number of recent writers argue, labeling it the "information channel"), then a direct statement of such beliefs might also influence the market. And it seems distinctly quixotic for Robert Rubin to have gone to such lengths as he describes in his recent book (Rubin 2003, 184) to avoid statements that might disturb the market if oral intervention had no effects.

In fact, Fratzscher's careful tests find that both forms of intervention have had measurable effects.[10] He also finds very clear evidence that traditional intervention has been largely abandoned as a policy instrument by both the Federal Reserve and the European Central Bank (and its de facto predecessor, the Bundesbank) in recent years. Intervention policy now consists essentially of oral intervention, except in Asia.

In the other paper (chapter 10), Christopher Kubelec argues that intervention works increasingly well the further the exchange rate is from its equilibrium value. Governments that use intervention to try to influence the equilibrium value of the exchange rate are doomed to fail. In contrast, as the exchange rate gets carried further away from equilibrium by chartists following "technical" trading strategies, the proportion of traders starting to worry about the possibility of losing money as the rate reverts back to equilibrium increases. In his formal model, an increasing number of traders find it worthwhile to invest in costly equilibrium-discovery activities (like buying research reports). Because of that, there is an increasing chance that an act of intervention will have a strategic impact in tipping the market from an errant path to an equilibrium-reverting path. His empirical tests suggest that intervention indeed becomes more and more effective as the central bank tries to combat a larger and larger misalignment.

Martin Evans, one of the pioneers of the new micro modeling of the foreign exchange market, commented on the papers by Fratzscher and Kubelec (his comment appears at the end of part IV). He outlines how this type of model works, and he confirms that in principle it would provide scope for an impact on the exchange rate of either of the mechanisms modeled by Fratzscher and Kubelec. Incidentally, Evans questions whether intervention could have these effects if the macro models of exchange rate determination told us everything there is to know about the issue. But, while acknowledging that Fratzscher had provided statistical evidence that oral intervention is effective, Evans questions whether the evidence really supports a significant impact, noting that in both early 1998 and early 2002 a series of statements in support of a strong dollar had no obvious impact on the dollar-euro rate. He also suggests that Kubelec's evidence is inconclusive. Nevertheless, he concedes that the findings of both researchers provide suggestive evidence that at least under some circumstances intervention can be effective.

What can one conclude about the usefulness of intervention in generating a set of exchange rates that would promote adjustment? At least three observations can be made. First, the point emphasized at the earlier conference remains valid: At a minimum, governments ought to stop intervening in a way that is designed to thwart the adjustment process. A reasonable corollary might be that the international system should include rules that place an

---

10. This is consistent with Rubin's boast that all the interventions undertaken during his time at the Treasury Department were effective (Rubin 2003, 187).

obligation on the IMF to seek a mutually consistent view of what countries should be aiming at and then pressure them into abiding by those objectives.

Some analysts, including Goldstein in this volume, essentially argue that the IMF already has this power through the injunction against "exchange rate manipulation" in its existing Articles of Agreement. Others point out that this provision has never been interpreted to preclude pegging an exchange rate and suggest that an amendment that explicitly endorses the ability to prohibit pegging at a disequilibrium rate would be in order.

Second, if oral intervention is now the predominant way in which policy is exercised, it needs to be subject to the same international discipline as the more traditional forms of intervention. Treasury secretaries should not be free to voice their support for a "strong dollar" when the dollar is already too strong by any reasonable measure, especially once that measure has been endorsed by the IMF. If they nonetheless insist on doing so, they should be contradicted by the managing director of the IMF—just as he has indeed contradicted them on numerous occasions concerning the appropriateness of US fiscal policy. Officials need to say they favor their exchange rates moving toward equilibrium, which will sometimes mean appreciation and sometimes depreciation (and occasionally will mean no movement at all).

Third, conventional intervention should be limited to occasions when the exchange rate is misaligned and the misalignment is harming the adjustment process. Even if no guarantee can be given that intervention will be effective, it stands more chance of working under these conditions than when used to defend a disequilibrium parity.

Conclusions

In summing up the conference, Fred Bergsten pointed to the stalemate that the system has reached. There is general agreement that the United States needs to curb quite substantially the size of its current account deficit. Most observers acknowledge that doing this will require a sizable depreciation of the dollar. That implies a need for other currencies to appreciate against the dollar. Some currencies have already done so: the euro, the pound, the Swiss franc, the Canadian dollar, and the Australian and New Zealand dollars. (Indeed, some participants felt that several of these currencies might have overshot, although it is hard to believe that this remains true after the renewed strengthening of the dollar in early 2004.) Despite these corrections, the US dollar remains very substantially overvalued.

One thing the conference did not reach agreement on is the magnitude of the current dollar overvaluation. Wren-Lewis went straight to estimates of equilibrium bilateral exchange rates, but if one weights and averages these, one would estimate on his measure that the dollar was overvalued by a little under 10 percent at the time of the conference. The figure of Bénassy-Quéré and her colleagues would seem to be about 4 percent, if one looks at their estimate of the dollar's real effective overvaluation, although weighting their estimates of bilateral misalignments with the Federal Reserve's weighting system would suggest a rather larger figure, again approaching 10 percent. O'Neill's preferred estimate would also seem to be about 10 percent.

Mussa, conversely, asserted that a further dollar depreciation of about 20 percent or more would be needed to complete the adjustment process. Mann (2004) is even more alarmist, predicting that an immediate adjustment of close to 20 percent (enough to bring the Fed's broad real index down to an index value of 85, as against its July 2004 value of 101.5) would do little more than stabilize the size of the US current account deficit. And to prevent the deficit growing again in future years, the initial depreciation would need to be followed by a secular depreciation of about 10 percent a year (to offset the Houthakker-Magee asymmetry in the import elasticities and the growing deficit on the investment income account as the United States piles up foreign indebtedness, and to allow for an initial situation in which the value of imports vastly exceeds that of exports). What one can conclude is that the dollar is currently overvalued by at least 10 percent or so, and possibly by substantially more.

Yet the world has run out of volunteers for currency appreciation. Japan has already undertaken some appreciation, and its authorities fear that much more might derail the incipient recovery that looks as though it may finally be under way. China has a fixed nominal exchange rate with the dollar, and its officials parrot phrases about "keeping the yuan stable around a rational and balanced level" (ignoring the facts that stability in the bilateral rate against the dollar implies instability in what really matters, the effective exchange rate, and that the present rate is by no stretch of the imagination reasonable and balanced). Other Asian countries resist substantial appreciation, even when their exchange rates are nominally floating, when this would also mean losing competitiveness against China. Canada and the eurozone are both relieved that the full appreciation of 2003 did not stick. Latin American countries seem determined not to repeat their past mistake of acquiescing in overvalued exchange rates, and they may well be tempted to err in the opposite direction.

In this situation, there is an acute need to reach some measure of international understanding about a consistent set of balance of payments objectives and the resulting policy implications. Yet this is one responsibility that the International Monetary Fund, the institution that is supposed to be in charge of supervising the adjustment process, seems singularly reluctant to fulfill. The G-7 and G-20 should tell the IMF that it is high time for it to accept its responsibility to negotiate an agreed-on and mutually consistent set of current account objectives. Unless the Institute's conference was chronically mistaken, these objectives will have as a corollary an obligation to orchestrate a concerted Asian appreciation against the dollar, and to encourage countries with both deficits and surpluses to make the needed complementary adjustments in their policies regarding domestic demand.

No one doubts that adjustment will eventually happen. The sooner it starts, the less the chance that it will take a catastrophic form. If and when the worst happens, the world will surely not look back forgivingly at the present generation of officials who told themselves reassuring stories about the omniscience of markets while they allowed the disequilibria to explode.

References

Bergsten, C. Fred, and John Williamson, eds. 2003. *Dollar Overevaluation and the World Economy.* Washington: Institute for International Economics.

Dooley, Michael P., David Folkerts-Landau, and Peter Garber. 2003. *An Essay on the Revived Bretton Woods System.* NBER Working Paper 9971. Cambridge, MA: National Bureau of Economic Research.

Goldstein, Morris. 2003. China's Exchange Rate Regime. Testimony before the Subcommittee on Domestic and International Monetary Policy, Trade, and Technology, Committee on Financial Services, US House of Representatives, Washington, October 1.

Mann, Catherine L. 2003. How Long the Strong Dollar? In *Dollar Overevaluation and the World Economy,* ed. C. Fred Bergsten and John Williamson. Washington: Institute for International Economics.

Mann, Catherine L. 2004. Managing Exchange Rates: Achievement of Global Re-balancing or Evidence of Global Co-dependency? *Business Economics* (July): 20–29.

Rubin, Robert, with Jacob Weisberg. 2003. *In an Uncertain World: Tough Decisions from Wall Street to Washington.* New York: Random House.

Wren-Lewis, Simon, and Rebecca L. Driver. 1998. *Real Exchange Rates for the Year 2000.* POLICY ANALYSES IN INTERNATIONAL ECONOMICS 54. Washington: Institute for International Economics.

II

HOW MUCH ADJUSTMENT?

2

Current Account Objectives: Who Should Adjust?

JOHN WILLIAMSON

Not long ago, an article in *The Economist* likened the world economy to an airplane that flies on only one engine, with the United States being the sole growth pole that was injecting additional demand into the global economy. More recently, a paper by Michael Dooley, David Folkerts-Landau, and Peter Garber (2003) pictured the Asian countries as constituting a fixed exchange rate periphery to the US role as the permanent-deficit center country of a revived Bretton Woods system.[1]

In both cases, the notion seems to be that any correction of the US current account deficit would risk global demand deflation because there is no other region able and inclined to substitute for the United States as the source of additional global demand. This chapter asks whether that is true and, if not, where the additional demand could come from.

The question of where sufficient additional demand would come from to keep the world economy expanding if and when the United States does initiate a serious effort to correct its external deficit is of course an important one. A US adjustment that did not have a counterpart demand expansion

John Williamson is a senior fellow at the Institute for International Economics. The author is indebted to C. Fred Bergsten and participants in the conference for comments on a previous draft and to Jacob Kirkegaard for research assistance.

1. The United States actually had a current account surplus most years while the Bretton Woods system—one of whose basic rules was that a country was supposed to adjust its exchange rate if it was in "fundamental disequilibrium"—was in operation. What the authors appear to confuse with the Bretton Woods system is the Dollar Standard, which for a time looked as if it would emerge from the Bretton Woods system as the latter was breaking down. (In fact, this perversion of the Bretton Woods system did not last long.)

in the present surplus countries might succeed in correcting the US external deficit, but if so it would be at a severe cost in the level of global output. An adjustment achieved at the cost of global growth could be a cure worse than the disease.

This chapter therefore seeks a way to allocate the reduction in current account surpluses[2] among non-US countries that would be implied by a smaller US current account deficit. A successful adjustment process will require that these countries expand their internal demand by a sum greater by the programmed reduction of their current account balance than they otherwise would. Without such expansion, adjustment would come at the cost of net global demand deflation. (This may seem obvious to some, but there are still people who seem to believe that recognition of the importance of exchange rates in facilitating adjustment implies blindness to the importance of anything else. My view is the mainstream one that both relative demand and real exchange rates are important determinants of payments positions.)

There is no reason to expect that a reduction in current account surpluses would in general be undesirable to the countries in question. In a recent paper (Williamson 2003) that aimed to rationalize the notion of export-led growth, I postulated that growth depends on investment and that the desire to invest is stimulated by a more competitive exchange rate. This is the sort of mechanism that Dooley, Folkerts-Landau, and Garber appeal to as rationalizing the growth strategies of the East Asian periphery. But, unlike both them and the self-styled "Keynesians" at Cambridge, I also recognized that there is a potential disadvantage from the standpoint of growth in an undervalued exchange rate: that the resulting current account surplus diverts resources away from absorption into reserve accumulation. The desire to invest (demand side) may be greater, but the ability to invest (supply side) is diminished. The growth-maximizing exchange rate is that at which these two forces are balanced at the margin.

When (as in China) investment is already well over 40 percent of GDP, one may reasonably question whether it is desirable to increase investment further or whether the marginal productivity of investment is low because of a constraint on absorptive capacity. But even if one answers that further increases in investment are for that reason undesirable, it is difficult to believe that a country's government is doing its citizens a service by investing so many resources in low-yielding reserves, rather than encouraging consumption of the current generation to rise faster. Future growth need be no slower, and current consumption could be higher, with a different macroeconomic strategy that resulted in a lower current account surplus or a shift into a deficit sufficiently small to be financed prudently. Certainly

---

2. In principle, one should add "or increase in current account deficits," because it is conceivable that some countries that already run current account deficits ought to aim at larger current account deficits.

Table 2.1 Current account balances, 2004 (billions of dollars)

Economy, group, or region	IMF forecast	Change	Targets	GDP
Advanced economies				
United States	−496	246	−250	
Euro area	68	−68	0	9,266
Japan	144	−73	71	4,760
New industrial economies	77	−19	58	1,228
Other advanced economies	23	−23	0	6,167
Total	−184	63	−121	
Developing economies				
Africa	−8	0	−8	610
China	25	−24	1	1,583
Other developing Asia	26	−22	4	1,449
Middle East	44	−11	33	734
Western Hemisphere	−7	0	−7	1,978
Total	80	−57	23	
Economies in transition	6	−6	0	1,824
Discrepancy	−98	0	−98	

Sources: International Monetary Fund, *World Economic Outlook*, April 2004, appendix tables 26 and 28; assumptions described in the text; and IMF data bank for GDP figures.

it is difficult to conceive of a model other than the crudest Keynesian one, with no supply side, under which growth is increased by hoarding low-yielding reserves.

I therefore do not believe that reduced current account balances outside the United States need be inimical to the welfare of those countries. On the contrary, except in a situation of global excess demand (like the early 1970s) or excess supply (like the 1930s), my presumption is that countries' national interests are consistent. We have no rigorous way of establishing what an optimal pattern of payments imbalances would be, so the approach adopted here is to explore ad hoc rules that appear to give reasonable results that respect the interests of all countries in achieving sustainable payments positions and high-growth, high-employment domestic outcomes.

Computations

The first set of numbers in table 2.1 shows the latest (April 2004) IMF forecasts of the current account balances of the principal economies and regions in the current year, 2004. The US deficit is projected as $496 billion. That is more than 50 percent offset by surpluses in other advanced economies, which are disaggregated in the table into the euro area, Japan, the new industrial economies (Hong Kong, South Korea, Singapore, and Taiwan), and other advanced economies (consisting of Australia, Canada, Cyprus, Denmark, Iceland, Israel, New Zealand, Norway, Sweden, Switzerland,

and the United Kingdom). A further 16 percent of the US deficit finds its counterpart in net current account surpluses in the developing countries. After allowing for a small net surplus of the transition economies, there is a $98 billion expected statistical discrepancy. This is the current account deficit that the world runs with itself because the statisticians are unable to figure out to whom $98 billion in receipts is accruing (or, less probably, who is reporting larger payments than they are really making).

How large a correction in the US current account deficit would it be reasonable to seek in the coming years (say, within a time horizon of about three years)? Halving the measured deficit would seem a reasonable objective. That would still leave a substantial measured deficit, of nearly $250 billion, or some 2.5 percent of GDP. This is probably equal to a real deficit (an increase in the net indebtedness of the United States toward the rest of the world, ignoring changes in asset values) of something over $200 billion (a little under 2 percent of GDP), after attributing a reasonable proportion of the world statistical discrepancy to the United States. That would suffice to end the increase in the ratio of the US net international investment position (NIIP) to GDP at a reasonable value, even if in future years the statisticians do not revalue assets and liabilities in such a way as to offset much of the increase in the NIIP caused by the current account deficit, as they did in 2003.

Of course, this would not guarantee that the United States would not at some point encounter a crisis. Most crises arise from circumstances that are not foreseen, so one cannot assert with any confidence that a particular deficit is sustainable for a given length of time. What one can say is that the *probability* of a crisis increases as the debt/GDP ratio rises, in which case an end to the trend increase in the debt/GDP ratio would prevent a further increase in the likelihood of a crisis.

How could the counterpart deterioration in the current account balances of the rest of the world be distributed? In principle, there are of course an infinite number of ways, but consider the following approach. The two deficit regions (Africa and the developing countries of the Western Hemisphere) are not asked to participate in the adjustment process. The remaining regions' GDP totals $29,599 billion. The $246 billion target change amounts to 0.83 percent of that change. A change of 0.83 percent of their GDP would push the euro area, other advanced economies, and the economies in transition into deficit. These regions are therefore assigned a target of eliminating their current account surpluses. That provides for $97 billion of the desired $246 billion of adjustment.

There remains $149 billion of adjustment to divide among the remaining areas, whose GDP totals $9,754 billion. That is, countries on average need to adjust by 1.528 percent of GDP. If that is distributed proportionately to GDP, all these regions could remain in surplus (although the Chinese surplus would be marginal). That is the adjustment that is shown in the middle two columns of the table, with one column showing the changes and the other the proposed targets.

Are the Targets in the Interest of the Adjustees?

Would those targets be reasonable ones, in the sense that they give "reasonable results that respect the interests of all countries in achieving sustainable payments positions and high-growth, high-employment domestic outcomes"? Or are there reasons to think that their pursuit would impose unreasonably onerous obligations on some of the countries or regions, either because it would preclude their achieving full employment or high growth, or because it would interfere with their legitimate external objectives? The chapter proceeds to consider each of the countries or regions in turn.

Euro Area

The euro area has been a surplus region for most of the past decade, the exception being 2000, with the nine-year average surplus being $47 billion. But it would face no external problem if its external surplus were to vanish. A reduction of $68 billion would amount to under 1 percent of GDP, a sum that most economists probably believe could easily be offset by a relaxation of monetary policy to expand internal demand by $68 billion. (However, the model of the European Central Bank, or ECB, apparently attributes almost no impact on internal demand to changes in the interest rate, which in that model achieves its impact almost entirely by influencing the euro's exchange rate. Perhaps this implausible modeling explains why the ECB has been so reluctant to cut interest rates during the recent recession.) I therefore see no difficulty in Europe making its suggested contribution to the adjustment process.

Japan

In contrast, Japan has experienced severe problems in expanding internal demand during the past decade. However, the Japanese economy is now recovering from its prolonged bout of weakness (see chapter 8 in this volume), and so the factor that has for some years argued for exempting Japan from full participation in the adjustment process is no longer present. Taking William Cline's central estimate that each 1 percent appreciation in the yen's real effective exchange rate reduces the Japanese current account surplus by $2.3 billion (Bergsten and Williamson 2003, 192), a $68 billion decline in Japan's current account surplus would require an appreciation of just over 30 percent in the real effective exchange rate. If many of its trading partners also appreciate against the dollar, then the yen's rate against the dollar will need to appreciate by substantially more than this (although a part of the adjustment has already occurred). Even so, these are very large changes, and so it may be important to treat such a target as a longer-run one than most of the others discussed in this chapter.

New Industrial Economies

The new industrial economies were more or less in current account balance before the Asian crisis. However, one of the messages they took from that crisis was that they needed to build up their reserves to a much higher level to avoid any danger of a repetition. They have now abundantly accomplished that objective: Their collective reserves rose from $263 billion in 1996 to over $540 billion in late 2003. Accordingly, it would now be quite consistent with their continued economic security to stop stockpiling reserves and revert to a policy that would involve something close to current account balance. The decline in external demand that would need to be replaced by expanded internal demand would be more than 6 percent of their collective GDP if they were to go over time to this objective. The adjustment that is proposed in the short run (the next two or three years) is much smaller than this. While it would be sensible for them in due course to stimulate their internal demand so as to replace a much larger proportion of their external surplus, one might not want to envisage such a large adjustment in the short run.

Other Advanced Economies

One would look to the surplus countries in the motley group of other advanced economies (Canada, $17 billion, projected in 2004; Denmark, $6 billion; Norway, $31 billion; Sweden, $20 billion; and Switzerland, $34 billion—a total of $108 billion) to generate the reduction of $23 billion to put the group as a whole in current account balance. That would require a reduction in their collective surplus of only 21 percent, and an offsetting expansion in internal demand of less than 1 percent of their GDP. This seems eminently feasible.

Africa

The "target" for Africa is a collective deficit of $8 billion (the projection of the International Monetary Fund for 2004), which may be compared with the average deficit of the region of a similar sum over the past nine years. There is nothing obviously infeasible here.

China

The target involves virtual elimination of China's $25 billion current account surplus.[3] This is, if anything, on the modest side, because (1) the

---

3. Its bilateral surplus with the United States is, of course, totally irrelevant to this exercise.

current account surplus would be larger were it not for the fact that the Chinese economy is currently overheated; (2) the surplus is likely to grow in coming years as a result of the elimination of the Multi-Fiber Arrangement; and (3) China's capital imports (mainly of foreign direct investment) have on average been quite significant in recent years (on average, something like $40 billion). China would do itself a favor if it were to reduce its buildup of the low-yielding US Treasury bills that are forming the base of the speculative bubble that is growing and that constitutes the main threat to continued rapid Chinese growth. The adjustment asked of them is less than 2 percent of GDP, which should be a welcome (though possibly inadequate) way to relieve excess demand rather than something that needs replacing by more stimulatory policies.

Other Developing Countries of Asia

The other developing countries of Asia are another region that developed a surplus in the wake of the Asian Crisis (it was in significant deficit before that). The reserve buildup that resulted was a sensible precautionary move, but it has surely now gone far enough in most of the countries: Reserves increased from $134 billion at the end of 1996 to more than $250 billion in late 2003. Accordingly, it seems reasonable to ask this group of countries to accept a $23 billion deterioration in their collective current account position, which would be equivalent to less than 2 percent of their collective GDP. Most of them could use these resources productively in increased domestic investment, although there may again be the odd case in which, like China, it would make more sense to expand consumption.

The Middle East, Including Turkey

For 2004, the IMF is projecting an $8 billion deterioration in the current account surplus of the Middle East, including Turkey, to a $44 billion surplus. This is above the nine-year average of this group of countries, which suggests that it would be reasonable to adopt a smaller figure for the medium-run target. As long as the oil price stays unusually high, however, one should encourage this group of countries to maintain a current account surplus as a way of saving for the day when conditions turn more adverse.

The Western Hemisphere

The IMF is projecting a current account deficit of $7 billion for the countries of the Western Hemisphere in 2004, which is substantially less than the nine-year average of a $46 billion annual deficit. One can certainly argue (e.g., see Kuczynski and Williamson 2003) that in the past these countries have allowed themselves to become excessively dependent on foreign savings, and accordingly that a substantially lower target than the actual past medium-term average is called for. A somewhat larger deficit than the target of $7 billion would, however, seem consistent with prudence.

Economies in Transition

The IMF projection has the economies in transition maintaining a small collective current account surplus in 2004, which is a little above their nine-year average of a small ($2 billion) current account deficit. There seems every reason to regard current account balance as a sustainable medium-term position. Indeed, it may be that with continuing capital inflows a number of additional countries could benefit by moving into current account deficit.

Conclusions on the Feasibility of Adjustment

In sum, it seems difficult to justify the agony about whether the rest of the world could adjust to a lower US current account deficit. The adjustment that I postulated could be accommodated rather comfortably by the rest of the world, with the possible exception of Japan.

Of course, certain conditions would need to be satisfied for such a benign outcome to materialize. First, it would be necessary for the counterpart adjustment to be widely distributed, as in the above scenario, rather than concentrated on a handful of countries. In particular, this means that the Asian countries now need to be brought into the adjustment process, instead of it all being concentrated on Europe and the old dominions of the British Commonwealth. This need not be difficult for them if they move collectively, but so far all one hears is that change is impossible in the absence of a move by China. Second, it would be necessary for the countries that would lose foreign demand (except perhaps China, which currently has a problem of excess demand) to be able and willing to replace the lost demand by deliberately expanding domestic demand.

Indeed, a somewhat larger adjustment could be envisaged without imposing unreasonable burdens on some countries. The new industrial Asian economies could, and indeed should, contemplate a bigger adjustment in the medium term. Some of the other advanced economies, like Canada, Scandinavia, and Switzerland, could afford lower surpluses and would not have any difficulty in expanding internal demand. China and other developing economies in Asia could, and probably should, go into deficit rather than simply eliminating their surpluses. And as was pointed out above, there is scope for more adjustment by the Western Hemisphere.

A *much* larger adjustment, however, could be problematic, especially in the absence of much stronger economies in Europe and Japan, or else larger capital flows to emerging markets that both authorities and markets were confident would be sustained over time. These things may come to pass in due course, but a prudent adjustment strategy for the next few years should concentrate on reducing the US deficit to a level that does not imply an ever increasing debt/GDP ratio in the United States. In the absence of this, it is all too easy to imagine a scenario in which at some point the dollar collapses due to some shock or other and the United States is thus forced into precipitate adjustment. This might pose dangers to the US economy, for example, from the inflationary pressures that would arise. But perhaps the graver danger is that the rest of the world would not be able to accommodate the counterpart adjustment, thus creating a world recession. This chapter has argued that it does not have to happen that way.

References

Bergsten, C. Fred, and John Williamson. 2003. *Dollar Overvaluation and the World Economy.* Washington: Institute for International Economics.

Dooley, Michael P., David Folkerts-Landau, and Peter Garber. 2003. *An Essay on the Revived Bretton Woods System.* NBER Working Paper 9971. Cambridge, MA: National Bureau of Economic Research.

Goldstein, Morris, and Nicholas Lardy. 2003. Two-Stage Currency Reform for China. *Asian Wall Street Journal,* September 12.

Kuczynski, Pedro-Pablo, and John Williamson. 2003. *After the Washington Consensus: Restarting Growth and Reform in Latin America.* Washington: Institute for International Economics.

Williamson, John. 2003. Exchange Rate Policy and Development. Paper presented at a conference on the Initiative for Policy Dialogue, Barcelona, June.

3

The Needed Changes in Bilateral Exchange Rates

SIMON WREN-LEWIS

This chapter presents sets of bilateral exchange rates consistent with alternative assumptions about "sustainable" current accounts.[1] It makes no direct attempt to assess what sustainable current accounts might be. Instead, it examines what exchange rates are implied by alternative assumptions about sustainable current accounts in the medium term.

The results presented here update work presented in Wren-Lewis (2003) that was part of the UK Treasury's assessment of entry into the European Monetary Union. The methods used are similar to that in Driver and Wren-Lewis (1998), and they have been applied extensively by a number of researchers, including John Williamson and economists at the International Monetary Fund. The approach goes under a variety of names, including fundamental equilibrium exchange rates (FEERs), dynamic equilibrium exchange rates (DEERs), and the macroeconomic balance approach. However, the results presented here are derived from a new global model (the five-area bilateral equilibrium exchange rate, or FABEER, model), which for the first time implements this approach by simultaneously determining equilibrium bilateral values for the dollar, yen, euro, and pound sterling.

The main text of the chapter focuses on the key results, and a more academic discussion of technical issues is contained in the appendices. The second section briefly outlines the key concepts behind the model. The third section presents medium-term equilibrium rates for the major four curren-

Simon Wren-Lewis has been a professor at Exeter University since 1995.

1. "Sustainable" here means the current account that is implied by medium-term (cyclically adjusted) private- and public-sector savings behavior. The concept is discussed further below.

cies under alternative assumptions about sustainable current accounts. The fourth section looks at three relatively minor currencies: the Australian and New Zealand dollars, and the Chinese renminbi. The fifth section extends the model to look at the implications for sustainable current accounts of two US-based macroeconomic shocks: a technology shock and a fiscal shock.

Key Concepts and the FABEER Model

In this chapter, I present medium-term estimates for bilateral exchange rates. Although "medium term" in macroeconomics can simply refer to a time period (e.g., five years), it can be given a more counterfactual interpretation, which is where the economy would be if there were no Keynesian frictions (nominal inertia). This is the meaning of "medium term" as used here.[2]

Within this medium-term time frame, it also makes sense to abstract from other, relatively short-lived effects. For example, I ignore the consequences of expectations errors. In addition, I abstract from any lags that may occur before changes in activity or competitiveness feed through into trade prices or volumes.

The main way that the business cycle influences actual exchange rates is through interest rates. An economy that is cyclically strong is likely to have relatively high interest rates, which will appreciate the exchange rate. By abstracting from this effect, I also calculate exchange rates that are independent of monetary policy.

A key assumption behind the calculations presented here is that the economy as a whole faces a downward-sloping demand curve for its production. Aggregate equations for exports and imports have traditionally found this to be the case, and more recently the "new international macroeconomics" (see Lane 2001) has focused on theoretical models based on imperfectly competitive goods markets for traded goods.

Appendix 3A sets out the theoretical basis for my estimates in more detail. They can be described in two, mutually consistent ways. The first is to say that I calculate a set of bilateral rates that will be consistent with the current accounts implied by medium-term savings behavior. (These are labeled "sustainable" current accounts.) The second is to describe the bilateral exchange rate estimates as matching the medium-term demand for domestic production with its supply.

Abstracting from cyclical effects allows me to describe my calculations as delivering estimates of medium-term equilibrium exchange rates. They

---

2. An alternative description might be cyclically adjusted exchange rates. Woodford and others use the term "natural" to describe a similar idea.

differ from long-run equilibrium rates, because long-run equilibrium refers to a position in which asset stocks are constant. Because sustainable current accounts may be nonzero in the analysis, asset stocks could well be changing. The approach in this chapter is very similar to Williamson's fundamental equilibrium exchange rate: Abstracting from the Keynesian business cycle is similar to assuming that economies are in "internal balance." As a result, this approach is often referred to as the macroeconomic balance approach, and it has been widely used by both individual authors and institutions such as the IMF (for an example of the latter, see Isard and Farquee [1998]).

A key feature of the calculations presented here is that I make no attempt to estimate what the sustainable current account is for each country. Instead, I use the model to calculate the set of bilateral rates that are consistent with exogenous projections for these sustainable current accounts. In this sense, the model and analysis are a partial equilibrium exercise.

Partial equilibrium models are not fashionable in macroeconomics. Why not estimate a complete model, which predicts sustainable current accounts as well? (The problem with a partial equilibrium approach is that it may ignore feedback from exchange rates to medium-term savings behavior; see Driver and Wren-Lewis [1999].) The simple answer is that knowledge of what determines consumption and investment in the medium term is far more imprecise than the understanding of aggregate trade relationships. Below, I do examine a general equilibrium version of the model, but this chapter looks only at simulations rather than forecasts.

Traditionally, this partial equilibrium approach to calculating equilibrium exchange rates has been implemented on an individual-country basis, and it has involved in the first instance estimating an effective exchange rate for each country. In a study of the Group of Seven (G-7), Driver and Wren-Lewis (1998) convert these effective exchange rate numbers into bilateral rates. In this chapter, I use the FABEER model, which simultaneously determines bilateral exchange rates for the four major currencies: the dollar, euro, yen, and pound sterling. Appendix 3B outlines the specification of the model in detail. Appendix 3C describes some of the main features of the model's calibration.

The macroeconomic balance approach is quite different from calculations of equilibrium exchange rates based on purchasing power parity (PPP). (Driver and Westaway [2003] present a recent and extensive discussion of alternative equilibrium exchange rate measures.) PPP implies a constant equilibrium exchange rate (EER) independent of shifts in demand or supply, whereas the macroeconomic balance approach would imply a constant EER only if trade competitiveness elasticities were infinite. Barisone, Driver, and Wren-Lewis (2004) suggest that FEER-type calculations track medium-term movements in exchange rates for the G-7 better than does PPP.

Equilibrium Rates for the Four Major Currencies

As a pedagogical device, the equilibrium exchange rate calculation can be split into two stages. In the first stage, the "underlying current account" conditional on actual exchange rates is calculated. This involves cyclical adjustment (i.e., eliminating the business cycle), but it also involves eliminating dynamic and erratic elements in trade. At this first stage, exchange rates are kept at their historical values. The second stage involves moving the exchange rate to its EER to eliminate the gap between the underlying current account and the sustainable current account. The advantage of this two-stage presentation is that the first stage is independent of any assumption about sustainable current accounts, yet it gives a strong indication of the implications for the EER of assuming alternative values for domestic savings and investment.

Underlying Current Accounts

Calculating the underlying current account involves stripping out from the actual current account those elements that are due to the business cycle, and other erratic or temporary effects. In particular, this approach calculates the full implications of any historical change in exchange rates (for given asset stocks). For example, suppose a current account deficit suggests that a currency is overvalued. The J curve tells us that a depreciation might initially lead to a deterioration in the current account. A naive assessment might conclude that a further depreciation was required to achieve a sustainable current account. However, the deterioration following the J curve is temporary, and the model allows one to see past these dynamics.

The danger in using a model to calculate the underlying current account is that the model may be misspecified. Suppose, for example, that there is a permanent but unexplained upward shift in a country's export share. The model on its own will treat this shift as temporary, and ignore it when calculating the underlying current account. As a result, the underlying current account will persistently look worse than the actual data, and the EER will be incorrectly estimated.[3]

Table 3.1 shows the actual and underlying current accounts for the five blocs of FABEER in 2002. (Data for 2003 for some key variables, particularly asset stocks, are incomplete.) The US underlying deficit in 2002 is close to the actual. However, this reflects some offsetting factors. Actual rest of

---

3. Some partial equilibrium macroeconomic balance calculations calculate underlying current accounts by adjusting actual data to take out the effects of the business cycle (i.e., cyclically correcting) and dynamic effects (e.g., Brooks and Hargreaves 2000). This avoids the problem outlined above, but it will also retain any unexplained movements in trade that are in fact temporary. Which method is better amounts to a judgment about how stationary are errors in trade equations.

Table 3.1 Actual and underlying current accounts for FABEER blocs, 2002

Bloc	Actual	Underlying
United States (percent of GDP)	−4.6	−4.6
Japan (percent of GDP)	2.8	4.3
Euro area (percent of GDP)	1.1	3.1
United Kingdom (percent of GDP)	−1.8	−3.5
Rest of world[a] (billions of dollars)	334.9	237.9

FABEER = five-area bilateral equilibrium exchange rate model

a. Including the global statistical discrepancy (i.e., this figure matches exactly the sum of the current accounts of the four major blocs).

Source: OECD Economic Outlook 2003 and author's calculations.

the world (RoW) imports are assumed to be 7 percent below trend levels in 2002, leading to an improvement in the underlying current account based on trend RoW imports. However, we also assume a positive US output gap; underlying output is above actual, so this raises imports. There is also an interesting puzzle associated with recent US export behavior, which is discussed in box 3.1.

In Japan, the underlying surplus is significantly larger than actually recorded. There are three main reasons for this:

■ Despite a large increase in the value of overseas assets in 2002, actual interest receipts did not rise (both as a share of GDP). The model assumes that underlying receipts were higher. Very roughly, this adds 0.5 percent to the underlying surplus.

■ In 2002 the underlying export volume share was well above actuals. This result seems robust to alternative competitiveness elasticities. This adds about 0.5 percent to the underlying surplus.

■ Underlying exports in 2002 are boosted by the fact that underlying RoW imports are well above actual levels, which adds about 0.5 percent to the underlying surplus.

The underlying euro area surplus in 2002 was also significantly larger than the actual surplus. More than 1.5 percent of this is due to higher RoW imports; this figure is well above the impact on Japan and the United States because exports are a much larger share of GDP for the euro bloc.

The underlying UK deficit is larger than the actual, despite the RoW factor (which reduces the underlying deficit by 0.8 percent of GDP). This reflects

■ higher interest receipts than would be expected from the net assets position, worth more than 1 percent in 2002 (preliminary figures for 2003 suggest a much smaller interest payments surplus);

Box 3.1 Recent US export behavior

The model's export equations determine the share of exports in world trade (where world trade is a weighted average of imports from the other blocs of the model) as a function of manufacturing price competitiveness (export prices relative to competitors' export prices). Figure 3.1 shows the actual and predicted values for the volume of US exports of goods and services, where the constant and competitiveness elasticities are estimated by static ordinary least squares during the 1980–2002 period (the latter is 0.96). The equation systematically underpredicts by about 10 percent during the past few years. One could reduce the underprediction by reducing the competitiveness elasticity, but then the equation would fail to track the mid-1980s period (see figure 3.1).

Because the equation is static, short-term errors are explicable, but large systematic errors are problematic. One possible explanation is that the variety of goods produced in the United States has expanded in recent years as the result of a US-based technological shock. I have allowed for this in a simple way by shifting the constant in the equation from the late 1990s onward. However, if this judgment proves incorrect, the model may be significantly underestimating the underlying US current account deficit, and therefore overestimating the equilibrium dollar.

- import volumes that appeared to be unusually low in 2002 (but this appears to have continued in 2003); and

- actual export volumes that were higher than underlying levels in 2002 (although probably much less so in 2003).

Both these last two effects could represent attempts by UK producers to counteract the effects of a perceived temporary appreciation in the exchange rate. Overall preliminary figures for 2003 suggest much less of a gap between actual and underlying deficits, suggesting that perhaps 2002 was somewhat erratic.

These figures give a good indication of the direction that bilateral EERs would move relative to actual exchange rates in 2002. Unless the sustainable Japanese surplus is very high, one would expect an appreciation in the yen, and likewise an appreciation in the euro. In contrast, both the dollar and pound sterling look overvalued.

Alternative Equilibrium Exchange Rates for Different Sustainable Current Account Assumptions

The second and final stage in calculating EERs is to choose some value for sustainable current accounts and to solve for the set of bilateral exchange rates that will produce these sustainable current accounts. However, choosing values for sustainable current accounts, which is difficult at the best of times, seems particularly hazardous at the moment. This is because of two factors, both involving the United States. First, some part of recent US deficits could well be the result of a positive technology shock. Second, it is very difficult to evaluate the trend US fiscal position. Both factors are discussed and modeled below.

Figure 3.1   Actual and predicted US export volumes, 1980–2002

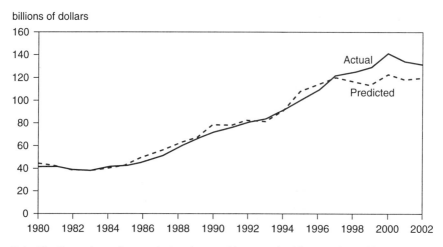

billions of dollars

Note: The figure shows the constant and competitiveness elasticity as estimated by static ordinary least squares.
Source: OECD *Economic Outlook 2003* and author's calculations.

Several tables below show the relationship between exchange rates and a variety of sustainable current accounts. For single-country EER studies, this is reasonably straightforward, because one can look at effective rates and not worry about where any change in surplus or deficit goes. In FABEER, it is necessary to be explicit about the allocation of changes in sustainable current accounts.

In table 3.2, I look at alternative values of the US sustainable deficit using the following simple rule: For each 1 percent increase in the sustainable US deficit, we have an equivalent 0.75 percent increase in the Japanese surplus, and a move to surplus of 0.5 percent in the UK and euro bloc. This allocation means that a larger US deficit is also accompanied by an increase in the RoW surplus.

The table shows the pattern of dollar bilateral rates that would be consistent with different US deficits using the assumed allocation across blocs. In all cases, the sustainable US deficit, and the sustainable Japanese surplus, are smaller than actual current accounts for 2002, and so the equilibrium value of the yen relative to the dollar appreciates substantially compared with actual values.

In addition, the sustainable RoW surplus is much smaller than actual 2002 values. The model does not invent a RoW exchange rate, but it does include a measure of RoW export prices (in dollars), which adjust along with exchange rates to achieve sustainable current accounts (see appendix 3B). In all three cases shown in table 3.2, RoW export prices are much higher than recorded levels in 2002. Implicit, therefore, is a substantial appreciation of

Table 3.2 Equilibrium exchange rates for alternative US sustainable deficits, 2002

US current account (percent of GDP)	Euro area plus UK current account (percent of GDP)	Japan current account (percent of GDP)	Rest of world[a] current account (billions of dollars)	Equilibrium rate		
				Yen-dollar	Dollar-euro	Dollar-pound
Sustainable						
−1.0	0.5	0.75	3	79	1.26	1.70
−2.0	1.0	1.50	23	88	1.18	1.59
−3.0	1.5	2.25	59	98	1.09	1.49
Actual						
−4.6	1.1, −1.8	2.80	337	125	0.94	1.50

a. Including statistical discrepancy. Note that this residual is based on equilibrium exchange rates, not actual exchange rates.

Source: OECD Economic Outlook 2003 and author's calculations.

other currencies against the dollar required to achieve sustainable current accounts. One example of such a currency would be the renminbi, which we examine in the next section.

Table 3.3 varies the sustainable current account for individual blocs relative to the second set above, assuming an offsetting change in the rest of the world (i.e., keeping sustainable current accounts in the other blocs constant).

Increasing the sustainable US deficit from 2 to 3 percent of GDP, with a corresponding increase in the RoW surplus, leads to an appreciation in the dollar of 5.1 percent against the yen, 6.4 percent against the euro, and 5.4 percent against the pound sterling. The euro depreciates against the yen because of relatively stronger Japan–United States links, and likewise for the United Kingdom. (The sensitivity of the euro-sterling cross rate to developments in the United States is highlighted in Wren-Lewis 2003.)

Eliminating the sustainable euro surplus appreciates the euro against the dollar by about 3 percent, with a similar appreciation against the yen. An increase in the sustainable Japanese surplus depreciates the yen by nearly 8 percent. The difference between these two numbers largely reflects the greater openness of the euro area. The United Kingdom is similar to the euro area in this respect. Table 3.4 presents additional cases of surplus/deficit combinations.[4] In the first row, case A, we set the sustainable current account

---

4. Although the model is used to produce table 3.4, as a fairly good approximation we could use tables 3.2 and 3.3 as a "ready reckoner" by assuming linearity and symmetry. For example, using these tables, a 3 percent US deficit combined with a 2.5 percent Japanese surplus would imply a depreciation of 13 percent in the yen relative to the dollar compared with the base case, or a rate of about 100, whereas a model simulation gives a depreciation of 13.5 percent.

Table 3.3   Equilibrium exchange rates for alternative sustainable current accounts, 2002

US current account (percent of GDP)	Euro area current account (percent of GDP)	United Kingdom current account (percent of GDP)	Japan current account (percent of GDP)	Current account for rest of world[a] (billions of dollars)	Equilibrium rate		
					Yen-dollar	Dollar-euro	Dollar-pound
−2.0	1.0	1.0	1.5	23	88.3	1.177	1.592
−3.0	1.0	1.0	1.5	139	92.8	1.106	1.510
−2.0	0.0	1.0	1.5	107	88.2	1.212	1.604
−2.0	1.0	0.0	1.5	40	88.3	1.180	1.629
−2.0	1.0	1.0	2.5	−25	95.3	1.183	1.593

a. Including statistical discrepancy. Note that this residual is based on equilibrium exchange rates, not actual exchange rates.

Source: OECD Economic Outlook 2003 and author's calculations.

equal to the actual current account for 2002. If the trend deficit were equal to the actual deficit in that year, then the equilibrium exchange rate would equal the actual exchange rate. Case A therefore gives us another indication of the extent to which actual current accounts were a misleading indication of trend current accounts. The most notable example is the yen, where the equilibrium rate is ¥113.5/$1, compared with an actual rate for that year of ¥125/$1. This accords with table 3.1, where the underlying surplus in Japan for 2002 is well above the actual surplus, so an appreciation in the yen is required to bring the large trend surplus back to the actual. The euro is also stronger against the dollar, for similar reasons. The second row, case B, simply sets the sustainable current account at half the actual recorded current account. The dollar depreciates substantially relative to actual recorded rates, as we would expect.

Case C of table 3.4 is close to the numbers assumed in Wren-Lewis (2003). This allows for a high sustainable US current account deficit, partly reflecting the impact of a favorable technological shock (see below), with corresponding surpluses for the euro area and Japan. However, there appear to be no grounds for assuming a sustainable UK deficit. The yen is at 100, while the euro is much stronger than it was in 2002, but closer to its actual value in 2003. Case D of the table is based on chapter 2 of this volume by John Williamson; compared with case C, the US sustainable deficit is slightly smaller, and there is no euro area surplus. As a result, the dollar depreciates relative to case C, particularly against the euro.

Other Countries

In this section, I calculate equilibrium bilateral rates for three other currencies: the Australian dollar, the New Zealand dollar, and the Chinese

Table 3.4 Additional cases of equilibrium exchange rates for alternative sustainable current accounts, 2002

| | Current account (percent of GDP) | | | | Equilibrium rate | | |
Case	United States	Japan	Euro area	United Kingdom	Yen-dollar	Dollar-euro	Dollar-pound
A	−4.6	2.8	1.0	−1.8	113.5	0.985	1.451
B	−2.3	1.4	0.5	−0.9	88.8	1.177	1.645
C	−3.0	2.5	1.0	0.0	100.2	1.114	1.547
D	−2.5	2.5	0.0	0.0	97.6	1.185	1.601
Actual exchange rate (2002)					125.0	0.940	1.500
Actual exchange rate (2003)					118.0	1.120	1.627

Source: OECD Economic Outlook 2003 and author's calculations.

renminbi. There is one important difference between the way these currencies are modeled compared with the major four. The major four were modeled simultaneously, so that movements in one currency would have implications for all the others. The three bilateral rates considered here are modeled recursively, so their movements have no impact on the major four.

Australia and New Zealand

Australia and New Zealand are both major commodity exporters. However, commodities account for only about one half of their exports, the remainder being manufactured goods and services. As a result, the demand for these countries' aggregate production will still be sensitive to the real exchange rate, so the overall approach of the model remains valid. Appendices 3A and 3B show how the specification of the model needs to change to allow for a significant proportion of commodity exports.

Both Australia and New Zealand have run large current account deficits in recent years. In both cases, I make the fairly arbitrary assumption that the sustainable deficit is 4 percent of GDP. Although I assume that developments in these two economies do not influence the major four currencies, I do allow interaction between the two.

Table 3.5 presents rates for the Australian and New Zealand dollars against the four major currencies, based on the sustainable current accounts for the major four set out in case C of table 3.4. Both currencies were undervalued against the US dollar in 2002. However, the subsequent depreciation of the US dollar has completely reversed this position, with both currencies appreciating strongly. Against a basket of currencies, both the Australian and New Zealand currencies appeared close to their equilibrium value in 2002, so they have become significantly overvalued (against all of the major four) in 2003 and 2004 (for

Table 3.5 Selected equilibrium bilateral exchange rates for New Zealand and Australian dollars, 2002
(actual rates for 2002 in parentheses)

Currency	New Zealand dollar	Australian dollar
US dollar	1.96 (2.16)	1.65 (1.84)
New Zealand dollar		0.84 (0.85)
Australian dollar	1.19 (1.18)	
Euro	2.19 (2.03)	1.84 (1.72)
Pound sterling	3.03 (3.23)	2.56 (2.76)
Yen	0.02 (0.02)	0.02 (0.01)

Source: OECD Economic Outlook 2003 and author's calculations.

more details, see Wren-Lewis 2004). Note, however, that the two currencies were close to equilibrium against each other in 2002; the two tend to move together.

Because both are "commodity currencies," it is interesting to note how changes in commodity prices would influence the two equilibrium rates. Wren-Lewis (2004) shows that a sustained 10 percent increase in all commodity prices would lead to an appreciation in both currencies (in effective terms) of 5 percent. This is toward the lower end of the range estimated in Chen and Rogoff (2003). There are two main effects at work here. First, higher commodity prices raise the value of exports and improve the underlying current account. Second, higher export prices raise the profitability of commodity production, which diverts labor toward this sector and away from other traded goods production. Lower output of noncommodity traded goods implies a higher price.

China

Calculations for China are more uncertain, for two reasons. First, I have fewer data for Chinese trade, with no breakdown of values into volumes and prices.[5] Second, the Chinese economy is more likely to be subject to structural change.

For China, I have calibrated the trade value equations with the following properties: an imposed import competitiveness elasticity of 0.5,[6] an activity elasticity for imports of 1.6 (which, given the above, fits data from

---

5. Data come from the International Monetary Fund, *International Financial Statistics*. The model therefore includes equations for export and import values, which simply combine the specifications for trade prices and volumes; see appendix 3B.

6. Assuming that a 1 percent increase in world prices will raise import prices by 0.7 percent.

Table 3.6   Putting China's current account to trend, 2002
           (percent of GDP)

Aspect	Current account
Actual	2.9
Excluding erratic trade	2.6
World activity to trend	3.0
World activity and commodity prices to trend	3.4

Source: OECD Economic Outlook 2003 and author's calculations.

1990 to 2003), a competitiveness elasticity of exports of –2,[7] and a trend rise in the export share of about 11 percent a year (which again fits the 1990–2003 period).

Once again the calculation was split into two stages. First, I calculate the underlying current account using actual exchange rates. Second, I consider the implications of alternative values for the sustainable current account. Table 3.6 shows that in 2002, the underlying current account surplus was a little larger than the actual surplus. This is partly because actual imports in the RoW were below trend, and partly because trend oil prices were below actual.

The underlying surplus in 2003 is likely to be larger still. The depreciation of the renminbi in 2002 and 2003, following the US dollar, helped lead to a large increase in exports. The actual current account surplus did not rise substantially, but this is mainly due to a very rapid increase in imports. This increase in imports cannot be explained by higher activity or competitiveness, and so it is likely to be erratically high. As a result, the underlying surplus for 2003 is likely to be substantially higher than the actual.

Table 3.7 looks at an equilibrium exchange rate against the dollar, euro, and yen for 2002 either assuming a 1 percent sustainable surplus or current account balance. (For contrasting views on whether the sustainable current account for China is a small surplus or a deficit, see Bosworth [2004] and Goldstein and Lardy [2003].) Even with a 1 percent surplus, the analysis suggests a 20 percent depreciation against the dollar.

Global Implications of Two US Shocks

Above, I identified two major uncertainties associated with the sustainable US current account. The first was in assessing the implications of a US-

---

7. Assuming that a 1 percent increase in world prices will raise export prices by 0.7 percent. This high value relative to those assumed for the major 4 seems justified given that, at this stage of development, the economy is likely to be producing relatively homogenous manufactured goods.

Table 3.7 Renminbi equilibrium exchange rate with alternative sustainable current accounts, 2002

Sustainable current account	US dollar	Euro	Yen
Actual	8.28	7.79	0.066
Assuming 1 percent surplus	6.71	7.47	0.067
Assuming current account balance	6.47	7.21	0.065

Source: OECD Economic Outlook 2003 and author's calculations.

based technology shock. The second was in judging the size and impact of future government budget deficits. Both issues are examined here. To do so, we transform our partial equilibrium model into a general equilibrium model of the four major currency blocs.

Completing the model requires specifying the determinants of domestic demand: consumption and investment. The consumption functions split consumers into two types: those who are credit constrained, who consume all their current income; and those who are not, whose spending depends on discounted lifetime income and financial wealth (see appendix 3B for the details). The discount rate used by non-credit-constrained consumers exceeds the real rate of interest because of uncertainty, including uncertainty about the time of death. (This is the Blanchard-Yaari formulation, where there are no bequests.) We therefore have two departures from Ricardian Equivalence.

The investment equations are based on a Tobin q model, with share prices depending on expected future profits. There are therefore two forward elements in the model: expected future labor income and expected future profits.

A US Fiscal Shock

Examining the global implications of a US fiscal shock is something of a "standard simulation" for global models; for example, see Ralph Bryant (1995). However, these simulations have often focused on the short-term dynamics associated with Keynesian multipliers. Instead, FABEER looks at the medium term.

The fiscal shock used here is a tax cut, worth 1 percent of GDP in 2004, which declines by 0.05 percent of GDP each year. Overlaid on this is a reaction function for tax, which raises taxes in response to higher government debt. Tables 3.8 and 3.9 give figures for tax and debt as a share of GDP.

It is instructive to look at a preliminary simulation, where real interest rates are fixed (table 3.8). Fixed real rates imply fixed investment, output, and capital. The absence of Ricardian Equivalence means that consumption increases by about half the decrease in taxes. The increase in consumption,

**Table 3.8   US fiscal shock with fixed interest rates,
selected years** (percent of GDP)

	2004	2010	2015
US tax	−0.91	−0.37	−0.13
US debt	0.88	3.26	3.22
US consumption	0.39	0.15	0.02
US current account	−0.45	−0.23	−0.11
Dollar appreciation against:			
Yen (percent)	2.2	0.7	0.2
Euro (percent)	3.0	0.8	0.1
Pound (percent)	2.6	0.7	0.1

Source: OECD Economic Outlook 2003 and author's calculations.

coupled with an appreciation in the dollar, generates a deterioration in the trade balance, leading to a current account deficit of about half the size of the tax cut. This is the familiar twin deficits story. The size of the current account deficit depends critically on the degree on non-Ricardian behavior. In the main case, the proportion of income going to credit-constrained consumers is 30 percent; reducing this to 10 percent would halve the current account effect.

The current account deficit is associated with an appreciation of the dollar against all currencies. The appreciation is slightly greater against the euro than the yen, reflecting the factors discussed above. The depreciation of nondollar currencies reduces real incomes and consumption in those countries, leading to small surpluses. It is interesting to note that the relationship between US deficits and exchange rate changes from the partial equilibrium model shown in tables 3.2 and 3.3 still holds to a first approximation in this general equilibrium version of the model.

Once one endogenizes interest rates, some of the quantitative conclusions change substantially. US real interest rates do not rise by much: just 6 basis points initially, with a gradual reduction thereafter. This is very much at the lower end of the range noted in Mühleisen and Towe (2004), although not as low as one estimate by the George W. Bush administration. However, it is enough to substantially dampen the increase in US consumption and current account deficit, with a correspondingly smaller appreciation in the dollar.

A US Technology Shock

Table 3.10 shows the impact of technical progress, which added 0.2 percent to GDP each year from 1996 to 2000, so that GDP is at least 1 percent higher from 2000 onward. The simulation starts in 1995, implying that the full

Table 3.9 US fiscal shock with endogenous interest rates, selected years (percent of GDP)

	2004	2010	2015
US tax	−0.91	−0.36	−0.12
US debt	0.90	3.36	3.32
US consumption	0.15	0.08	0.03
US interest rates (basis points)	6	4	3
US current account	−0.15	−0.10	−0.06
US GDP (percent)	0.00	−0.01	−0.02
Dollar appreciation against:			
Yen (percent)	0.7	0.3	0.1
Euro (percent)	0.8	0.4	0.1
Pound (percent)	0.7	0.4	0.1

Source: OECD Economic Outlook 2003 and author's calculations.

1 percent gain is anticipated from 1995. Anticipation is very important in assessing the current account implications of this technical progress shock.

The US current account goes into deficit following the technology shock principally because consumers and firms anticipate higher future incomes and production. (Consumption remains higher as a share of GDP after 2000 in this simulation because taxes are cut following a reduction in the debt/GDP ratio.) The majority of consumers attempt to smooth consumption, and therefore consumption rises in advance of the increase in GDP. Firms invest to build the capital stock, although the parameters in the model imply that the increase in investment is fairly slow.

However, both effects are significantly dampened by an increase in US interest rates. The short-term reduction in US net savings puts significant pressure on global financial markets, leading to an increase in US interest rates of nearly 20 basis points. Without this increase in interest rates, the current account deficit as a share of GDP in 1995 would have been more than 0.6 percent of GDP, compared with the 0.2 percent shown in table 3.10.

In the model, the dollar depreciates as a result of this shock. The reason is that higher GDP leads to an increase in imports, but there is no corresponding rise in overseas demand to raise exports. As a result, a real depreciation is required. The depreciation is modest to begin with, but it rises to between 1.5 and 2.0 percent in the medium term.

The model produces this result because it implicitly assumes that higher US GDP involves producing more of the same type of goods, so those goods have to be made cheaper to create additional demand. In this particular context, it makes more sense to assume that the United States is producing new types of goods, which would lead to an autonomous increase in exports. (See box 3.1 on p. 42 for some evidence on this.) If this shift in the demand for US exports were enough to leave the long-run

Table 3.10   US technical progress shock, selected years

Aspect of shock	1995	1998	2000	2005
US GDP (percent)	0.00	0.61	1.02	1.05
US consumption (percent of GDP)	0.18	0.12	0.08	0.08
US interest rates (basis points)	18.00	17.0	0.00	−1.00
US current account (percent of GDP)	−0.19	−0.04	0.08	0.07

Source: OECD Economic Outlook 2003 and author's calculations.

value of the dollar unchanged, then the short-term appreciation of the dollar due to higher consumption and investment might be about 1 percent.

Conclusions

Simulations of a general equilibrium version of FABEER confirm that an anticipated technology shock and a fiscal expansion in the US will both increase the value of the sustainable current account deficit. However, the model also suggests that both shocks will lead to increases in US interest rates that significantly dampen this current account effect.

The results are of course sensitive to the calibration of the model. However, they do provide a guide to the qualitative significance of both shocks. If the technology shock that hit the United States had been large enough, it could have accounted for a good part of the increase in the deficit observed at the end of the 1990s and early 2000. However, this current account effect is significant only during the period in which the technology shock is anticipated but not yet realized. It seems unlikely that it could justify a deficit continuing into the second half of the decade, particularly because the technology gain is likely to be dispersed to other countries. A sustainable deficit in the second half of this decade would be a consequence of the US fiscal expansion during the period, although a maximum figure here would seem to be about 1 percent of GDP.

References

Alberola, E., S. Cervero, H. Lopez, and A. Ubide. 1999. *Global Equilibrium Exchange Rates: Euro, Dollar, "Ins," "Outs," and Other Major Currencies in a Panel Cointegration Framework*. IMF Working Paper WP/99/175. Washington: International Monetary Fund.

Anderton, B., B. Pesaran, and Simon Wren-Lewis. 1992. Imports, Output and the Demand for Manufactures. *Oxford Economic Papers* 44: 175–86.

Barisone, G., R. Driver, and Simon Wren-Lewis. N.d. Are Our FEERs Justified? *Journal of International Money and Finance*, forthcoming.

Bosworth, B. 2004. Valuing the Renminbi. Brookings Institution, Washington. Photocopy (February).

Brooks, A., and D. Hargreaves. 2000. *A Macroeconomic Balance Measure of New Zealand's Equilibrium Exchange Rate*. Reserve Bank of New Zealand Discussion Paper 2000-10. Wellington: Reserve Bank of New Zealand.

Bryant, Ralph C., ed. 1995. *International Coordination of National Stabilisation Policies*. Washington: Brookings Institution Press.

Chen, Y., and K. Rogoff. 2003. Commodity Currencies. *Journal of International Economics* 60: 133–60.

Driver, R., and P. Westaway. 2003. Concepts of Equilibrium Exchange Rates. In *Exchange Rates, Capital Flows and Policy*, ed. R. Driver, P. Sinclair, and C. Thoenissen. London: Routledge.

Driver, R., and Simon Wren-Lewis. 1999. FEERs: A Sensitivity Analysis. In *Equilibrium Exchange Rates*, ed. R. MacDonald and J. Stein. Boston: Kluwer Academic Publishers.

Dvornak, N., M. Kohler, and G. Menzies. 2003. *Australia's Medium-Term Exchange Rate: A Macroeconomic Balance Approach*. Canberra: Reserve Bank of Australia Discussion Paper 2003-03.

Goldstein, M., and N. Lardy. 2003. A Modest Proposal for China's Renminbi. *Financial Times*, August 26.

Houthakker, H., and S. P. Magee. 1969. Income and Price Elasticities in World Trade. *Review of Economics and Statistics* 51: 111–25.

Isard, P., and H. Farquee, eds. 1998. *Exchange Rate Assessment: Extensions of the Macroeconomic Balance Approach*. IMF Occasional Paper 167. Washington: International Monetary Fund.

Lane, P. 2001. The New International Macroeconomics: A Survey. *Journal of International Economics* 54: 235–66.

Lane, P. R., and G. M. Milesi-Ferretti. 2002. External Wealth, the Trade Balance, and the Real Exchange Rate. *European Economic Review* 46: 1049–71.

Mühleisen, M., and C. Towe, eds. 2004. *US Fiscal Policies and Priorities for Long-Run Sustainability*. IMF Occasional Paper 227. Washington: International Monetary Fund.

Williamson, John. 1985. *The Exchange Rate System*. Washington: Institute for International Economics.

Williamson, John. 1994. *Estimating Equilibrium Exchange Rates*. Washington: Institute for International Economics.

Woodford, Michael. 2003. *Interest and Prices: Foundations of a Theory of Monetary Policy*. Princeton, NJ: Princeton University Press.

Wren-Lewis, Simon. 2003. *Estimates of Equilibrium Exchange Rates for Sterling Against the Euro*. London: UK Treasury.

Wren-Lewis, Simon. 2004. *A Model of Equilibrium Exchange Rates for the New Zealand and Australian Dollar*. Reserve Bank of New Zealand Discussion Paper. Wellington: Reserve Bank of New Zealand.

Wren-Lewis, Simon, and Rebecca, Driver. 1998. *Real Exchange Rates for the Year 2000*. Washington: Institute for International Economics.

Appendix 3A
Microfoundations

This appendix outlines the microfoundations of the FABEER implementation of the macroeconomic balance approach. This approach to estimating equilibrium exchange rates dates back at least as far as Williamson (1985) and has at its heart aggregate trade equations that have an even longer pedigree (e.g., Houthakker and Magee 1969). However, it would be a mistake to condemn this approach as "old-fashioned." In fact, it fits in with one of the central characteristics of the new international macroeconomics (Lane 2001), which stresses the importance of imperfect competition in the market for traded goods.[8]

A Baseline Model

Consider the following, deliberately simple, small open economy. There are two goods, one produced overseas (subscript w) and one produced domestically (subscript z). Assume that all domestically produced goods are exported, so that only overseas goods are consumed. Production only requires labor, and the production function is simply

$$Y_z = a_z L_z = a_z L \tag{3A.1}$$

where Y is output and L total labor supply. For simplicity, assume that labor supply is fixed. Producers face a demand curve for their product, given by

$$Y_z = A(p_z/p_w)^{-\theta} \tag{3A.2}$$

where $\theta > 1$, and p_z/p_w are the terms of trade, both measured in a common currency.

If we assume a time period in which prices are fully flexible, such that demand and supply are equal ("internal balance"), then we have

$$a_z L = A(p_z/p_w)^{-\theta} \tag{3A.3}$$

This equation determines the terms of trade. A country-specific increase in labor productivity will require a depreciation (a fall in p_z) to sell the additional goods, while an increase in world demand (A) will generate an appreciation. Viewing the real exchange rate as a relative price equating domestic aggregate supply and demand is a key characteristic of the macroeconomic balance approach.

---

8. A macroeconomic balance approach can be rationalized using more traditional microfoundations using perfect competition, as in Dvornak, Kohler, and Menzies (2003).

We can define three measures of the real exchange rate in this economy:

- the terms of trade,
- the price of output at home relative to overseas, and
- the price of consumption at home relative to overseas.

In this very simple model, the first two definitions are equal, while the third is always unity, if we assume the economy is small so that overseas consumers mainly consume good w.

The consumption real exchange rate becomes endogenous if we add nontraded goods, denoted by subscript N. Consumer preferences across the two goods are given by

$$U = c_N^\epsilon c_W^{1-\epsilon} \qquad (3A.4)$$

so we get the standard result that the share of each good in total consumption is constant, that is,

$$c_N p_N = \epsilon(c_N p_N + c_W p_W) = \epsilon(Y_N p_N + Y_Z p_Z) \qquad (3A.5)$$

assuming no savings.

The markup in the export-producing sector from profit maximization is given by

$$p_Z = \frac{w}{a_Z} \frac{\theta}{\theta - 1}. \qquad (3A.6)$$

If wages are equal for labor in the traded and nontraded sectors, then relative prices will be given by

$$\frac{p_Z}{p_N} = \frac{a_N}{a_Z} B(..) \qquad (3A.7)$$

where a_N represents productivity in the nontraded sector, and $B(..)$ will be a function of variables such as demand elasticities. Given the demand function for nontraded goods (and $C_N = Y_N$), we can write

$$a_Z L = A(p_Z/p_W)^{-\theta} B'(\epsilon, \theta, ..). \qquad (3A.8)$$

Once again, the terms of trade move to equate domestic demand and supply. The output price real exchange rate will move with the terms of trade, but it will also depend on relative productivity movements between traded and nontraded goods.

Given preferences, the consumer price index (CPI) will be given by

$$CPI = p_N^\epsilon p_W^{1-\epsilon}. \qquad (3A.9)$$

We can immediately see that the consumer price real exchange rate will no longer be constant but will depend on the terms of trade (with an elasticity ϵ). In addition, relative productivity movements between traded and nontraded goods will influence this definition of the real exchange rate, which is the Balassa-Samuelson effect.

The macroeconomic balance approach is often described as finding the real exchange rate that brings about a particular current account. In this simple economy with no financial assets, the current account is always zero. Exports are given by the demand function in 3A.2 above, while imports are given by the demand curve

$$c_W p_W = (1 - \epsilon)(Y_N p_N + Y_Z p_Z). \tag{3A.10}$$

Equating exports and import solves for the terms of trade in exactly the same way as equation 3A.8. Export equations typically used in macroeconomic balance models are exactly of the form of equation 3A.2, where A is some measure of world trade or world demand. Import equations typically take the traditional form

$$c_W = M(Y, p_W/p_D) \tag{3A.11}$$

where Y is a measure of total output and p_D is the price of that output. This formulation again follows naturally from equation 3A.10.[9]

In this simple model, export prices are a markup on domestic costs, and import prices (in overseas currency terms) are exogenously determined overseas. Empirical data for the major industrial economies strongly suggest a more complex picture, where export prices are influenced in part by competitors' prices, and import prices depend in part on the price of domestically produced goods. If p_{MD} and p_{XD} respectively denote the price of actual imports and exports, we can write

$$p_{MD} = p_W^\gamma p_D^{1-\gamma}, $$
$$p_{XD} = p_W^\delta p_D^{1-\delta}. \tag{3A.12}$$

The trade balance can then be written as

$$p_{XD} A (p_{XD}/p_W)^{-\vartheta} - p_{MD} M(Y, p_{MD}/p_D). \tag{3A.13}$$

Assuming some value for the trade balance, world demand A and total domestic output Y, we can use expressions 3A.12 and 3A.13 to solve for the output price exchange rate p_D/p_W.

---

9. Once we allow for saving, so that the current account may not be balanced, then whether the activity term should be total output or total domestic demand becomes an issue.

Adding Commodity Trade

Not all trade in advanced industrial countries can be characterized as selling differentiated goods in imperfectly competitive markets. However, if we identify such trade as involving commodities (i.e., not manufactured goods or services),[10] then the proportion of such goods in imports is typically small: often about 10 percent and rarely exceeding 25 percent. In such cases, a very simple way to incorporate such trade into the macroeconomic balance framework is to define *total* import and export prices, p_M and p_X, as

$$p_M = p_{MD}^{\kappa} p_C^{1-\kappa}$$
$$p_X = p_{XD}^{\lambda} p_C^{1-\lambda}$$

(3A.14)

where p_C are world commodity prices, and $1 - \kappa$ and $1 - \lambda$ are the share of these commodities in total trade. The trade balance can then be written as

$$p_X A (p_{XD}/p_W)^{-\vartheta} - p_M M(Y, p_{MD}/p_D)$$

(3A.15)

where it is assumed that trade in commodities is demand inelastic. This is how commodity production is treated in the FABEER model.

Although this approach may be an appropriate simplification when commodity production is small, it becomes problematic when a significant proportion of exports involves commodities. In Australia and New Zealand, nearly half of exports are commodities.

If *all* domestic exports involved commodities, then the macroeconomic balance approach would no longer be an appropriate way to determine real exchange rates. The price of exported goods would now be determined on world markets, and so the terms of trade would be exogenously given by world conditions. Shifts in domestic supply would have no impact on the terms of trade. Note, however, that PPP would not hold for such an economy, because shifts in the price of exported commodities would influence nontraded goods prices and therefore the CPI.

The more interesting case (at least for Australia and New Zealand) is where there is mixed commodity/differentiated goods production. In one extreme case, adding commodity production would make no difference to the way we model trade—if the proportion of labor going to produce commodity exports was fixed. The terms of trade for differentiated goods production (p_{XD}/p_{MD}) would still move to equate demand for exports with supply, where supply was now some fixed proportion of total labor. However, this extreme case is unlikely to be realistic; an increase in the

---

10. Of course, in reality, some manufactures or services may be fairly homogenous goods and some national commodity production may be facing a downward-sloping demand curve.

price of commodities relative to differentiated exports goods would attract labor into the commodity-producing sector.

An alternative extreme case is where the production function for commodities is linear. In this case commodity prices would effectively set wages and, given equation 3A.6, the price of differentiated goods exports. The demand curve for these goods would simply give the proportion of labor in this sector, with any residual labor used to produce commodities.

A more likely case is where commodity production is subject to decreasing returns to scale. As a simple example, suppose commodity production (denoted by subscript O) is governed by the following production function:

$$L_O = a_{O1}Y_O + \frac{a_{O2}}{2} Y_O^2. \tag{3A.16}$$

Wage equalization implies

$$Y_O = \frac{1}{a_{O2}} \left(\frac{\theta - 1}{\theta a_z} \frac{p_O}{p_z} - a_{O1} \right). \tag{3A.17}$$

Total exports now become

$$p_X \left[A(p_{XD}/p_W)^{-\vartheta} + \frac{1}{a_{O2}} \left(\frac{\theta - 1}{\theta a_z} \frac{p_O}{p_z} - a_{O1} \right) \right]. \tag{3A.18}$$

This is a hybrid demand and supply relationship. The volume of total exports continues to be influenced by world demand and competitiveness, but now the share of differentiated goods production in total exports reduces their impact. A rise in relative commodity prices *for a given level of differentiated goods competitiveness* will raise total exports, by shifting labor into the commodity-producing sector. In the model as a whole, of course, such a relative price shift would reduce the supply of differentiated goods production, requiring a rise in its price to choke off demand.

Data Availability and Model Specification

For the four major blocs in the FABEER model, trade is determined by equations of the form 3A.12, 3A.14, and 3A.15. Data on noncommodity trade prices are not generally available, so we use manufacturing trade prices as a proxy. The GDP deflator is used as a measure of P_D.

In the case of Australia, data on manufacturing trade prices were not available. However, a series for the price of manufacturing output is published, denoted by P_I. It seems reasonable that we can augment expression 3A.12 in the following way:

$$p_{MD} = p_W^\gamma p_I^{1-\gamma}$$

$$p_{XD} = p_W^\delta p_I^{1-\delta} \qquad\qquad (3A.12a)$$

$$p_I = p_W^\kappa p_D^{1-\kappa}.$$

As a result, we can substitute P_I for P_{XD} and P_{MD} in the trade volume equations.

In the case of China, the IMF publishes data on trade values only. However, we can write out value equations by simply combining the specifications for price and quantity discussed above. The details are set out in appendix 3B.

The Partial Equilibrium Approach

The system just described represents one part of a complete macroeconomy; for the complete model, we need to add equations for domestic output and overseas demand, as well as determinates of the capital flows that have to match any trade balance. In fact such a structure does represent many if not most large macroeconometric models (e.g., see Williamson 1994). However, the partial equilibrium approach to calculating equilibrium exchange rates treats these variables as exogenous inputs.

For such a partial equilibrium approach to be completely valid, the economy would have to have a recursive structure, where the real exchange rate did not influence medium-term capital flows or the trend level of output. There are a number of economic mechanisms that mean that this assumption is bound to be false; the key issue is rather whether it represents a useful approximation. There is a partial discussion of this issue in Driver and Wren-Lewis (1999). Above, this chapter suggests that feedback from the equilibrium exchange rate to the sustainable current account is not strong enough to make the partial equilibrium calculations grossly misleading.

Appendix 3B
FABEER Model Specification

This appendix describes the basic structure of the five-area bilateral equilibrium exchange rate model.

Notation

Let X_i denote variable X for country/bloc i. Two "atypical" blocs are the rest of the world ($i = r$) and the United States ($i = u$). Suppose there are n blocs, including r and u.

Exchange Rate Determination

Suppose, for simplicity, that export prices for country i = domestic prices for i. For each country, we define p_i as an index of domestic prices in dollars. The trade balance for country i in nominal dollars is given by

$$p_i x_i(p_i, all\ p_j\ j \neq i) - pm_i(all\ p_j\ j \neq i)m_i(p_i, all\ p_j\ j \neq i) \qquad (3B.1)$$

where $x_i(..)$ are real exports (measured in base year dollars), $pm_i(..)$ the import deflator, and $m_i(..)$ real imports for i. (We ignore all other arguments in these functions for simplicity, and we take the standard homogeneity assumptions as given.) The sum of each of these expressions across all i (including $i = r$) must equal zero, or whatever the world current account balance is (which we take as exogenous). As a result, we can drop one of these expressions (specifically $i = r$), which will then be determined by the residual. We lose no information by doing this, although it also allows us to avoid issues of cross-equation restrictions, which may or may not be a good thing.

Suppose that for each bloc we have some exogenous projection for the current account/GDP ratio = cay, and also assume interest flows are zero (so trade balance = current balance). We could then write $n - 1$ equations of the form

$$cay_i = \{x_i(p_i, all\ p_j\ j \neq i) - pm_i(all\ p_j\ j \neq i)m_i(p_i, all\ p_j\ j \neq i)/p_i\}/y_i \qquad (3B.2)$$

where y_i is real GDP (also exogenous). For each country, we also define pdc_i as domestic prices *in domestic currency terms*, which we also assume is exogenous. (The exogeneity of pdc is innocuous, for the model is essentially defined in real terms.[11]) Thus we have

---

11. One can also think of monetary policy as targeting output price inflation, so the exogeneity assumption may not be unreasonable.

$$p_i = ex0_i \, pdc_i / ex_i \qquad\qquad\qquad (3B.3)$$

where ex_i is the dollar exchange rate (currency per dollar), and $ex0$ this value in the base year, for all i—except u.

Equation 3B.2 represents $n-1$ independent equations determining $n-1$ unknowns ex_i. This includes an equation for cay_u, which can be thought of as an equation "determining" ex_r, although of course all equations determine all unknowns simultaneously.[12] The model therefore determines all bilateral dollar rates, with no need to work backward from effective rates to bilaterals (e.g., as in Wren-Lewis and Driver [1998], or as reduced-form studies like Alberola et al. [1999] need to do).

One problem may appear to be that ex_r does not in practice exist. However, we simply omit equation 3B.3 for $i = r$, and 3B.2 still determines p_r. Data for p_i may exist, but we could use instead a measure of export prices—see below.

The Trade Model for Each Country

For each country except $i = r$, we need to elaborate on our model of trade determination. We drop the assumption above about export prices, and we introduce three new variables: px, the export price deflator; qx, the manufacturing export price; and qm, the manufacturing import price—defined in dollars for each i. We assume that each deflator is a function of the manufacturing price and a country-specific weighted commodity price index:

$$px = qx^a cx^{(1-a)} \qquad\qquad\qquad (3B.4)$$

$$pm = qm^b cm^{(1-b)} \qquad\qquad\qquad (3B.5)$$

where cx and cm are the commodity price bundles, a and b are parameters that can be derived from data on the composition of trade, and we drop the i subscript because these equations are common across all i, $i \neq r$. (These equations will in practice need constants and possibly trends, reflecting measurement errors and trade in services.)

For both qx and qm, we assume that prices are a weighted average of domestic prices and other countries' export prices; that is,

$$qx_i = p_i^c \left(\sum_{j \neq i} wx_{ij} qx_j \right)^{1-c} \qquad\qquad\qquad (3B.6)$$

$$qm_i = p_i^d \left(\sum_{j \neq i} wm_{ij} qx_j \right)^{1-d} \qquad\qquad\qquad (3B.7)$$

---

12. Using iterative solution techniques here may be tricky, because p_i does not appear on the left-hand side of any of these equations.

where c and d are again parameters (to be calibrated), and wx and wm are weights summing to 1 (which can be derived from direction of trade statistics). Finally, we have the specification of the two volume equations. For imports, we have

$$m = m(y, qm/p). \tag{3B.8}$$

The function $m(..)$ is partly calibrated, but its constant at least is estimated. There are three problematic issues here. The first is using y as the activity measure. It could be replaced by TFE (i.e., $y + m$) or by a weighted demand variable. The second is the log-linear specification, which is not consistent with a log-linear model for the demand for domestic output (see Anderton, Pesaran, and Wren-Lewis 1992). The third is that qm/p is not an ideal measure of competitiveness, because p contains many non-traded goods, and traded goods that are not subject to strong competitiveness effects (like commodities). One possibility here is to define an additional domestic price variable (e.g., a price of domestic manufactures), and add a linking equation between this and the GDP deflator p. The disadvantage of this is that domestic manufacturing prices are likely to depend on overseas prices to some extent, so the system becomes complex in terms of simultaneity.

For exports, we have

$$x_i \Big/ \Big(\sum_{j \neq i} wd_{ij} m_j \Big) = f \Big[qx_i \Big/ \Big(\sum_{j \neq i} wc_{ij} qx_j \Big) \Big]. \tag{3B.9}$$

The function $f(..)$ is calibrated, but its constant is estimated. Here wd and wc are weights (based on direction of trade statistics) reflecting the direction of exports and third-party competition respectively. The equations say that the share of exports in a weighted demand variable is a function of export price competitiveness.

Exchange Rate Determination Revisited, and the RoW Bloc

Specifying the trade equations allows us to delineate more precisely how countries interact. There are two forms of interaction: (1) Changes in imports in one country influence exports in another; and (2) changes in export prices in one country influence other countries both by changing import prices and through export competitiveness.

Output prices only influence other countries via these two effects. As a result, it is not necessary to define output prices for the rest of the world. Instead, the endogenous "exchange rate" variable for this bloc will be qx: manufacturing export prices.

What about RoW imports? In this exercise, they are treated exogenously, although in Wren-Lewis (2003) they did vary with qx.

Interest Flows

The IMF publishes data on the stock of overseas assets held by domestic residents and domestic assets held by overseas residents. We can calculate an implicit rate of return by combining this information with recorded interest flows (*ipd*). Modeling these flows involves two major problems. First, the composition of assets by type is diverse, and so modeling the return is likely to be very difficult. A nominal deposit will attract the (short) nominal interest rate. There will be an inflation loss on these assets, but this is not recorded in the official data. An indexed deposit will suffer no inflation loss and will return a real interest rate. Shares will receive dividends, which appear in the data, plus some capital gain that is not recorded there. Direct investment returns a profit stream. Ex ante, arbitrage should ensure that the total return on all these assets should be equal after allowing for risk premia. However, the data do not measure the total return (i.e., they exclude capital gains), and ex post there will be unexpected gains and losses.

The second major problem involves modeling changes in the asset stock. Historic estimates of EERs have normally been conditional on actual stocks (the EER is a flow equilibrium, not a stock equilibrium concept), so at first sight no modeling may appear necessary. However, overseas assets will be held in different currencies, and it is important to allow deviations in the EER from actual rates to influence asset stocks. Uncovered interest parity (UIP) should ensure that expected capital gains are offset by interest rate differentials, but the data only record the latter and there will be unexpected gains and losses.

Tackling the first problem for a simple model involves making heroic assumptions that do the least damage to the EER estimates. A key aspect of EER estimates is that they abstract from cyclical effects. Because the economic cycle is likely to influence interest rates as much as output, it would be inconsistent to use actual interest rates in modeling *ipd*, although this has been the approach normally adopted in the literature. Instead, what we do here is construct a synthetic "smoothed world *ipd* return" time series, and then relate *ipd* returns for each country to this rate, using a simple linear relationship:

$$ipd\ return_{it} = a + b\ world\ ipd\ return_t \tag{3B.10}$$

This enables us to take account of any permanent differences that appear to occur in individual countries' rates of return (see Lane and Milesi-Ferretti 2002) and knock out any cyclical effects. However, any persistent but temporary idiosyncratic movements in returns will be lost.

We also want the dollar value of assets to move in simulations with changes in the exchange rate. We can define a simple "deviation from base" equation as

$$a_i = \hat{a}_i \sum_j w_{ij} p_j / \hat{p}_j \tag{3B.11}$$

where a "hat" over a term denotes the base value, and w is a set of weights reflecting the proportion of currency j assets in total assets for country i.

Previous FEER studies have implicitly treated these weights w as equal to the weights in the effective exchange rate index, although in some studies a percentage of US overseas assets is assumed to be in dollars. Equation 3B.11 offers greater flexibility.

Smaller Countries

The specification of the New Zealand (NZ) bloc is very similar to the typical non-US bloc, with two key exceptions. First, neither NZ imports nor export prices are involved in the weighted world trade or price variables discussed above. This makes the NZ bloc recursive.

The same is true for the Australian bloc, although Australian imports and export prices do influence New Zealand variables and vice versa. However, Australia differs from New Zealand in that there are no manufacturing export or import price series. Instead, we define an additional variable, domestic manufacturing prices. This variable depends on total domestic output prices, plus a trend. The variable then replaces the two missing manufacturing trade price series in determining import volumes, total import prices, total export prices, and export volumes, as well as NZ manufacturing export and import prices.

The second difference in the Australian and New Zealand blocs is in the aggregate export equation. This adapts equation 3B.9 above in two ways. First, the coefficient on world trade and price competitiveness is halved, to allow for the fact that only about half these countries' exports are relative price and demand sensitive. Second, we add a term in the relative price of commodity production to manufacturing exports. If this term rises, commodity production becomes more profitable, and labor moves into commodity production and away from other export goods. (See appendix 3A for more details on this derivation.)

For the China bloc, there is no volume/price split at all. Instead, the model has reduced-form equations for total values (exports and imports). Specifically, the share of exports in total GDP is given by

$$
px_i \cdot x_i / p_i y_i = qx_i^a cx_i^{1-a} \sum_{j=majors} wd_j \cdot m_j \left(\frac{qx_i}{\sum_{j=majors} wc_j \cdot qx_j} \right)^\beta \Big/ p_i y_i
$$

$$
= \left(p_i^c \left(\sum_{j=majors} wc_j \cdot qx_j \right)^{1-c} \right)^{a+\beta} cx_i^{1-a} \sum_{j=majors} wd_j \cdot m_j \left(\sum_{j=majors} wc_j \cdot qx_j \right)^{-\beta} \Big/ p_i y_i
$$

(3B.12)

and similarly for imports.

Endogenizing the Sustainable Current Account

Above, this chapter extended FABEER to endogenize the sustainable current account. This involves adding equations for medium-term consumption and investment. We treat fiscal policy as exogenous, although we make sure the government's intertemporal budget constraint holds. We also endogenize real interest rates. This involves at the national level ensuring that UIP holds, and at the global level ensuring that global saving and investment match.

Consumption

Our model is based on two sets of consumers: intertemporal maximizers of the Blanchard-Yaari type, and rule-of-thumb consumers who consume all of their current income. Consumption as a percentage share of GDP is then given by

$$cy_t = ccc\left(\frac{p_t}{pm_t}\right)^{cs} 100(1 - ps - tr_t) + mpc\left(hy_t + \left(\frac{p_t}{pm_t}\right)^{cs} wy_t\right) \qquad (3B.13)$$

where ccc is the proportion of income going to credit-constrained consumers, cs is the share of imports in total consumption, ps is the share of profits in total income (assumed constant), tr is the tax rate, mpc is the propensity for non-credit-constrained consumers to consume out of total wealth, hy is the ratio of human capital to income, and wy is the ratio of financial wealth to income. (Because all variables refer to an individual economy, we drop the country subscript but add a time subscript.)

Human wealth (as a percentage share of GDP) is given by

$$hy_t = \frac{hy_{t+1}}{rrc_t} + (1 - ccc)\left(\frac{p_t}{pm_t}\right)^{cs} 100(1 - ps - tr_t) \qquad (3B.14)$$

where rrc is a discount factor that adds a risk premium to the real interest rate. Financial wealth (as a percentage share of GDP) is given by

$$wy_t = 100 \cdot rsp_t \cdot \frac{k_t}{y_t} + dy_t + ay_t - ly_t \qquad (3B.15)$$

where rsp is the real share price, k is capital (related to investment in the standard way), dy is the government debt to income ratio, and ay and ly are the overseas asset and liability ratios already discussed.

Investment

Investment is given by

$$i_t = k_{t-1}(c_0 + c_1 rsp_t)$$ (3B.16)

and the real share price is given by

$$rsp_t = \frac{rsp_{t+1}}{rrrf_t} + ps \frac{y_t}{k_t}$$ (3B.17)

where $rrrf$ is a discount factor. This is a Tobin q–type formulation: Share prices depend on expected, discounted future profits, and investment responds to the ratio of share prices to the book value of the capital stock.

Appendix 3C
A Bilateral Global Model: Calibration

For most model variables, calibration is based on data from the Organization for Economic Cooperation and Development's (OECD's) *Economic Outlook* for December 2003.

Output Gap Estimates

FABEER models output assuming a Cobb-Douglas production function, with a parameter of 0.3 on capital. In the partial equilibrium model, historical EERs are computed using actual values for the labor force and the capital stock. The main judgment involves assessing the output gap in some reference year, and assuming some value for trend productivity growth. In the results in this chapter, I have followed the OECD's calculations for the output gap in 2000. My assumptions about trend productivity growth are very similar but not identical to the OECD's figures, so my output gap figures for 2003 are slightly different. The details are set out in table 3C.1.

Trade Volume Equations

All equations have a constant estimated using static ordinary least squares (OLS) over a period in which the equation appears stable. In addition, the elasticity on output in the import equations is estimated in the same way, as are some of the competitiveness elasticities (table 3C.2).

Trade Price Equations

The price of imports or exports of goods and services is a weighted average of commodity prices and manufacturing prices. Manufacturing prices depend on domestic output prices and competitors' prices. The majority of parameters, and always the trend and constant, are estimated using static OLS (table 3C.3).

Manufacturing export prices are mainly influenced by domestic output prices, with (unsurprisingly) the largest weight for the United States, and the smallest for the United Kingdom. Again, it is not unexpected that domestic prices have a large influence on manufacturing import prices in the United States and the euro area, but the low weight for Japan is more surprising.

Table 3C.1 Output gap estimates (actual and trend, percent)

Bloc	OECD, 2000	OECD, 2003	Wren-Lewis (2003)	Implied TFP growth (percent)
Euro area	0.9	−2.2	−2.5	1.0
Japan	−1.1	−1.9	−1.5	1.0
United Kingdom	1.2	−1.4	−1.4	1.5
United States	2.2	−1.5	−1.3	1.2

TFP = total factor productivity

Sources: OECD Economic Outlook 2003 and author's calculations.

Table 3C.2 Elasticities in import and export equations

Bloc	Activity	Competitiveness	Estimation period
Exports			
United States	1.0	.89[a]	1980–2003[b]
Japan	1.0	.80	1988–2003
Euro area	1.0	1.00	1986–2003
United Kingdom	1.0	.87[a]	1975–2002[c]
Imports			
United States	1.80[a]	.73[a]	1975–2002[c]
Japan	1.73[a]	.80	1990–2003
Euro area	1.87[a]	.40	1980–2002[c]
United Kingdom	1.45[a]	.80	1980–2003

a. Estimated from a static regression.
b. Also includes a shift dummy worth 10 percent from 1999; see box 3.1.
c. Using data from *OECD Economic Outlook 2002,* taken from Wren-Lewis (2003).

Sources: OECD Economic Outlook 2003 and author's calculations.

Table 3C.3 Trade prices

Bloc	Aggregate		Manufacturing	
	Coefficient on commodity prices	Trend (percent per annum)	Coefficient on domestic prices	Trend (percent per annum)
Exports				
United States	0.12	0.8	0.88	−2.8
Japan	0.02	−1.6	0.68	0.6
Euro area	0.10	0.0	0.72	−1.0
United Kingdom	0.14	0.4	0.39	−0.1
Imports				
United States	0.20	0.2	0.54	−1.8
Japan	0.28	1.0	0.15	−0.4
Euro area	0.17	0.1	0.56	−1.0
United Kingdom	0.10	0.3	0.34	−1.0

Sources: OECD Economic Outlook 2003 and author's calculations.

4

Burden Sharing and Exchange Rate Misalignments Within the Group of Twenty

AGNÈS BÉNASSY-QUÉRÉ, PASCALE DURAN-VIGNERON, AMINA LAHRÈCHE-RÉVIL, and VALÉRIE MIGNON

Major changes in external imbalances have occurred in the world since the late 1990s. The most acknowledged one has been the growing size of the US current account deficit. This movement has been compensated for with rising surpluses in East Asia, in Russia, and in the Middle East, and with the vanishing of the aggregate deficit of Latin America. In 2003, individual imbalances grew to −4.9 percent of GDP in the United States, −6 percent in Australia, +10 percent in Taiwan, +11 percent in Hong Kong, +8.9 percent in Russia, and +12.9 percent in Saudi Arabia. Hence, the mirror of US imbalances has increasingly been located in emerging-market countries.

Another feature of the past decade has been the rise of foreign direct investment to developing Asia, and the subsequent buildup of foreign exchange reserves in this region. Indeed, Chinese official reserves have become the second largest in the world (after Japan), with 12.5 percent of world reserves at the end of December 2003, compared with only 6.4 percent of world reserves at the end of December 1996.[1]

Consistently, emerging-market countries have been increasingly included in the debate on exchange rate misalignments. This concern was manifest in

Agnès Bénassy-Quéré is a professor at the University of Paris X and deputy director of the Centre d'Etudes Prospectives et d'Informations Internationales. Pascale Duran-Vigneron is a PhD student at Thema-CNRS, University of Paris X. Amina Lahrèche-Révil is an economist at the Centre d'Etudes Prospectives et d'Informations Internationales. Valérie Mignon is a professor at University of Paris X and is affiliated with Thema-CNRS. The authors are grateful to Emmanuel Dubois for invaluable computer assistance and to Takatoshi Ito and John Williamson for helpful remarks.

1. These data are from the International Monetary Fund and national sources. We are grateful to Bronka Rzepkowski for providing us with these data.

the Boca Raton (Florida) statement of the Group of Seven (G-7) finance ministers on February 6–7, 2004: "In this context, we emphasize that more flexibility in exchange rates is desirable for major countries or economic areas that lack such flexibility to promote smooth and widespread adjustments in the international financial system, based on market mechanisms."[2]

This statement was not followed by action in Asian countries—especially China—that have continued de facto or de jure to run fixed pegs on the US dollar despite current account surpluses and capital inflows. However, the G-7 was perhaps not the best group to issue such a statement, because none of the Asian countries belongs to it. As Fred Bergsten (2004) has argued, the right group would instead be the Group of Twenty (G-20), which was created in 1999 to "promote cooperation to achieve stable and sustainable growth that benefits all." Inasmuch as persistent exchange rate misalignments could be the source of a misallocation of resources, this should be an issue discussed in G-20 meetings. Hence, Bergsten argues that "the G-20 should gradually but steadily succeed the G-7 as the informal steering committee for the world economy in addressing topics such as these, for reasons of both effectiveness and political legitimacy."[3]

Following this view, one is left with the difficult problem of providing exchange rate benchmarks for the G-20 countries. In this chapter, we present equilibrium effective exchange rates for a set of industrial as well as developing countries, based on a methodology close to that used by Enrique Alberola and colleagues (2002) and Alberola (2003), where the real exchange rate is jointly determined by external balance as well as internal balance. We then calculate equilibrium bilateral exchange rates against the US dollar. Finally, we investigate the size of bilateral misalignments depending on the number of flexible currencies within the G-20.

Real Effective Exchange Rates for the G-20

Research on real equilibrium exchange rates has followed two main avenues. The first was launched by John Williamson (1983): The fundamental equilibrium exchange rate (FEER) is defined as the real exchange rate that allows both internal and external equilibrium. Internal equilibrium can be defined using the concept of the nonaccelerating inflation rate of unemployment. External equilibrium is more difficult to operationalize, because it corresponds to a "sustainable" current account surplus or deficit. In practice, it is necessary to define a current account target for each country. This method has been widely applied (see, in particular, Wren-Lewis and Driver 1998). Its main advantage is that the methodology is transparent and openly normative. Its main drawback is that it relies on price elasticities of trade that

---

2. This quotation can be found at http://www.g7.utoronto.ca/finance/fm040207.htm.

3. Bergsten (2004, 5). See also O'Neill and Hormats (2004).

are difficult to estimate, and on current account targets that can be seen as ad hoc assumptions. In addition, as Ronald MacDonald (1997, 7) puts it, "The FEER approach per se does not embody a theory of exchange rate determination. Nonetheless, there is the implicit assumption that the actual real effective exchange rate, q, will converge over time to the FEER."

The second research avenue relies on observed long-run relationships between the real exchange rate and its determinants. This approach has been proposed by MacDonald (1997) and Peter Clark and MacDonald (1998). The behavioral equilibrium exchange rate (BEER) contains no assessment on the sustainability of the exchange rate path. It is an equilibrium rate only in the sense that the observed real exchange rate tends to come back to the BEER after a shock, in the sense of the cointegration literature. The misalignment is the difference between the actual exchange rate and the exchange rate provided by the permanent part of the model, which can incorporate a wide array of theories of exchange rate determination.

A number of researchers have developed approaches of the equilibrium exchange rate that fall between the FEER and the BEER. This is the case, for instance, of the natural real exchange rate approach (NATREX) introduced by Jerome Stein (1994). As in the FEER approach, the NATREX is the exchange rate that permits the attainment of both internal and external equilibrium. However, the current account is modeled as the result of saving and investment behavior, as in a BEER approach. Because consumption is a positive function of the net foreign asset position (through a wealth effect), it is possible to derive the equilibrium exchange rate by holding the ratio of net foreign assets to GDP constant in the long run. The NATREX also depends on productivity, which drives investment in the short run but growth and savings in the long run.

Carsten Detken and colleagues (2002), among others, have applied the NATREX methodology to the euro equilibrium exchange rate. The model developed by Hamid Faruqee, Peter Isard, and Paul Masson (1999) also falls between the two approaches, in that the current account target is determined by econometric estimation of saving and investment behavior rather than a sustainability calculation.

Finally, a Balassa-Samuelson effect can be introduced either in the FEER or in the BEER, by assuming the existence of two sectors in the economy. The external equilibrium requirement then only applies to the tradable sector, whereas internal equilibrium must include a long-run productivity drift on top of short- to medium-run demand effects.[4]

Here we follow a methodology close to that used by Alberola and colleagues (2002) and Alberola (2003), where the real exchange rate is jointly determined by external balance as well as internal balance. The real exchange rate is defined as the relative price of foreign currencies; hence,

---

4. See, e.g., Edwards (1989). Egert (2003) provides a recent review of equilibrium exchange rate estimations for transition countries, which generally include a Balassa-Samuelson effect.

it rises when the domestic currency depreciates in real terms. The price index at home and abroad is the geometric average of the price indices of the tradable sector and of the nontradable sector. Assuming the share of each sector is the same across countries, the real exchange rate can be written as the geometric average of the foreign-to-domestic relative price in the tradable sector and of the "internal" real exchange rate, that is, the ratio of domestic nontradable-to-tradable relative price to foreign nontradable-to-tradable relative price.

The equilibrium relative price in the tradable sector is defined as the one that allows the current account to reach a level that is consistent with desired capital outflows or inflows, the latter being proportional to the discrepancy between the desired and observed levels of the net foreign asset (NFA) position.

The equilibrium internal real exchange rate stems from a Balassa-Samuelson effect; that is, the relative price of domestic nontradable goods rises when productivity in the tradable sector rises relative to world productivity. This very simple model leads to the following testable relationship:

$$q_t = f(nfa_t, relp_t) \tag{4.1}$$

where q_t denotes the real effective exchange rate, nfa_t is the net foreign asset position, and $relp_t$ stands for relative productivity in the tradable sector compared to the nontradable sector, as a ratio of foreign relative productivity. We expect q_t to fall (the real exchange rate to appreciate) when the NFA position rises, because a lower trade account is needed to reach a given current account due to higher interest receipts, and because desired capital outflows are likely to diminish when the NFA position rises. The real exchange rate is also expected to appreciate when $relp_t$ rises, because this leads to a price increase in the nontradable sector, which experiences wage increases without productivity gains.

We consider 15 currencies corresponding to Argentina, Australia, Brazil, Canada, China, the eurozone, India, Indonesia, Japan, Mexico, South Africa, South Korea, Turkey, the United Kingdom, and the United States.[5] Data are annual and cover the period 1980 to 2001. The (log of the) real effective exchange rate for each country is calculated as a weighted average of real bilateral exchange rates, with consumer price indices.[6] The weights rely on the average geographic distribution of imports and exports of goods and services during the period 1999–2001. We do not want to use the "rest of the

---

5. Hence, our sample covers all G-20 countries except Russia and Saudi Arabia; France, Germany, and Italy are grouped into the euro area.

6. Nominal exchange rates are taken from the IMF, *International Financial Statistics* database, except the Chinese rate, which is taken from World Bank (1994) in order to include the nonofficial exchange rate before 1994. The consumer price indices are from the World Bank, *World Development Indicators*. For Argentina and Brazil, bilateral real exchange rates are taken from the CHELEM database of the Centre d'Etudes Prospectives et d'Informations Internationales.

world" as a residual that would implicitly participate in the correction of G-20 imbalances, despite its own balance of payments pattern. Introducing the rest of the world as a residual would be especially misleading given the world imbalance,[7] and it is beyond the scope of G-20 meetings.[8] Hence, trade weights here are normalized to sum to 1.

The NFA position is obtained from the Lane and Milesi-Ferretti database.[9] The stock data are updated using current accounts for 2000 and 2001. We use the ratio of the NFA position to GDP. Finally, relative productivity is proxied by the ratio of the consumer price index (CPI) to the producer price index (PPI), denoted rpi_t in logarithms.[10] This widely used approximation stems from the idea that nontradable goods are included in the CPI but not (or not much) in the PPI. Therefore, the Balassa-Samuelson effect, which passes productivity growth differentials to the relative price of nontradable to tradable goods, should be caught through this variable.

The euro nominal exchange rate before 1999 is calculated as a weighted average of the 12 eurozone members. The weights used are the share of each country in GDP at current exchange rates for each year of the sample. The same calculation is performed for price levels. The NFA position is taken from the European Commission (net international investment position) from 1998. Before 1998, the variable is obtained by subtracting the current account of the eurozone aggregate.

Panel unit root and cointegration tests were performed using the various methodologies proposed in the literature (see, e.g., Pedroni 1996; Kao and Chiang 2000). The series are found to be integrated of order 1 and cointegrated in the panel (see appendix 4A). Table 4.1 reports the cointegration vector obtained either with ordinary least squares (OLS) or the fully modified OLS method (FM-OLS) introduced by Peter Phillips and Bruce Hansen (1990). The two variables are significant and correctly signed; a rise in the NFA position or in the CPI/PPI ratio leads to a real exchange rate appreciation. Moreover, the value of the parameter associated with rpi is close to –1, as expected.

Using a unique panel equation for calculating equilibrium exchange rates relies on the very strong assumption that the same behavior applies to all countries. However, country-by-country estimates would be of poor econometric significance because there are only 22 observations per country. More important, the estimation period may not be representative of long-term behavior in some countries. For instance, the "desired" NFA position may in fact have moved in emerging-market countries, following capital liberalization or structural reforms. This could well have led to a positive rela-

---

7. Summing world current accounts tends to produce a world deficit.

8. This is true in the same way as China's misalignment is out of the scope of G-7 meetings.

9. This database can be found at www.tcd.ie/iiis/plane/data.html.

10. PPIs are taken from the International Monetary Fund, *International Financial Statistics*. For Argentina, Brazil, and Turkey, wholesale prices from national sources are used.

Table 4.1 Cointegration vector obtained with either ordinary least squares (OLS) or fully modified OLS (FM-OLS) estimation in a panel context with fixed effects

Variable	OLS	FM-OLS
q	1.0	1.0
nfa	−0.4323 (−3.80)	−0.6398 (−6.28)
rpi	−0.8755 (−9.08)	−0.9349 (−10.61)

q = real effective exchange rate
nfa = net foreign asset
rpi = relative productivity index

Note: t-statistics are given in parentheses.

Source: Authors' calculations.

tionship between *nfa* and *q* (a fall in the NFA position being concomitant with exchange rate appreciation). In a similar way, price liberalization may have polluted the relationship between *rpi* and *q*. Such specific behaviors in some countries in the past may have little to say about the future.

In addition, for world consistency, it is not possible to say that a rise in the NFA position leads with opposite exchange rate reactions in two different countries, just because the NFA of one country should be reflected in the NFAs of its partners. For all these reasons, we believe that working on a single, panel equation is more appropriate for deriving a set of consistent equilibrium exchange rates.[11]

In figure 4.1, the real equilibrium exchange rate calculated with the FM-OLS panel estimation is compared with the observed rate in each of the 15 countries. By construction, the average of both series over the whole 1980–2001 period is the same. This is due to the fact that the residuals of the estimation have a zero average. Hence, it is implicitly assumed that the real effective exchange rate was at its equilibrium level, on average, over this period. The misalignments observed at any point in time are conditional on this assumption.

For the whole period 1980–2001, the equilibrium real exchange rate appears relatively stable in Canada, Mexico, the United States, and South Africa. The result obtained for the United States may appear puzzling. It stems from the offsetting effects of a fall in the NFA position (which depreciates the equilibrium exchange rate) and of a rise in the CPI/PPI ratio (which induces an appreciation), especially in the second half of the period. Consistent with common wisdom, the US dollar appears overvalued from 1983 to 1986. It is undervalued from 1988 to 1995, and overvalued again

---

11. Further discussion of "in-sample" versus "out-of-sample" estimations of equilibrium exchange rates can be found in Egert, Lahrèche-Révil, and Lommatzsch (2004).

Figure 4.1 Real effective exchange rates calculated using FM-OLS, 1980–2001

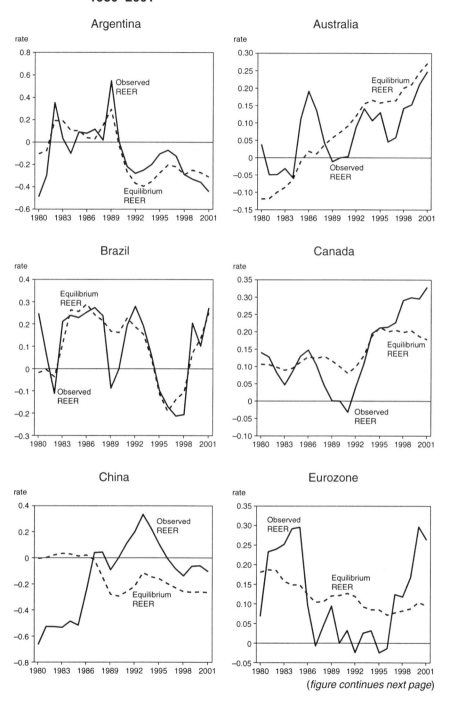

(*figure continues next page*)

Figure 4.1   Real effective exchange rates calculated using FM-OLS, 1980–2001 (*continued*)

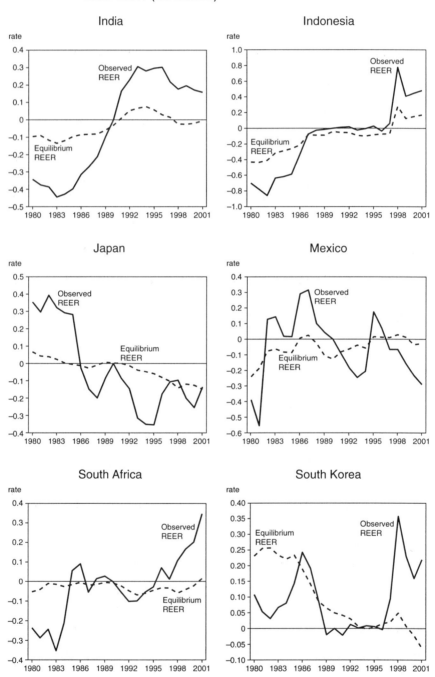

Figure 4.1 (*continued*)

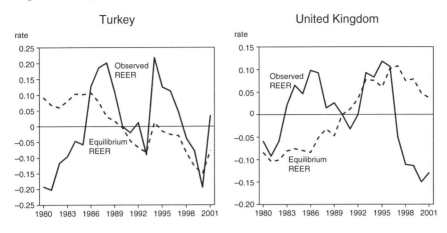

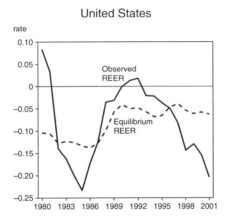

FM-OLS = fully modified ordinary least squares
REER = real effective exchange rate
Note: Rise = depreciation.

from 1997 to 2001. The Mexican peso also appears to be overvalued at the end of the period, whereas the Canadian dollar is undervalued due to a sharp depreciation from 1996 to 2001.

Conversely, the real equilibrium exchange rate tends to appreciate during the period in Argentina, China, Japan, South Korea, Turkey, and the eurozone. This movement stems from rising NFAs in the eurozone, from a rising CPI/PPI ratio in Argentina and Turkey, and from both effects in China, Japan, and South Korea.

Finally, the depreciation of the equilibrium exchange rate during the period is sizable in Australia, India, Indonesia, and the United Kingdom. In all cases, the CPI/PPI ratio declines over the period. In all cases but the

Table 4.2   Real exchange rate misalignments, 2001
(percent)

Overvalued currencies		Undervalued currencies	
Argentina	−13.0	Brazil	2.2
Australia	−2.3	Canada	15.1
United Kingdom	−16.6	China	16.2
Mexico	−26.2	Indonesia	31.4
United States	−14.2	India	16.4
		Japan	1.3
		South Korea	28.2
		Turkey	11.2
		South Africa	33.1
		Eurozone	16.8

Source: Authors' calculations.

United Kingdom (where a hump shape is observed), the NFA position also declines over the period.

The case of Brazil is particular in that, except in 1989–1990, the equilibrium exchange rate seems to closely follow the observed exchange rate. This movement mimics the CPI/PPI fluctuations, which are much larger than in other countries. The results for Brazil should be handled with care.

The misalignments obtained for 2001 are summarized in table 4.2. There is a symmetry between, on the one hand, the overvaluation of the US dollar (14 percent) and of the pound sterling (17 percent), and on the other hand, the undervaluation of the euro (17 percent), the Canadian dollar (15 percent), the Chinese renminbi (16 percent), and the Indian rupee (16 percent). The table shows a very large undervaluation in Indonesia and South Korea, whereas the yen appears close to equilibrium in 2001.

As noted by Alberola and colleagues (1999), among others, the results for effective equilibrium exchange rates, although interesting, are uninformative as regards the equilibrium position between pairs of countries. This problem has become especially topical since the end of the 1990s, with Asian countries coming back to de facto pegs on the US dollar. Hence, we now proceed to the calculation of equilibrium bilateral exchange rates.

Equilibrium Bilateral Exchange Rates

The methodology for deriving bilateral exchange rates basically consists in multiplying the vector of effective rates by the inverted matrix of the weights (see appendix 4B). When necessary, the vector of bilateral rates against the numeraire is ultimately converted into exchange rates against the US dollar.

Because we work in a closed, G-20 framework, there is no "rest of the world." Hence, each of the 15 effective exchange rates is a weighted average of 14 bilateral rates. This means that, when moving to bilateral rates, one of the 15 currencies must be selected as the numeraire. In the derivation of bilateral rates, the misalignment in effective terms for this currency will not be accounted for. Hence, the choice of the numeraire is of high importance. In the following, we successively use different numeraires and compare the results.

The Dollar as the Numeraire

Here we calculate equilibrium bilateral exchange rates against the dollar when taking the dollar as the numeraire. It should be kept in mind that this amounts to neglecting the misalignment of the effective rate of the dollar in the calculation. The results are displayed in figure 4.2. Contrasting to effective rates, there is no equality between average equilibrium and average observed bilateral rates. For instance, one currency can be systematically undervalued against the US dollar (provided it is systematically overvalued against another currency). However, in practice, the shape of equilibrium bilateral rates against the US dollar is generally close to that of the effective rate. The United Kingdom is an exception, with a stable equilibrium rate against the US dollar despite the depreciating trend in effective terms.

Table 4.3 reports the bilateral misalignments in 2001. All currencies but the Mexican peso appear undervalued against the US dollar, which means that the US dollar is overvalued against all currencies but the peso. We then calculate the bilateral real exchange rate variations between 2001 and 2003 to obtain an estimate of misalignments in 2003, provided the equilibrium exchange rate stayed at its 2001 level. Given its strong appreciation between 2001 and 2003, the euro appears undervalued by only 7.6 percent in 2003 compared with 30.5 percent in 2001. Canada, Indonesia, and South Korea also reduce their amount of undervaluation. The British pound switches from undervaluation in 2001 to overvaluation in 2003, whereas the undervaluation of the yen remains stable at about 22 percent. The large undervaluation of the Chinese currency (44.0 percent) was slightly larger still in 2003 (47.3 percent), given the peg on the dollar and low inflation differential between China and the United States over this period. Finally, the case of Argentina is puzzling, with a huge undervaluation due to the fall of the currency after the crisis. The hypothesis of a constant equilibrium exchange rate between 2001 and 2003 is likely to be violated in this country, invalidating the 2003 estimated misalignment.

Alternative Numeraires

As was argued above, the effective misalignment of the numeraire currency is not taken into account in the derivation of bilateral misalignments.

Figure 4.2 Equilibrium bilateral exchange rates against the dollar, 1980–2001

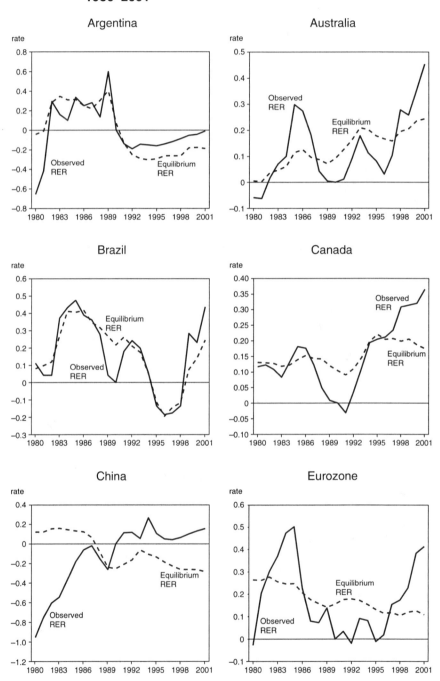

Figure 4.2 (*continued*)

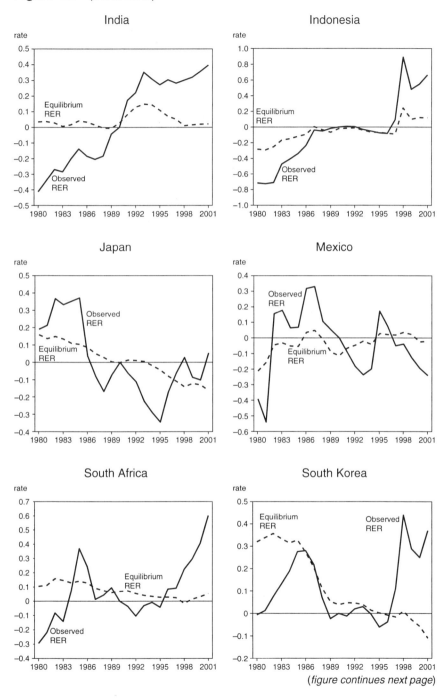

India

Indonesia

Japan

Mexico

South Africa

South Korea

(*figure continues next page*)

Figure 4.2   Equilibrium bilateral exchange rates against the dollar, 1980–2001 (*continued*)

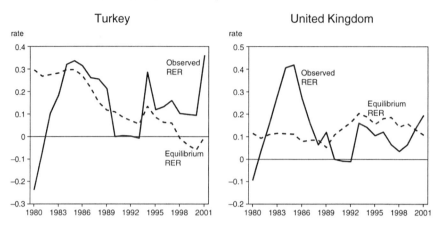

RER = real exchange rate
Note: Rise = depreciation.

This means that using the US dollar as the numeraire may lead to misleading results, because the dollar appears overvalued in effective terms in 2001 (table 4.2).

To quantify this problem, we calculated two additional sets of equilibrium bilateral rates. The first one uses the euro as the numeraire. The second one uses the Turkish lira. Turkey is the country with the smallest share in the trade of its other G-20 partners (and it also appeared close to equilibrium in 2003; see table 4.3). Hence, not accounting for Turkish misalignments is unlikely to have a major distortionary impact on other bilateral rates. For the sake of comparability, all bilateral rates are ultimately converted into bilateral rates against the US dollar using the corresponding equilibrium dollar-euro or dollar-lira exchange rate. In fact, the misalignments obtained with the euro and with the Turkish lira as the numeraire are very close to each other. Hence, table 4.4 reports only the misalignments with the euro as the numeraire in 2001 and 2003 (along with the results already presented in table 4.3).

When the euro is used as the numeraire, the dollar-euro rate appears at equilibrium in 2003, whereas a slight undervaluation of the euro remains in 2003 when the dollar is used as the numeraire. This difference can be related to the fact that the amount of euro undervaluation in effective terms in 2001 is lower than the amount of dollar overvaluation (table 4.2); hence, neglecting euro undervaluation in effective terms leads to lower euro undervaluation against the dollar than when the dollar's effective overvaluation is neglected.

Another reason for this difference is the fact that the (normalized) share of the United States in eurozone trade (28.9 percent) is higher than the share

Table 4.3 Bilateral misalignments against the US dollar, 2001 and 2003 (percent; numeraire = US dollar)

Country or region	Misalignment in 2001	Real exchange variation between 2001 and 2003	Misalignment in 2003 based on 2001 equilibrium rate
Argentina	17.8	74.7	92.5
Australia	21.0	−24.5	−3.5
Brazil	19.2	8.3	27.4
Canada	19.0	−11.2	7.8
China	44.0	3.3	47.3
Eurozone	30.5	−22.9	7.6
India	37.6	−5.5	32.0
Indonesia	54.6	−31.7	22.9
Japan	21.8	0.3	22.1
Mexico	−22.0	8.9	−13.1
South Africa	54.9	−22.9	32.0
South Korea	48.0	−10.4	37.5
Turkey	36.3	−35.6	0.7
United Kingdom	8.8	−13.3	−4.4

Note: A positive sign denotes an undervaluation.

Source: Authors' calculations.

of the eurozone in US trade (19.3 percent). Hence, a smaller adjustment in the dollar-euro exchange rate is needed to reach the equilibrium effective rate of the euro than the equilibrium effective rate of the dollar. For other countries, the difference between the two calculations is quite small.

The Number of Adjustees

As was stressed at the start of the chapter, one central argument in the debate on exchange rate misalignments is the fact that the lack of adjustment in some countries may magnify the burden of the adjustment for other countries. Indeed, the equilibrium bilateral exchange rate calculations proposed in the previous section implicitly assume that all exchange rates adjust simultaneously. In this section, we try to quantify the impact of some countries' refraining from letting their real exchange rate adjust.

To this end, several sets of equilibrium bilateral exchange rates are calculated depending on the number of currencies that are flexible. Equilibrium bilateral rates are calculated in the same way as in the previous section. However, the country that does not allow for exchange rate adjustment is removed from the calculations: Its effective real exchange rate does not participate in the correction of imbalances; remaining bilateral exchange rates adjust to move remaining effective exchange rates to their equilibrium values. Five scenarios are compared:

- S0 is the benchmark scenario where all currencies adjust.

- S1: All currencies but the renminbi adjust.

Table 4.4 Bilateral misalignments against the US dollar, 2001 and 2003 (percent)

Country or region	Misalignment in 2001		Real exchange variation between 2001 and 2003	Misalignment in 2003 based on 2001 equilibrium rate	
	Dollar as numeraire	Euro as numeraire		Dollar as numeraire	Euro as numeraire
Argentina	17.8	12.8	74.7	92.5	87.5
Australia	21.0	17.3	−24.5	−3.5	−7.2
Brazil	19.2	15.1	8.3	27.4	23.4
Canada	19.0	18.1	−11.2	7.8	6.9
China	44.0	40.8	3.3	47.3	44.1
Eurozone	30.5	22.0	−22.9	7.6	−0.9
India	37.6	33.2	−5.5	32.0	27.6
Indonesia	54.6	51.1	−31.7	22.9	19.4
Japan	21.8	18.8	0.3	22.1	19.1
Mexico	−22.0	−22.7	8.9	−13.1	−13.9
South Africa	54.9	49.6	−22.9	32.0	26.7
South Korea	48.0	44.9	−10.4	37.5	34.5
Turkey	36.3	29.6	−35.6	0.7	−6.0
United Kingdom	8.8	2.6	−13.3	−4.4	−10.7

Note: A positive sign denotes an undervaluation.

Source: Authors' calculations.

■ S2: The currencies of emerging-market Asian countries (China, India, Indonesia, and South Korea) do not adjust.

■ S3: Asian currencies (China, India, Indonesia, South Korea, and Japan) do not adjust.

■ S4: Only G-7 currencies (US dollar, Canadian dollar, euro, yen, and pound sterling) adjust.

As in the previous section, we proceed by inverting the system of equilibrium effective rates. We assume that nonadjusters have fixed exchange rates against the US dollar. As is detailed in appendix 4B, when the US dollar is used as the numeraire, this amounts to removing both the rows and the columns corresponding to nonadjusters, which means that their effective misalignment is no longer taken into account in the calculation, and that their bilateral rates against the numeraire (the US dollar) are fixed.

When the euro is used as the numeraire, the bilateral rates to be held constant are not bilateral rates against the numeraire (e_i) but bilateral rates against the US dollar ($e_i - e_D$). For instance, the renminbi-euro rate (e_Y) moves exactly like the dollar-euro rate (e_D). Once again, the rows and columns corresponding to nonadjusters must be removed. But now, the corresponding weights must be transferred to the US dollar column (see appendix 4B).

Table 4.5 Bilateral misalignments against the US dollar in the various scenarios (percent)

Country or region	Scenario	Misalignment in 2001		Real exchange rate variation between 2001 and 2003	Misalignment in 2003	
		Numeraire = euro	Numeraire = dollar		Numeraire = euro	Numeraire = dollar
Canada	S0	18.1	19.0	−11.2	7.0	7.8
	S1	18.2	17.5	−11.2	7.0	6.3
	S2	18.2	17.6	−11.2	7.0	6.4
	S3	18.2	17.1	−11.2	7.0	5.9
	S4	18.2	17.9	−11.2	7.0	6.7
Eurozone	S0	22.0	30.5	−22.9	−0.9	7.6
	S1	32.4	24.9	−22.9	9.6	2.1
	S2	32.2	25.7	−22.9	9.3	2.8
	S3	38.4	24.0	−22.9	15.5	1.2
	S4	31.3	27.2	−22.9	8.5	4.3
United Kingdom	S0	2.6	8.9	−13.3	−10.7	−4.4
	S1	9.2	3.7	−13.3	−4.1	−9.6
	S2	9.0	4.4	−13.3	−4.2	−8.8
	S3	12.9	2.8	−13.3	−0.4	−10.5
	S4	8.7	5.8	−13.3	−4.6	−7.5
Japan	S0	18.8	21.8	0.3	19.1	22.1
	S1	16.1	14.0	0.3	16.4	14.3
	S2	16.4	14.9	0.3	16.6	15.2
	S3	16.5	15.6	0.3	16.7	15.8

Note: A positive sign denotes an undervaluation.

Source: Authors' calculations.

The impact of the lack of adjusters on remaining misalignments is ambiguous. Suppose, for instance, that the renminbi is fixed against the US dollar. When depreciating toward equilibrium, the dollar must depreciate more against the euro because it does not depreciate against the renminbi. To put the same point a different way, the euro has to appreciate more against the dollar if the renminbi does not adjust. However, if the problem were that the dollar was undervalued, the euro would need to depreciate less against the US dollar when the renminbi appreciates with the dollar. In general, then, the impact of the lack of adjusters is an empirical question.

The results for the G-7 currencies with the two alternative numeraires are displayed in table 4.5. Consistent with the above reasoning, the overvaluation of the dollar against the euro is larger when some adjusters are lacking if the euro is taken as the numeraire, but smaller if the dollar is taken as the numeraire. The latter result comes from the fact that the euro is undervalued in effective terms: If the renminbi does not appreciate, then the needed appreciation of the euro against the US dollar (which is taken as the numeraire) is smaller because there is no depreciation against the renminbi.

Hence, the magnification or dampening effect of fewer adjusters depends on the numeraire chosen, that is, on whether the analysis focuses on an overvalued currency (the US dollar) or on an undervalued one (the euro). However, the sensitivity of the dollar-euro misalignment to the lack of adjusters is weaker in the dampening case than in the magnification one, so that it is likely that fewer adjusters will magnify the needed dollar-euro adjustment. This feature can be related to the fact that, as mentioned above, bilateral trade between the eurozone and the United States is more important for the eurozone than it is for the US economy. Hence, what happens in the rest of the world impacts more on the dollar-euro misalignments when focusing on the US imbalance (with the euro as the numeraire) than on the eurozone imbalance (with the US dollar as the numeraire).

It has been argued above that the dollar-euro exchange rate was close to equilibrium in 2003. This corresponds to the baseline scenario (S0). The lack of adjustment from China and other Asian countries leads to a residual undervaluation of the euro that can be as large as 16 percent in the calculation with the euro as the numeraire if the yen does not adjust. Interestingly, the bulk of this effect comes from China, because that is where undervaluation was largest in 2003 (see table 4.3). Indeed, scenarios S1 to S4 appear relatively close to each other in the second half of the period because they are dominated by the lack of adjustment in China. It is less the case in the 1990s where scenarios S1, S2, and S3 clearly fall between S0 and S4 (see figure 4.3).

Turning to other G-7 currencies, it is worth noting that with the euro as numeraire the lack of adjusters largely eliminates the overvaluation of the pound sterling against the US dollar found in the baseline scenario in 2003. In the case of Japan, the lack of appreciation in other Asian countries reduces the needed appreciation of the yen against the US dollar. This is because the effective exchange rate of the yen is close to equilibrium: If Asian currencies appreciate, then the yen needs to appreciate against the US dollar to keep the effective rate stable, but this is no longer necessary if Asian currencies do not appreciate. Finally, the impact of a reduced number of adjusters is negligible for Canada due to the overwhelming share of the US dollar in the effective exchange rates (81.7 percent in our normalized database), which leaves little room for an impact of other bilateral rates.

It has been found above that the lack of adjusters has an ambiguous impact on the equilibrium dollar-euro rate depending on the numeraire (euro vs. dollar), but that the magnifying effect is likely to dominate. This point can be checked by using a third currency as the numeraire. One candidate is the Turkish lira because Turkey's share in US and eurozone trade is small. Another candidate is the yen, which is the currency closest to its equilibrium level (in effective terms) in 2001. The results (table 4.6)

Figure 4.3   Adjustment scenarios for selected Group of Seven currencies (numeraire = euro, 1980–2001)

Canada

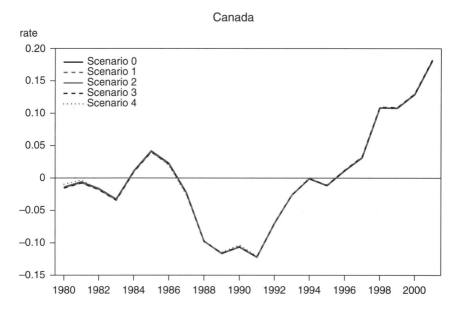

United Kingdom

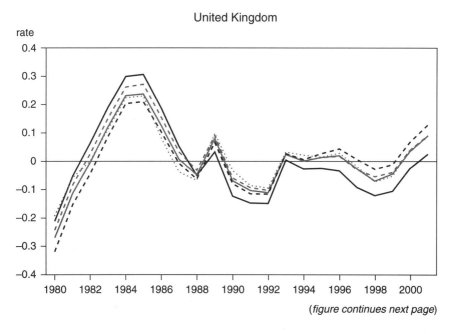

(*figure continues next page*)

Figure 4.3 Adjustment scenarios for selected Group of Seven currencies (numeraire = euro,1980–2001) (*continued*)

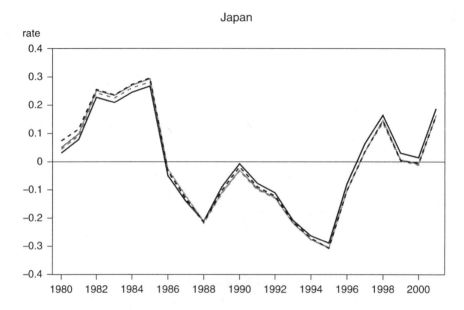

Japan

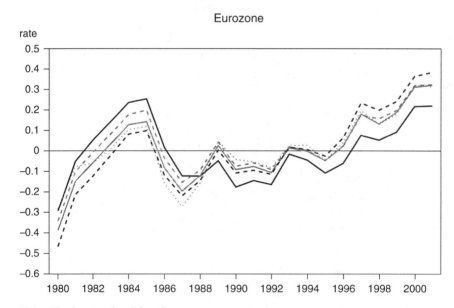

Eurozone

Notes: Key is same for all four figures.
     Rise = depreciation.
     Scenarios in Canada and Japan appear close to each other.
     Bilateral misalignments against the US dollar are based on panel estimations of equilibrium exchange rates.

Source: Authors' calculations.

Table 4.6 Bilateral misalignments against the US dollar
in 2001 depending on the numeraire

Country or region	Scenario	Numeraire			
		Euro	Dollar	Turkish lira	Yen
Canada	S0	18.1	19.0	18.2	18.2
	S1	18.2	17.5	18.2	18.1
	S2	18.2	17.6	18.2	18.1
	S3	18.2	17.1	18.2	n.a.
	S4	18.2	17.9	18.2	18.2
Eurozone	S0	22.0	30.5	23.8	27.5
	S1	32.4	24.9	30.7	27.2
	S2	32.2	25.7	30.6	27.4
	S3	38.4	24.0	34.7	n.a.
	S4	31.3	27.2	30.2	28.1
United Kingdom	S0	2.6	8.9	2.9	6.0
	S1	9.2	3.7	8.8	5.9
	S2	9.0	4.4	8.8	6.1
	S3	12.9	2.8	12.2	n.a.
	S4	8.7	5.8	8.5	6.7
Japan	S0	18.8	21.8	18.9	n.a.
	S1	16.1	14.0	16.0	n.a.
	S2	16.4	14.9	16.3	n.a.
	S4	16.5	15.6	16.4	n.a.

n.a. = not available

Source: Authors' calculations.

confirm that having fewer adjusters tends to raise the bilateral dollar-euro misalignment. As expected, the difference across the scenarios is smaller when the yen or the Turkish lira is the numeraire. The difference across the scenarios is especially small when the yen is used as the numeraire. Hence, one should not exaggerate the "burden-sharing" argument according to which a lack of adjusters magnifies the dollar-euro misalignment.

Conclusions

In this chapter, we have tried to produce a quantitative analysis of exchange rate misalignments in a closed G-20 framework. The first step consists in estimating real effective equilibrium rates based on the same model through a panel cointegration approach on 15 of the G-20 currencies. This first step is useful in that it provides a quantification of misalignments for each country. However, the policy discussion needs to translate effective misalignments into bilateral misalignments. This is the second step, which consists in deriving the full set of bilateral misalignments on the basis of effective misalignments.

This second step is difficult, because only $n - 1$ independent bilateral rates can be derived from a set of n effective rates. One solution is to add an nth currency representing the rest of the world. However, this solution means that G-20 countries transfer to third countries the burden of overall adjustment. Keeping the analysis within G-20 boundaries implies choosing one of the G-20 currencies as the numeraire, which means that the effective misalignment of this currency will be dropped in the calculation of bilateral rates.

By using various alternative numeraires, we can show the diagnosis of bilateral misalignments to be robust for most currencies. However, such diagnosis assumes a simultaneous adjustment of all G-20 currencies. One main point of debate in the early 2000s has been the lack of adjustment of some G-20 currencies. The last step of this chapter is to quantify the impact of such a lack of adjustment on bilateral misalignments for other currencies.

On the whole, the analysis suggests that the dollar-euro exchange rate was close to equilibrium in 2003, conditional on the acceptance, by China and other Asian countries, of a rather large undervaluation of their own currencies against the US dollar. We also show that the lack of adjustment in Asia tended to magnify the dollar's overvaluation in 2001, and to a lesser extent in 2003. However, this effect is less general than might be believed, because the lack of appreciation of Asian currencies also helps the euro to reach its equilibrium level in effective terms. And in the case of Japan, the lack of adjusters reduces the amount of the yen-dollar misalignment because the yen is found to be close to equilibrium in effective terms in 2001.

References

Alberola, E. 2003. *Misalignment, Liabilities, Dollarization, and Exchange Rate Adjustment in Latin America.* Banco de España documento de trabajo 0309. Madrid: Banco de España.

Alberola E., S. G. Cervero, H. Lopez, and A. Ubide. 2002. Quo vadis euro? *European Journal of Finance* 8, no. 4 (December): 352–70.

Bergsten, C. F. 2004. The G-20 and the World Economy. Speech to the Deputies of the G-20, Leipzig, Germany, March 4. www.iie.com/publications/papers/bergsten0304-2.htm.

Clark, Peter, and Ronald MacDonald. 1998. *Exchange Rates and Economic Fundamentals: A Methodological Comparison of BEERs and FEERs.* IMF Working Paper 98/671. Washington: International Monetary Fund.

Detken, C. A., A. Dieppe, J. Henry, C. Marin, and F. Smets. 2002. *Model Uncertainty and the Equilibrium Value of the Real Effective Euro Exchange Rate.* ECB Working Paper 160. Frankfurt: European Central Bank.

Edwards, Sebastian. 1989. *Real Exchange Rates, Devaluation and Adjustment.* Cambridge, MA: MIT Press.

Egert, Balasz. 2003. *Assessing Equilibrium Exchange Rates in Acceding Countries: Can We Have DEER with BEER Without FEER? A Critical Survey of the Literature.* Focus on Transition 2/2003. Vienna: Oesterreichische Nationalbank.

Egert, Balasz, A. Lahrèche-Révil, and K. Lommatzsch. 2004. The Stock-Flow Approach to the Real Exchange Rate of the EU Acceding Countries: In-Sample Versus Out-of-Sample Estimates. Centre d'Etudes Prospectives et d'Informations Internationales, Paris. Working paper (forthcoming).

Faruqee, H., P. Isard, and P. R. Masson. 1999. A Macroeconomic Balance Framework for Estimating Equilibrium Exchange Rates. In *Equilibrium Exchange Rates,* ed. R. MacDonald and J. Stein. Boston: Kluwer Academic Publishers.

Im, K. S., M. H. Pesaran, and Y. Shin. 2003. Testing for Unit Roots in Heterogeneous Panels. *Journal of Econometrics*, 115: 53–74.

Kao, C., and M. H. Chiang. 2000. On the Estimation and Inference of a Cointegrated Regression in Panel Data. In *Advances in Econometrics*, vol. 15, ed. B. Baltagi and C. Kao. Burlington, MA: Elsevier Science.

Levin, A., and C. F. Lin. 1992. *Unit Root Tests in Panel Data: Asymptotic and Finite Sample Properties.* Discussion Paper 56. La Jolla, CA: Department of Economics, University of California, San Diego.

MacDonald, R. 1997. *What Determines the Real Exchange Rate? The Long and the Short of It.* IMF Working Paper 97/21. Washington: International Monetary Fund.

Maddala, G., and S. Wu. 1999. A Comparative Study of Unit Root Tests and a New Simple Test. *Oxford Bulletin of Economics and Statistics* 61: 631–52.

Maeso-Fernandez, F., C. Osbat, and B. Schnatz. 2001. *Determinants of the Euro Real Effective Exchange Rate: A BEER/PEER Approach.* ECB Working Paper 85. Frankfurt: European Central Bank.

O'Neill, J., and R. Hormats. 2004. *The G-8: Time for a Change.* Global Economics Paper 112. New York: Goldman Sachs.

Pedroni, P. 1996. *Fully Modified OLS for Heterogeneous Cointegrated Panels and the Case of Purchasing Power Parity.* Working Paper in Economics. Bloomington: Department of Economics, Indiana University.

Pedroni, P. 2004. Panel Cointegration: Asymptotic and Finite Sample Properties of Pooled Time Series Tests with an Application to the PPP Hypothesis. *Econometric Theory* 20(3): 597–625.

Phillips, P. C. B., and B. E. Hansen. 1990. Statistical Inference in Instrumental Variables Regression with I(1) Processes. *Review of Economic Studies* 57: 99–125.

Saikkonen, P. 1991. Asymptotically Efficient Estimation of Cointegrating Regressions. *Econometric Theory* 58: 1–21.

Stein, Jerome. 1994. The Natural Real Exchange Rate of the US Dollar and Determinants of Capital Flows. In *Estimating Equilibrium Exchange Rates,* ed. John Williamson. Washington: Institute for International Economics.

Stock, J., and M. Watson. 1993. A Simple Estimator of Cointegrating Vectors in Higher-Order Integrated Systems. *Econometrica* 61: 783–820.

Williamson, John. 1983. *The Exchange Rate System.* POLICY ANALYSES IN INTERNATIONAL ECONOMICS 5. Washington: Institute for International Economics.

Williamson, John. 1994. Estimates of FEERs. In *Estimating Equilibrium Exchange Rates,* ed. John Williamson. Washington: Institute for International Economics.

World Bank. 1994. China GNP per Capita. Report 13580-CHA. Country Operations Division, World Bank, Washington, Document of the World Bank, December 15.

Wren-Lewis, Simon, and Rebecca Driver. 1998. *Real Exchange Rates for the Year 2000.* POLICY ANALYSES IN INTERNATIONAL ECONOMICS 54. Washington: Institute for International Economics.

Appendix 4A
Unit Root and Cointegration Results

Table 4A.1 Panel unit root tests

Variable	LM	*t*-bar	LL	MW
q	−0.2575	−0.6299	−0.0882	32.929
	(0.6016)	(0.2643)	(0.4648)	(0.3256)
nfa	0.8601	−0.7863	0.7692	36.955
	(0.1948)	(0.2158)	(0.7791)	(0.1784)
cpi/ppi	1.0819	−1.8343	−1.0167	52.384
	(0.1396)	(0.0333)*	(0.1546)	(0.0061)*

LL = Levin and Lin (1992) test
LM = Lagrange multiplier test (Im, Pesaran, and Shin 2003)
MW = Maddala and Wu (1999) test
t-bar = group mean *t*-bar test (Im, Pesaran, and Shin 2003)

Note: *p*-values are given in parentheses. An asterisk indicates the rejection of the unit root null hypothesis at the 5 percent significance level (*p*-value less than 0.05).

Source: Authors' calculations.

Table 4A.2 Pedroni panel cointegration tests

	Panel cointegration tests: $q = f(nfa, rpi)$				Group mean cointegration tests: $q = f(nfa, rpi)$		
v-test	ρ test	Nonparametric *t*-test	Parametric *t*-test		ρ test	Nonparametric *t*-test	Parametric *t*-test
2.9013*	−1.0187	−0.9223	−1.6543*		0.0204	−0.7972	−1.5402
(0.0018)	(0.1542)	(0.1782)	(0.0490)		(0.5081)	(0.2126)	(0.0617)

Note: *p*-values are given in parentheses. An asterisk indicates the rejection of the null hypothesis of no cointegration at the 5 percent significance level (*p*-value less than 0.05).

Sources: Pedroni (2004) and authors' calculations.

Appendix 4B
From Effective to Equilibrium Bilateral Exchange Rates

The logarithm of the real effective exchange rate for country i, q_i, is the trade-weighted average of the log of bilateral exchange rates of country i against trade partners j:

$$q_i = \sum_j w_{ij}(e_i - e_j) = e_i - \sum_{j \neq i} w_{ij} e_j \qquad (4B.1)$$

where e_i is the log of the bilateral exchange rate of country i against the numeraire currency, and w_{ij} denotes the share of country j in the trade of country i. Note that the sum of the weights is equal to 1, that is, $\sum_j w_{ij} = 1$.

Let Q be the vector of the 15 real equilibrium effective exchange rates previously estimated, and let E be the vector of the 15 equilibrium bilateral real exchange rates. As suggested by Alberola and colleagues (1999), it is possible to express Q, with the numeraire currency being the last element, in terms of E as follows:

$$Q = (I - W)E \qquad (4B.2)$$

where W is the (15×15) trade matrix and I is the identity matrix of order 15.

Because $(I - W)$ contains only 14 independent exchange rates, it must be singular. To circumvent this problem, we have to eliminate the redundant multilateral exchange rate. To do so, we remove the row and the column corresponding to the numeraire currency, and the remaining 14 multilateral exchange rates are expressed relative to the numeraire. We can write

$$Q^* = (I - W)^* E^* \qquad (4B.3)$$

where the asterisk indicates that the row and column corresponding to the numeraire currency have been removed. The vector of equilibrium bilateral real exchange rates, denoted as E^*, is thus given by

$$E^* = (I - W)^{*-1} Q^*. \qquad (4B.4)$$

Suppose that one country, z, keeps a fixed exchange rate against the numeraire. We have $e_z = 0$. According to equation 4B.1, we have

$$q_z = -\sum_{j \neq i} w_{zj} e_j. \qquad (4B.5)$$

The effective exchange rate of country z reflects only the exchange rates of third currencies against the numeraire. The effective exchange rates of other currencies q_i are also given by applying equation 4B.1:

$$q_i = e_i - \sum_{j \neq z} w_{zj} e_j. \qquad (4B.6)$$

Hence, the vector of flexible bilateral rates against the numeraire is obtained by inverting the system of 13 effective rates (14 currencies less currency i) $\tilde{Q}^*$ in terms of the 13 floating bilateral rates $\tilde{E}^*$:

$$\tilde{E}^* = \left(\tilde{I} - \tilde{W}\right)^{*-1} \tilde{Q}^* \tag{4B.7}$$

where a tilde ($\sim$) means that the row and column corresponding to the fixed currency have been removed. If more than one currency keeps a constant exchange rate against the numeraire, the same methodology applies with a reduced system size.

Now suppose that one country, z, fixes its exchange rate not against the numeraire but against a third currency, h. Hence, we have $e_z - e_h = 0$. In this case, the effective rate of z is given by

$$q_z = e_h - w_{zh}e_h - \sum_{\substack{j \neq z \\ j \neq h}} w_{zj}\, e_j. \tag{4B.8}$$

The effective rates of other currencies are given by

$$q_i = e_i - w_{iz}e_h - \sum_{\substack{j \neq i \\ j \neq z}} w_{ij}\, e_j. \tag{4B.9}$$

The $w_{iz}e_h$ term comes from the fact that currency z is no longer fixed against the numeraire. For instance, a depreciation of currency h against the numeraire (rise in e_h) does not have a one-for-one impact on the effective rate of h (q_h) because currency h does not depreciate against z. The vector of bilateral rates is now given by the following 13×13 system:

$$\tilde{E}^* = \left(I - \tilde{Y} - \tilde{W}\right)^{*-1} \tilde{Q}^* \tag{4B.10}$$

where $\tilde{Y}$ is a matrix with zeros everywhere but in a column containing the share of z in trade of each country in row (w_{iz}). This column is located in the same place as the column containing the share of h in the trade of each country (w_{ih}) in $\tilde{W}$:

$$\tilde{Y} = \begin{pmatrix} 0 & \cdots & w_{1z} & 0 \\ 0 & & w_{2z} & 0 \\ \cdots & \cdots & \cdots & \cdots \\ 0 & & w_{13z} & 0 \end{pmatrix}. \tag{4B.11}$$

This correction of the system amounts to considering an "h monetary zone," which includes currency z and whose impact on each effective rate q_i depends on the sum of the cumulated weights of h (w_{ih}) and of z (w_{iz}). The same methodology applies to more than one nonadjuster: The corresponding rows and columns are removed, and the weights are added to that of the anchor currency h in the trade matrix.

Comment

ELLEN HUGHES-CROMWICK

The three chapters in part II of this book address important questions about exchange rate adjustments, particularly that of the US dollar, in light of the present disequilibria. What all the authors implicitly conclude is that adjustments are warranted, especially in the US dollar value, because the United States has an unsustainable current account deficit. That there appears to be a consensus on that conclusion is undeniable.

In that vein, John Williamson's approach to the "problem" in chapter 2 should surely be the envy of both engineers and international economists. I liken his approach to the Wizard of Oz behind the curtain—it only needs the pull and push of a few levers to achieve the desired outcome. Never mind that several key macroeconomic policy developments may stand in the way of the behavior required to generate the rebalancing that is outlined in his chapter. The allocation of the reduction in the US current account deficit, as he points out, could be done in any number of ways. His logical approach, summarized in table 2.1, distributes the burden of adjustment among several countries, with Japan and the euro area accounting for nearly 60 percent of the proposed change in the US current account balance.

The conclusion of Williamson's chapter is that the adjustment can be accommodated "rather comfortably by the rest of the world, with the possible exception of Japan." Further research on this subject to augment this conclusion should focus on whether the policy mix—particularly in the euro area and Japan—is conducive to such adjustment in the near term. Furthermore, policies to induce this adjustment, especially in the United

---

Ellen Hughes-Cromwick directs the corporate economics group at Ford Motor Company.

States, are not at all self-evident. As for Japan, its aggressive exchange rate policy in the form of currency intervention likely delayed the process of adjustment, with costs borne by US producers (lost production) and consumers (jobs) relative to what would have been most likely if Japan had faced its restructuring head-on without resorting to currency manipulation.

Other policies to induce the adjustment are not very attractive. For example, it is unlikely that any economist would wish for a productivity slump, inflation acceleration, or inappropriate monetary policy to induce a dollar adjustment of 20 percent. Nevertheless, Williamson's chapter is very helpful in advancing discussion on the likely options as the dollar realignment emerges in the years ahead.

The vexing questions remain, for both policymakers and those in the private sector: How long can a US current account deficit of the present size be sustained? And what are the factors supporting the view that the present deficit in the United States is unsustainable? These questions were outside the scope of Williamson's research agenda for his chapter; however, they are questions that require answers before policy proposals are made. In light of strong productivity growth and other positive features of US fundamentals, what level of the US current account deficit is sustainable? As good essays do, Williamson's places on our radar important further questions to consider.

The modeling prowess of Simon Wren-Lewis and Agnès Bénassy-Quéré and her colleagues in chapters 3 and 4, respectively, is welcome in a book dedicated to the discussion of exchange rate adjustments. Both of these efforts give ample backbone to the discussion. Wren-Lewis's chapter includes some intriguing results pertaining to two major uncertainties in the United States—a fiscal shock and a technology shock. That both shocks, in his simulations, increase the level of the US current account deficit is an important result. This raises the important question of whether the United States could sustain a deficit larger than the present consensus of 2 to 3 percent. Though Wren-Lewis likely did not intend to infer this, the fiscal expansion shock that thereby induces a larger medium-run deficit may well imply abrupt and likely painful adjustment in the decade following 2010. This will also be the period during which the United States will experience the first major wave of baby boomer retirements. A fiscal expansion shock would be a recipe for crisis beyond 2010, for the federal government cannot afford to be ill prepared for the consequences of the unfunded liabilities associated with the Medicare program. This particular shock scenario is worthy of further investigation because of the likely policy backdrop that will confront global investors in the 2010–20 period.

Finally, I offer a few comments on the chapter by Bénassy-Quéré and her colleagues—another solid contribution to this volume. Of particular note are the renminbi results. In light of data reliability and capital controls in China, estimates of renminbi misalignment are very difficult to obtain, as may be illustrated by the big difference between the results from the two approaches used in the chapter. The renminbi range of undervaluation is somewhere from 4.7 percent to upward of 28 or 30 percent. The chapter appropriately concludes that the patient (the dollar) is overvalued and the "diagnosis of bilateral misalignments [is] robust for most currencies." The large undervaluation of China's and other Asian countries' currencies relative to the dollar is the culprit. Oddly, Japan is not significantly out of line according to their calculations, at least as of 2001 (when the nominal yen-dollar value averaged nearly 125 for the year).

I took away from this chapter a reinforced conclusion that exchange rate misalignments are evident and fairly large, especially in US-Asian bilateral rates. I drew less comfort on how these misalignments will be resolved in the near term.

Comment

JIM O'NEILL

To begin, it is good to note how much progress appears to have been achieved by leading academic researchers in the short time since September 2002. At a meeting at that time, I had remarked on the fact that quite a lot of the analysis had been stuck in the style of the 1980s, not recognizing the dramatic changes that had taken place in the world economy and US trade relationships around the world.

All three chapters in part II of this volume recognize these changing patterns, as evidenced by not having the euro and yen as the only counterparts to further dollar adjustment. It is important to recognize these issues. As can be deduced from table II.1, the modern trade-weighted dollar for the Group of Seven (G-7) currencies has a weight of 51.4 percent, with many developing countries now becoming increasingly important. The combined weight of the Chinese renminbi and the Mexican peso, at close to 22 percent, is bigger than the weight of the euro. In this context, moves in the dollar against each of these currencies might be just as important as moves against the euro in the effect of dollar adjustment.

To illustrate how further changes in this direction are likely as time passes, figure II.1 depicts how the world may look in the future. This figure envisages a world in which China is the largest economy and India is third, with the United States sandwiched between them.

Most European countries are somewhere behind. Of course this is only dreaming, but dreams can sometimes become true. Already, some aspects of

Jim O'Neill has been managing director and head of global economic research at Goldman Sachs since September 2001.

Table II.1   Trade-weighted US dollar, 2004

Economy or region	Weight	Economy or region	Weight
Euro area	18.53	Thailand	1.43
Canada	16.50	Australia	1.28
Japan	11.13	Philippines	1.16
Mexico	11.03	Sweden	1.09
China	9.78	India	1.08
United Kingdom	5.23	Israel	1.05
South Korea	3.86	Indonesia	0.99
Taiwan	3.05	Russia	0.75
Malaysia	2.28	Saudi Arabia	0.63
Singapore	2.17	Chile	0.51
Hong Kong	1.98	Argentina	0.44
Brazil	1.86	Venezuela	0.40
Switzerland	1.43	Colombia	0.37

Source: US Federal Reserve data.

China's and India's influence on the world are becoming clear, and it is vital to consider their role in any fundamental assessment of dollar adjustment going forward. In this regard, it was especially pleasing to see the scope and vision of Agnès Bénassy-Quéré and her colleagues in chapter 4.

Chapter 2 by Williamson

Turning to each chapter individually, I strongly support the basic contention in chapter 2, by John Williamson, that a decline in the dollar does not necessarily have to be deflationary for the world. Indeed, on the contrary, the dollar's decline since early 2002 has been one of the main reasons that the world has been in somewhat better shape. Its decline has contributed to a much-needed improvement in US financial conditions and pressurized other major nations into more accommodative policies to provide an offset. According to the Organization for Economic Cooperation and Development, financial conditions have been easier since the dollar started its decline (figure II.2).

Japan is an especially interesting case. As Fred Bergsten remarked to me 20 months ago, there was considerable debate about whether Japan was in a position to cope with the yen's strength. Today, it can be argued that the persistent pressure for an ever-strengthening yen could have been a major contributor to the more expansive policies pursued by the Bank of Japan and has added to the evidently healthier economic environment in Japan.

This illustration may also be pertinent to the current case of the eurozone and its ability to cope with more dollar weakness. Superficially, I—probably like many others—respond with suspicion to the idea presented in Williamson's chapter that as a counterpart to the proposed (and assumed

Figure II.1 The world economy in 2050

GDP (in trillions of 2003 dollars)

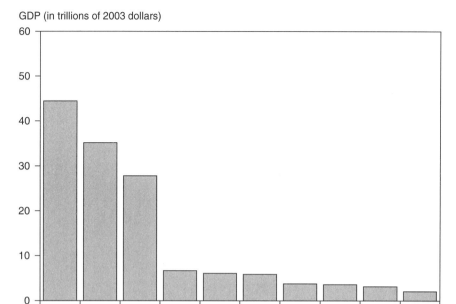

Source: Wilson and Purushothaman (2003).

necessary) halving of the US current account deficit to 2.5 percent of GDP within 3 years, the eurozone would need to lose 0.83 percent of GDP through trade. At the time we met for the conference on which this book is based, it was just a week or so after Germany reported that the value of its March nominal retail sales was lower than 11 years ago (figure II.3). This is a rather incredible outcome that most would presume impossible in a developed economy, highlighting Europe's difficulties in coping with US current account adjustment.

Nonetheless, the notion that this necessarily always has to be the case is clearly incorrect. Given the size of Europe—supported by the European Union's expansion—it is quite possible, as well as appropriate, that the euro-zone will develop more ambitious fiscal and monetary policy regimes, and it should certainly not persist with inward-looking ones. If the US current account is to adjust, the eurozone clearly needs to serve as a counterpart.

What is one to make of Williamson's basic premise that a reduction of the US current account by half is necessary? Goldman Sachs has strong sympathies with this notion. Early in 2004, it published a paper by the present author and Hatzius arguing that a US current account deficit of 3 percent of GDP might be more sustainable (O'Neill and Hatzius 2004). Under such a

Figure II.2   US Goldman Sachs Financial Conditions Index and OECD Financial Conditions Index

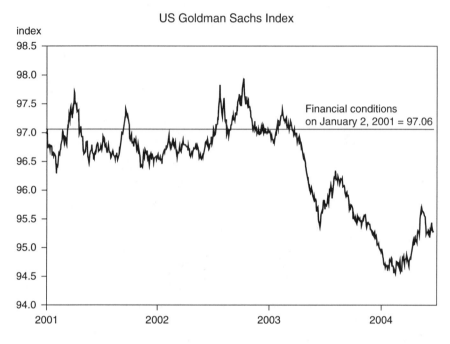

US Goldman Sachs Index

Financial conditions
on January 2, 2001 = 97.06

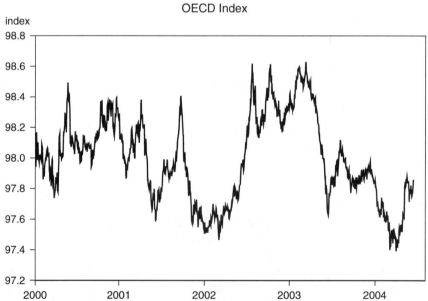

OECD Index

Rise = tightening conditions
Source: Goldman Sachs.

Figure II.3   Nominal retail sales in Germany, 1993–2004

index

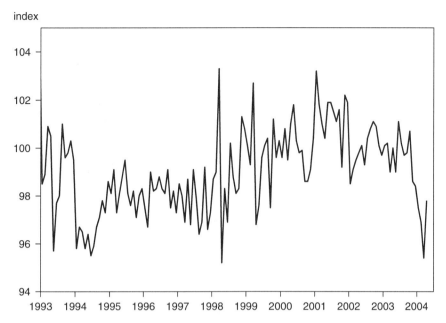

Source: Bundesbank.

scenario, the deficit would be matched by long-term capital flows. A decline from 5 to 3 percent is necessary to maintain a balance in the broader US "basic" balance. I defined a broad basic balance above as the current account balance plus net foreign direct investment (FDI) plus net portfolio flows, bonds, and equities. The sustainable current account is presumably the one that matches net FDI and portfolio flows over the longer term and that does not rely on hot capital short-term flows or foreign central bank intervention. Currently, the broad basic balance of payments is in deficit, and therefore either the current account deficit needs to decline or FDI and portfolio flows need to accelerate (figure II.4).

Given that the combined FDI and portfolio flows have averaged about 3 percent of GDP since the early 2000s, a slightly bigger current account deficit than Williamson suggests might be sustainable for a while. However, 0.5 percent of GDP is not of material difference.

Chapter 3 by Wren-Lewis

As a general comment on the potential size of a further dollar decline necessary to reduce the current account deficit to a sustainable level, our research is rather consistent with the tone of all three chapters in part II, and specifically with the results presented in chapter 3, by Simon Wren-Lewis. O'Neill

Figure II.4   United States: Basic balance of payments versus current account, 1999–2005

percent of GDP (fourth-quarter moving average)

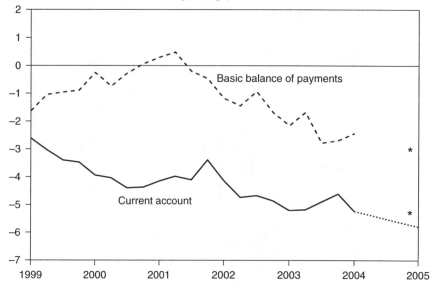

* = forecast for 2004
Sources: US Department of Commerce; Goldman Sachs.

and Hatzius concluded that the dollar, at a level of about 10 percent below its broad trade-weighted peak, may need to fall further by the same amount to reduce the current account deficit to 3 percent of GDP (O'Neill and Hatzius 2004). Such a decline might be spread across a different set of currencies from those that the dollar has declined against so far, and here O'Neill and Hatzius would broadly agree with the numbers implied by Wren-Lewis. It is particularly pleasing to see his conclusions that some revaluation of the Chinese renminbi is a necessary part of the adjustment process.

It was surprising to read that Wren-Lewis estimates the underlying current account surplus in the eurozone in 2002 to be as high as 3.1 percent of GDP. He explains that this estimate is consistent with the current account that might have prevailed if the euro had not strengthened sharply, and though a larger surplus might have existed, this estimate seems rather too high. There was little anecdotal evidence at the time to suggest that such a large surplus was in the making.

Another peculiarity of Wren-Lewis's chapter is the inclusion of research on both the Australian and New Zealand dollars. Although his results are interesting, it is unlikely to be the case that either is important to a dollar adjustment and the US current account deficit.

Figure II.5 US core consumer price index, 2000–04

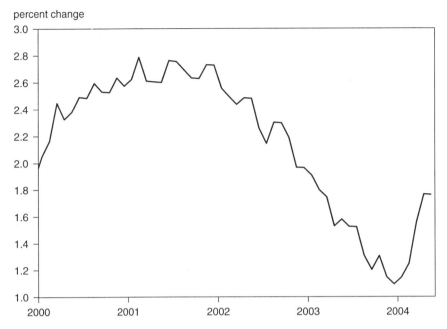

percent change

Source: US Department of Labor.

Another, more general point, noted by Wren-Lewis but also evident in chapters 2 and 4, is the lack of discussion of *internal* equilibrium in the US consistent with the desirability of a decline in the current account deficit. In its original presentation and most derivatives since, Williamson's model of the fundamental equilibrium exchange rate requires internal *and* external equilibrium. All three chapters in part II seem to focus mostly on the external balance. At the time of the Institute for International Economics conference in May 2004 (and becoming increasingly topical immediately afterward), there was some evidence that US inflation was starting to rise (figure II.5). If this indicates that the US output gap will be closed earlier than anticipated, it may follow that the United States is able to cope with a more delayed period of adjustment of its current account deficit. Certainly, a repeat of the dollar's decline since 2002 might have undesirable consequences if it coincides with, or contributes to, rising inflation in the United States.

Currencies and Productivity

The later sections of Wren-Lewis's chapter are its most interesting; there, he discusses simulations of the sustainable current account deficit based on both fiscal policy and technology shocks in the United States. He argues

Figure II.6 Dollar trade-weighted index versus GSDEER, 1984–2004

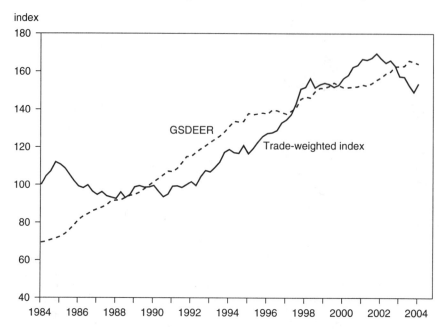

index

GSDEER

Trade-weighted index

GSDEER = Goldman Sachs dynamic equilibrium exchange rate
Rise = dollar appreciation

Source: Goldman Sachs.

that both raise the current account deficit, which may be financed more readily. This research is consistent with aspects of the O'Neill and Hatzius paper. It can be argued that though the US current account deficit is too big, a larger deficit may perhaps be financeable because longer-term capital flows to the United States are sustainable on a larger basis than in the past, due to evidence of stronger US productivity.

This strength in productivity can be linked to a technology shock. The so-called Goldman Sachs dynamic equilibrium exchange rate (GSDEER) model for estimating the equilibrium value of currencies is based on analyzing movements in the real exchange rate against movements in relative productivity. In recent years, the estimated GSDEER fair value for the dollar has risen both on a trade-weighted basis and against important bilateral currencies, such as the euro (figures II.6 and II.7).

This rise is due to the higher productivity performance of the United States against many other nations. Indeed, at the time of this writing, the specific Goldman Sachs trade-weighted estimate suggests that the dollar may be slightly *undervalued*.

This estimate appears to be at odds with comments above suggesting that the current account needs to decline to around 3 percent of GDP. For

Figure II.7 Dollar-euro GSDEER, 1980–2004

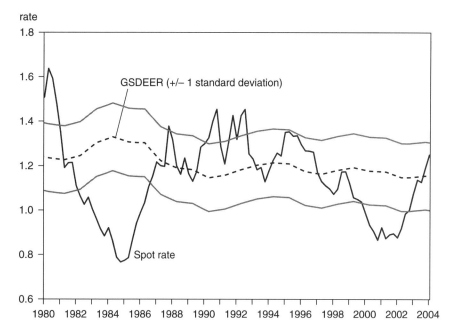

GSDEER = Goldman Sachs dynamic equilibrium exchange rate
Note: Fall = dollar appreciation
Source: Goldman Sachs.

the two approaches to be consistent, either long-term capital flows into the United States will have to rise considerably more, offsetting a persistently large current account deficit, or—and perhaps this is more likely—*future* productivity-driven estimates of fair value for the dollar will be lower.

Indeed, it is difficult to understand why and how a technology shock such as that in the late 1990s can permanently help the United States relative to other countries. Either the US productivity improvement will turn out to be temporary and/or there will be a productivity "catch-up" in other regions.

Of course, there is a strong case to be argued that the dollar *needs* to be undervalued against most conventional estimates of fair value. After all, the dollar was overvalued for much of the late 1990s and early 2000s. The case for an undervalued dollar is rather compelling, especially in view of the need to reduce the current account deficit to more sustainable levels. Indeed, some credible research that focuses on the long-term stability of the net foreign investment or net liability position would argue that the US current account needs to move into balance for a while (O'Neill, Ades, and Fuentes 2004; Lane and Milesi-Ferretti 2002). Such requirements would imply that the dollar needs to fall even more sharply.

Table II.2 Important weights in the trade-weighted dollar, 2004 (percent)

Currency	Weight
Euro	18.53
Canadian dollar	16.50
Japanese yen	11.13
Mexican peso	11.03
Chinese renminbi	9.78
British pound	5.23
Swedish krona	1.09

Source: US Federal Reserve data.

Chapter 4 by Bénassy-Quéré and Colleagues

Chapter 4, by Agnès Bénassy-Quéré and her colleagues, is especially interesting, given its sophisticated technical approach and its modern conceptual framework. In particular, its focus on the growth of bilateral US deficits with many emerging-market countries, especially China, warrants the method that Bénassy-Quéré and her colleagues employed. Only about 50 percent of the modern trade-weighted dollar carries weights with G-7 countries and much of the rest is with developing countries. The weight of the Chinese renminbi and the Mexican peso, combined around 22 percent, is bigger than the weight of the euro (table II.2). Therefore, the approach of Bénassy-Quéré and her colleagues is quite an advance over much of the previous research insofar as it recognizes that the US imbalances are no longer with the G-7 alone.

It is a shame that world policymakers cannot find a better club than the G-7/G-8 to help achieve some improvements in the US imbalances, and a correspondingly more optimal set of policies for the world economy. This is clearly acknowledged by Bénassy-Quéré and her colleagues. It is perhaps the key aspect of part II of this book, and it is something Goldman Sachs has been writing about recently (O'Neill 2001, Wilson and Purushothaman 2003, O'Neill and Hormats 2004). As was shown above, the future world economy may look very different than today (see figure II.1). Of course, projections for world GDP and its makeup in 2050 may turn out somewhat differently, but the growing roles of India, Russia, and especially China suggest that an improved structure for current world policymaking is necessary.

Linked to this theme, the chapter by Bénassy-Quéré and her colleagues very clearly shows how the consequences for the Group of Three currencies may vary, depending on whether some important emerging currencies share in any future dollar weakness. The results demonstrating the sensitivity of the euro to the consequences of a Chinese renminbi move

Figure II.8 Basic balance of payments versus current account for BRIC nations, 1997–2003

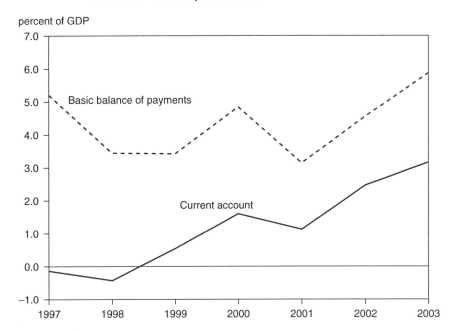

percent of GDP

BRIC = Brazil, Russia, India, and China
Sources: Goldman Sachs; national accounts.

against the dollar are especially useful, not least because this is a topical issue. A significant appreciation of the renminbi would almost definitely allow further euro strength against the dollar to be less damaging than otherwise.

Some observers may believe that the importance of China, India, and other countries to stimulate the reduction in the US current account deficit is overstated and/or that some of these countries should be allowed to run current account surpluses to help them reach their long-term potential. However, if the United States is to have any chance of reducing its growing broad basic balance of payments deficit, the major developing countries will need to reduce their growing broad balance of payments surpluses.

The overall broad basic balance—the aggregation of the current account, net FDI, and net portfolio flows—is a good guide to the net commercial supply and demand for a currency. Presumably, over repeated cycles, countries should be hoping to achieve a position close to zero. A current account deficit should ideally be offset by a similar-sized surplus in the other components of the broad balance, and a current account surplus should be offset by a similar-sized deficit. Currently, all four of the so-called

BRIC nations (Brazil, Russia, India, and China) are running surpluses on all three components of the broad basic balance (figure II.8).

This growing basic balance surplus of the BRIC countries suggests that their currencies may be too cheap, and certainly that they deserve to be part of any dollar depreciation in the future. This is clearly recognized more by Bénassy-Quéré and her colleagues than by many others, and they deserve congratulations for this research.

References

O'Neill, Jim. 2001. *Building Better Global Economic BRICs.* Global Economics Paper 66. New York: Goldman Sachs.

O'Neill, Jim, and Jan Hatzius. 2004. *US Balance of Payments: Unsustainable, But. . . .* Global Economics Paper 104. New York: Goldman Sachs.

O'Neill, Jim, and Robert Hormats. 2004. *The G-8: Time for a Change.* Global Economics Paper 112. New York: Goldman Sachs.

O'Neill, Jim, Alberto Ades, and Monica Fuentes. 2004. *An Alternative to a Further Necessary Modest US$ Decline: A Large Decline!* Global Markets Viewpoint 04/33. New York: Goldman Sachs.

Lane, P. R., and G. M. Milesi-Ferretti. 2002. External Wealth, the Trade Balance, and the Real Exchange Rate. *European Economic Review* 46: 1049–71.

Wilson, Dominic, and Roopa Purushothaman. 2003. *Dreaming with BRICs: The Path to 2050.* Global Economics Paper 99. New York: Goldman Sachs.

III

THE IMPACT OF A MAJOR DOLLAR REALIGNMENT

5

Exchange Rate Adjustments Needed to Reduce Global Payments Imbalances

MICHAEL MUSSA

The United States is now running a current account deficit that exceeds $500 billion a year—by far the largest international payments imbalance ever recorded by any country. Plausible estimates suggest that—at present exchange rates and with US economic growth continuing to exceed that of most other industrial countries—the US external deficit could reach $1 trillion by the end of this decade. The cumulative effect of these external deficits is reflected in the US net external liability position, which is now about 25 percent of annual GDP and which could rise to 50 percent within a decade and to more than 100 percent within the next 25 years.

On the other side of the US external payments position lies that of the rest of the world. Leaving aside the measurement problems associated with the global payments discrepancy, the combined current account surplus of the rest of the world amounts to about 1.5 percent of the GDP of the rest of the world (vs. about 5 percent of US GDP). This surplus tends not to be seen as a particular problem—at least until it is recognized that significant reduction in the US external payments deficit requires a corresponding reduction in the external surplus of the rest of the world and a corresponding negative impulse to output growth in the rest of the world.

Are the US external deficit, the associated buildup of US net foreign liabilities, and the corresponding developments in the rest of the world really important problems that require urgent attention? There are two extreme views on this question, each of which has (in its sophisticated and intellectually respectable form) a strong advocate among those asso-

Michael Mussa is a senior fellow at the Institute for International Economics.

ciated with the Institute for International Economics. On one side, the Institute's chair, Peter G. Peterson (in his new best-seller, *Running on Empty*), takes Chicken Little's "The sky is falling!" view that the US current account deficit and the US fiscal deficit are clearly on unsustainable paths and that serious damage to the US economy is likely to occur unless something is urgently done to correct these problems. On the other side, the chair of the Institute's Academic Advisory Panel, Richard N. Cooper, is an advocate of Alfred E. Newman's "What me worry?" view that US net foreign liabilities are only a small fraction of total US wealth (measured as the present value of US national income) and that the growth of these liabilities is unlikely to pose a serious problem as long as strong growth of the US economy continues to imply rapid increases in total US wealth.

The Institute's director, C. Fred Bergsten, is an advocate of "responsible excess" as a strategy for presenting the work of the Institute. However, with the extremes on the present issue already taken up, within the limits of intellectual respectability, by Peterson and Cooper, I am left with the alternative of being extremely moderate.

To that end, I argue in this chapter that there probably is a practical upper limit for US net external liabilities at something less than 100 percent of US GDP and, accordingly, that current account deficits of 5 percent or more of US GDP are not indefinitely sustainable. Conversely, the US current account deficit does not need to be eliminated to achieve external payments sustainability. For the United States, which is particularly attractive to foreign investors, current account deficits of up to 2 percent of GDP or slightly more, and net foreign liability ratios as high as 40 or even 50 percent of GDP, are probably sustainable without undue economic strain or risk of crisis.

Bringing the US current account deficit down from about 5 to 2 percent of GDP (and achieving a reverse change in the current account balance of the rest of the world) requires some key macroeconomic adjustments. Consistent with the focus of this volume, adjustments of exchange rates are particularly important. Specifically, it is argued below that a real effective depreciation of the dollar of about 30 percent (from the baseline of the period from mid-2000 to mid-2002) will probably be needed in connection with an improvement of about 3 percent of GDP in the US current account balance. Concerning the magnitude and timing of adjustments of individual exchange rates against the dollar, there is no sound basis for precise conclusions, but it is possible to reach some broad judgments about key individual exchange rate changes that might be expected to contribute to a 30 percent average real depreciation of the dollar over a time horizon of four to five years.

Exchange rate adjustments, however, are only one of three important classes of macroeconomic adjustments that must occur to address the problem of global payments imbalances represented by the large US current account deficit and rapidly growing net foreign liabilities. In addition, it is required that

- in the United States, domestic demand grow more slowly than domestic output to make room for an expansion of US net exports, and as logically necessary counterparts of this downward adjustment of US demand relative to output, there must be a corresponding improvement in the US national savings/investment balance and an equivalent reduction in the net use of foreign savings by the United States;

- in the rest of the world, domestic demand grow more rapidly than domestic output to allow for a reduction of net exports that corresponds to the improvement of US net exports.

And as logically necessary counterparts of this upward adjustment of demand relative to output, there must be a corresponding deterioration in the savings/investment balance and an equivalent reduction in the net outflow of capital to the United States from the rest of the world.

Indeed, from the perspective of challenges for economic policies around the world, the key issue is not primarily securing adequate adjustments of exchange rates. Those adjustments will eventually come, perhaps rapidly and disruptively, as the enthusiasm of foreign wealth holders (and central banks) for continued massive accumulation of United States–based assets begins to wane or even possibly reverses. The principal challenge for economic policy is to ensure that the exchange rate and other key macroeconomic adjustments essential to reducing global payments imbalances take place in a manner that allows economic output to remain near its potential in the United States and in the rest of the world.

As discussed below, for the United States, the most important policy adjustment necessary to contribute to a successful result is a gradual and cumulatively substantial reduction of the government deficit. This fiscal adjustment is needed fundamentally for its own sake—to put government finances in the United States on a more sustainable path. The main problem is political—agreeing upon and implementing the requisite changes in expenditure and revenue policies necessary to enforce meaningful fiscal consolidation.

In other industrial countries, the policy challenge is conceptually more difficult. The key problem is sustaining adequate growth of domestic demand to keep output and employment in line with its potential while offsetting the negative impulse associated with deteriorating current account balances. The relatively weak growth of domestic demand in most other industrial countries in recent years, the overextension of government budgets in most industrial countries, and the already easy stance of most monetary policies suggest important difficulties in designing measures to support more rapid growth of domestic demand.

In developing countries, the policy challenges are more mixed. For some countries, especially in emerging Asia, a change in exchange rate policies that have resisted currency appreciation against the dollar is clearly needed. In other countries, notably several in Latin America, the main need is for sound monetary and fiscal policies that will support sustainable recovery and instill confidence among domestic and foreign investors. Over time, success in these areas should permit some real currency appreciation and some widening of current account deficits to levels consistent with sustainable capital inflows and with a meaningful contribution to the reduction of key global payments imbalances.

The Sustainable Scale of External Imbalances

For nearly a quarter of a century, the United States has persistently run significant current account deficits. The cumulative consequence of these deficits is that the United States has been transformed from the world's largest net creditor to its largest net debtor—with a total shift in the US net asset position relative to GDP of about 50 percentage points since 1970. So far, the United States does not appear to have suffered significant ill effects from these developments, despite widely expressed fears of a "hard landing" in the 1980s and other dire warnings of catastrophe.[1] Nevertheless, this massive shift in the US net asset position and the persistent deficits that underlie it naturally give rise to the question: Is there any limit?

Plausible Limits to US Net External Liabilities

The alarmists of the Chicken Little school insist that there is a limit and that the threat that we may soon test that limit raises substantial risk of a foreign exchange crisis, or even of a broader financial crisis, for the United States and the global economy. Conversely, the unbridled optimists of the Alfred E. Newman school take the view that if there is a limit it is quite far off, and that, provided that the United States continues to perform well, it can go on piling up net external liabilities at a prodigious pace for a considerable time.

I take the middle ground between the fears of Chicken Little and the complacency of Alfred E. Newman. In particular, I broadly share the conclusions of Catherine Mann in the analysis she prepared several years ago.[2] There must be some upper limit on the amount of net claims that foreigners will wish to hold against the United States (and its resident businesses and

---

1. In popular discussions, it is often suggested that large US current account deficits result in high unemployment. This view, however, is fundamentally nonsense from a medium- or longer-run perspective. For instance, the unemployment rate in the United States in the second half of the 1990s was generally the lowest it has been since the late 1960s, notwithstanding the fact that the US current account deficit widened greatly between 1995 and 2001.

2. Catherine Mann, *Is the US Trade Deficit Sustainable?* (Washington: Institute for International Economics, 1999).

households) on terms that will be attractive both to the foreigners who hold these assets and to the US residents that have the obligations to service them.

There is, however, no indication yet that we may be approaching that upper limit. Nor, in my view, is there any way to estimate with precision and confidence where that limit might be. Nevertheless, there is good reason to suppose that US current account deficits of 5 percent or more of GDP cannot continue for a decade or longer and that there should be some urgency to fostering adjustments that would give evidence that US external payments are moving toward a more clearly sustainable path.

As a starting point for the analysis of this issue, it needs to be emphasized that achieving a zero current account deficit is not necessary to stabilize the US ratio of net external liabilities to GDP. This ratio, call it $n = N/Y$, stabilizes when the current account deficit as a share of GDP, call it $c = C/Y$, is equal to the rate of growth of GDP, call it g, multiplied by the net foreign liability ratio; that is, n stabilizes when $c = g \times n$. In this formula, N, Y, and C are all measured in nominal dollars, and g is the growth rate of nominal GDP. Because the issues concerning sustainability of the US external position are fundamentally longer-run issues, the relevant growth rate for nominal GDP, g, is the long-run average annual growth rate of Y. It is plausible to assume that g is about 5 percent a year—with about 3 percent coming from annual real GDP growth and about 2 percent coming from annual increases in the GDP deflator.[3]

At present, the US current account deficit is about 5 percent of US GDP; that is, $c = C/Y$ equals about 0.05. The ratio of net foreign assets to GDP, $n = N/Y$, is presently about 25 percent. Thus, c is presently greater than $g \times n$; $c = 0.05 > 0.25 \times 0.05 = n \times g$. The excess of c over $n \times g$ generally implies that the ratio of net foreign assets must be rising. Indeed (ignoring some complications to be discussed), the current account deficit is equal to the annual increase in US net foreign liabilities—presently running at about 5 percent of GDP. In contrast, an increase of net foreign liabilities of only one-fourth that amount (corresponding to the present ratio of N to Y) would be consistent with keeping the present ratio of N to Y constant.

We may further calculate that if the current account deficit were to be somehow stabilized at its present ratio to GDP (i.e., at 5 percent), then the ratio of US net foreign liabilities would continue to rise until it reached 100 percent of GDP. Using the same logic, we may calculate that if the US current account deficit were reduced to and stabilized at 3 percent of GDP, the US net foreign liability position would eventually level out at 60 percent of GDP; $c = 0.03$ is equal to $n = 0.6 \times g = 0.05$. Similarly, if the current account

---

3. Formally, working in continuous time, let $D(X)$ be the operator that takes the derivative of X with respect to time. Then $D(n) = D(N/Y) = (D(N)/Y) - (N/Y)g = (D(N)/Y) - ng$. Ignoring the issue of capital gains and losses on foreign assets and liabilities (to be addressed below), use the fact that the change in net foreign liabilities is equal to the current account deficit; i.e., $D(N) = C$. It follows that $D(N)/Y = C/Y = c$ and hence that $D(n) = D(N/Y) = c - ng$. Thus, the ratio of net foreign liabilities (N) to GDP (Y) is rising when $c > ng$, is falling when $c < ng$, and is stable when $c = ng$.

deficit were reduced to and stabilized at 2 percent of GDP, then US net foreign liabilities would be contained at 40 percent of GDP; $c = 0.02$ is equal to
$n = 0.4 \times g = 0.05$.

No one knows, or can estimate with great confidence, the outer limit of
US net foreign liabilities that would be tolerable both to US residents as net
debtors to the rest of the world and to residents of the rest of the world as
holders of claims on assets located in the United States. However, no country
of significant size has ever run up a net external liability position approaching 100 percent of its GDP. And for the world's largest economy (accounting
for about one-quarter of global GDP), there would be the special challenge
of persuading foreign investors to forgo diversification and vest an exceptionally large fraction of their total external investment in a single country.

Thus, while there is no absolute proof that there is an impenetrable upper
bound on US net external liabilities at about 100 percent of GDP, it is prudent to conclude that this boundary should not be tested. This, in turn,
implies that US current account deficits of 5 percent of GDP or larger are not
sustainable in the longer term.

Conversely, neither US residents nor foreign investors in United States–
based assets seem troubled at present by a net external liability ratio of
25 percent of GDP or by the likely prospect that this ratio will rise significantly in the next several years as a consequence of continuing, substantial
US current account deficits.

The decline in the foreign exchange value of the dollar against most
other industrial-country currencies since 2002, together with the shift of
foreign investment in the United States away from private investment and
toward official reserve accumulation, may suggest some slackening of foreign enthusiasm for US assets. However, the extent and pace of the dollar's downward correction do not indicate investor panic about either the
present scale or the likely near-term growth of US net external liabilities.
Thus, it would appear that net external liability ratios of perhaps 40 to
50 percent of GDP would not challenge long-term external payments sustainability. Correspondingly, continuing US current account deficits that
would decline gradually to about 2 percent of GDP (or slightly higher)
would appear to be sustainable in the longer term.

This conclusion recognizes that there are good reasons why the United
States is a particularly attractive place for foreigners to invest significant
fractions of their wealth. The United States has an exceptional record of
economic and political stability—unrivaled by any other large country
over the past two centuries.[4] Property rights are respected and protected.

---

4. Among the Group of Seven countries, the United States suffered economic turbulence and
substantial inflation in connection with the Civil War of 1861–65. But the United Kingdom lost
its empire in the 20th century and had about three times as much price inflation as the United
States. Canada became a self-governing commonwealth only in 1867. Germany and Italy did
not exist as national entities until 1871, and they, along with France and Japan, suffered substantial economic turbulence in connection with the world wars of the 20th century.

There is a wide diversity of assets available to foreign investors, including vast quantities of equities, real estate and other real assets, and privately issued bonds and mortgages, as well as highly secure government debt. Investors are generally well treated, and there is no record of any significant discrimination against foreign as compared with domestic investors.

These attractions for foreign investment in the United States are probably an important part of the explanation of why, with a net debtor position of already about 25 percent of GDP, the United States still seems able to secure inward foreign investment on terms (e.g., interest rates on bonds) that are below the returns that US residents earn on their investments abroad. However, as the US net debtor position rises higher and higher, the United States will probably need to offer more attractive terms to continue to attract large additional inflows of foreign investment.

This, in turn, should make US residents less enthusiastic about increasing their net foreign liabilities. When the situation reaches the point at which US residents are unwilling to offer the improved returns necessary to attract further increases in net foreign investment, the game will end. No one knows where this point is, though it appears to be well beyond the present ratio of US net foreign liabilities to GDP. My guess is that for the United States, a net external liability ratio of 40 percent of GDP, and probably up to 50 percent of GDP, is not a problem, but sustainability becomes highly questionable for ratios rising toward 100 percent of GDP.

Several Complexities and a Conclusion

The preceding discussion has bypassed a number of caveats and complexities that are of some practical importance in discussing external imbalances and exchange rate adjustments likely to be required to reduce these imbalances. A few of these are worthy of at least brief mention.

First, significant measurement error (and some important conceptual difficulties) infect reported figures for the current account balances of the United States and other countries. In particular, at the global level, whereas the sum of all countries' current account balances should be zero, the actual sum in recent years—the global current account discrepancy—has shown a significant global deficit. It is plausible that some of this global current account discrepancy is reflected in the measured US current account deficit, with the effect of raising the measured US deficit by one-quarter to one-half of 1 percent of US GDP. If there is such overstatement in the measured US current account deficit, then the adjustments necessary to reduce the true deficit to any particular level (e.g., 2 percent of US GDP) are correspondingly reduced.

Second, the effects of exchange rates and other variables on current account balances occur with varying lags and are estimated with considerable potential for error. For the United States, it appears that exchange rate changes take about two years to have the bulk of their effect on the current account. Thus, the current account result for 2004 still reflects, to a considerable extent, the very strong dollar of 2000–02, rather than the weaker dollar since 2002. It is unclear, however, how much downward adjustment of the current account deficit from its 2004 level should be assumed on the basis of the dollar's depreciation from 2002 to 2004. This uncertainty, in turn, adds to the uncertainty about how much further dollar depreciation will be needed to help reduce the US current account deficit to some specific level, such as 2 percent of GDP.

Third, the current account positions consistent with given patterns of exchange rates and growth rates of national economies are surely evolving over time, but in ways that are not perfectly predictable. In particular, for the United States, the Houthakker-Magee results (which have held up for more than three decades) suggest that because the US income elasticity of imports multiplied by the growth rate of US GDP is greater than the income elasticity of foreign demand for US exports multiplied by the growth rate of foreign income, the dollar must depreciate continually in real terms to sustain any given ratio of the current account deficit to GDP.

Recent estimates by Catherine Mann indicate that, taking account of this effect (and of the present large difference between the value of US imports and the value of US exports), the US current account deficit at present exchange rates would widen by about 1 percent of GDP per year to reach $1 trillion by 2010. If this is correct, then the adjustments required to reduce the US current account deficit to sustainable proportions will be correspondingly greater than suggested in the discussion below.

Fourth, the net foreign investment positions of the United States and other countries are measured with considerable uncertainty; and because of both conceptual issues and measurement problems, changes in these positions do not correspond to current account imbalances. For the United States, there is no comprehensive register of foreign investment (particularly by private individuals) and at least some foreign investors undoubtedly have strong incentives not to report their external investments to their own authorities. (For example, it is estimated that about half of the total US currency outstanding is held by foreigners, but who they are and where they are cannot be pinned down with confidence.) This uncertainty may lead, on balance, to undermeasurement of US assets held by foreigners.

Conversely, the concept of the current account balance excludes capital gains and losses as part of both US earnings on foreign assets and US payments to foreigners on their holdings of US assets. Standard estimates of the net foreign asset position of the United States are based on historical cost and also exclude such capital gains and losses; but other estimates that seek to reflect current market values take account of cumulative capital gains and losses. In general, US owners of foreign assets have enjoyed greater capital gains on their foreign assets (especially direct investments and portfolio equity) than foreigners have earned on their US assets (which are more heavily concentrated in debt instruments that return interest rather than capital gains). This factor has tended to keep the US net foreign liability position growing less rapidly than would be implied by the accumulation of US current account deficits.

Fifth, real capital losses from the effect of inflation eroding the value of nominal investments in bonds and similar instruments are not recorded in current accounts, either as losses for the holders of such instruments or as gains for their issuers. As a large net issuer of nominal instruments to the rest of the world, the United States undoubtedly enjoys a net unrecorded benefit from this source. Also, US debt instruments held by foreigners are predominantly denominated in US dollars, whereas US investments abroad are either real assets, equity, or debt instruments denominated to a significant extent in foreign currencies.

As William Cline emphasizes, this means that when the US dollar depreciates against foreign currencies, the US net foreign liability position tends to improve.[5] The dollar value of US gross investments in most foreign assets goes up, while the dollar value of a large volume of foreign gross investments in United States–based assets remains unchanged. The effect can be significant. Assuming (conservatively) that each 1 percent depreciation of the dollar generates a 1 percent capital gain on each dollar of US net foreign liabilities, then a 20 percent dollar depreciation operating on net foreign liabilities of 25 percent of GDP generates a gain of 5 percent of US GDP.

Finally, the sustainable level of the US current account deficit and of US net external liabilities is surely not invariant to key economic developments in the United States and elsewhere in the world economy. For example, the growth of the US current account deficit during the 1990s appears to have had benign—even beneficial—consequences in light of what was going on that helped to induce this deficit. Surely the acceleration of productivity growth in the United States was a good thing, even if it did not spread in equal measure to the rest of the world. The difficulties in other industrial countries and the catastrophic crises that afflicted emerging-market economies were not good things. However, given that these bad things happened, the widening of the US current account deficit and the appreciation of the dollar were favorable developments from the perspective of the performance of the world economy. Moreover, the widening of the US external deficit in the 1990s was clearly not the result of an irresponsible and unsustainable US fiscal policy; the US government budget moved into significant surplus for the first time in three decades.

Looking forward, if the next decade looks like a repeat of the 1990s—with the US economy driven by rapid productivity growth and the US budget moving to surplus while much of the rest of the world economy is mired in difficulty—then continuing large US current account deficits,

---

5. See William Cline, *The United States as a Debtor Nation: Problems, Policies, and Prospects* (Washington: Institute for International Economics, forthcoming).

financed by large voluntary foreign capital inflows, would probably also be a good thing. In contrast, if US economic performance is modest while the rest of the world booms, and if large US current account deficits persist because of a failure to address US fiscal problems, then this will not be a good thing. Moreover, in this latter situation, foreign wealth holders may well cease to be such enthusiastic investors in the US economy, with the result that the United States may experience significant difficulties in financing continued large external deficits.

Taking account of these complexities, I would still conclude that persistent US current account deficits of 5 percent of GDP or more (and net foreign liability ratios threatening to rise to 100 percent of GDP or higher) are not sustainable in the longer term. Conversely, US current account deficits of 2 percent of GDP or a little higher (with net foreign liability ratios rising to no more than about 50 percent of GDP) probably are sustainable—especially if it is perceived that timely adjustment in the next few years will put US external payments clearly on a path that will respect these limits.

The General Need for Dollar Depreciation

As was emphasized above, several important things will need to happen to reduce the US current account deficit to a sustainable level of about 2 percent of GDP. One of these things is that there must be a substantial depreciation of the dollar in real effective terms against the currencies of US trading partners. Such a depreciation is needed to shift the pattern of global demand toward goods and services produced by the United States and, correspondingly, away from goods and services produced by other countries—with the effect of raising US exports relative to US imports and thereby improving the US trade and current account balances.

What may reasonably be concluded about the extent of dollar depreciation that will be needed to contribute to the reduction of the US external deficit to sustainable proportions? A precise answer is not available, for at least two key reasons: The extent of the reduction in the US current account deficit needed to achieve external payments sustainability is not known with precision; and the (reduced-form) relationship between the real effective exchange rate of the dollar and the US current account deficit is neither precise nor invariant to other key developments that will affect global payments imbalances.

Real Effective Depreciation of the Dollar by About 30 Percent

Nevertheless, there is a reasonably stable empirical relationship between the real exchange rate of the dollar and the US current account deficit (with a lag of about two years). This relationship appears to be sufficiently reliable to give at least a broad idea of the extent of dollar depreciation that would be needed to reduce the US current account deficit by about 3 percent of GDP.

Indeed, though a variety of estimates of the sensitivity of the US current account to the dollar exchange rate are available, I like to use a simple relationship that says that a 10 percent real effective depreciation of the dollar (measured as a change in the natural logarithm of the Federal Reserve's broad exchange rate index for the dollar) will be associated with an improvement of about 1 percent in the ratio of the current account to GDP. This is a somewhat larger response than suggested by many estimates, but it is not out of the ballpark and is consistent with both the precision of our knowledge and the spirit of this exercise. Using this estimate, it follows that a 30 percent real depreciation of the dollar would be needed in connection with an improvement in the US current account of about 3 percent of GDP.

The average real effective exchange rate of the dollar between the middle of 2000 and the middle of 2002 is taken as the base from which the required depreciation needs to occur. This base (which corresponds closely to the peak value of the dollar since the mid-1980s) is selected because the normal two-year lag in the relationship between the exchange rate and the US current account balance indicates that the deficit of about 5 percent of GDP in 2003–04 is reflective of this base exchange rate.

Since its recent peak, the dollar has depreciated by a little more than 10 percent in real effective terms—with most of this downward correction occurring during 2003 and against the currencies of other industrial countries. This suggests that about one-third of the necessary downward correction in the value of the dollar has already taken place (as of mid-2004). It also suggests that about another 20 percent real dollar depreciation is still needed to help restore a sustainable US external payments position.

To achieve a substantial downward adjustment in the real effective foreign exchange value of the dollar, the value of the dollar obviously must decline against the currencies of most US trading partners. Given a requirement for a real effective depreciation of 30 percent (from the average level of mid-2000 to mid-2002), by how much should the dollar adjust against individual foreign currencies?

There is no reasonable and succinct way to answer this question. Indeed, little can be said with high confidence on this issue beyond three general principles. First, to achieve a real effective depreciation of 30 percent, the dollar must depreciate by 30 percent on average against the currencies of each of the other countries.

Second, though the magnitude and timing of exchange rate adjustments may vary considerably across different countries, significant depreciation of the dollar against the currencies of all significant US trading partners is likely to be needed and appropriate in the medium to longer term.

Third, the extent of downward correction of the foreign exchange value of the dollar against individual currencies should respect market forces and should appropriately reflect the strength of these countries' external payments positions. In particular, this means that countries facing upward market pressures on their exchange rates or giving other evidence of the undervaluation of their exchange rates should be expected to allow significant appreciations of their currencies against the dollar and, probably to a lesser extent, allow appreciation on a real effective basis. In contrast, countries with downward market pressures on their exchange rates or other indications of possible currency overvaluation should expect less appreciation (or, in some cases, possibly even depreciation) against the dollar.

Taking account of these three general principles, and without intending to be precise about the magnitude or timing of individual exchange rate adjustments, it is nevertheless useful for the purposes of this discussion to give some quantitative indication of the scale of exchange rate adjustments likely to be needed and appropriate in connection with the restoration of external payments sustainability for the United States. Let us do this first for industrial and then for developing countries.

Exchange Rate Adjustments Against Industrial Countries

The euro area (to which I attach Denmark, Sweden, and Switzerland for the purposes of this discussion) is the world's largest trading entity and approaches the United States in the size of its aggregate economy. Clearly, substantial depreciation of the dollar against the euro (from the average level of €1 equaling about $0.90 for the period mid-2000 to mid-2002) is an essential part of achieving a 30 percent real depreciation of the dollar. A significant appreciation of the euro has already occurred since mid-2002, taking the euro's exchange value to just above $1.20 in mid-2004.

Most of this appreciation was a reversal of the euro's somewhat surprising and ultimately excessive depreciation during the period 1999–2000. Although partly reflecting the relatively weak recovery from the world recession of 2001, the euro area has a relatively strong external payments position. Thus, it is reasonable to expect that further appreciation of the euro against the US dollar—to the range of $1.35 to $1.45 per €1—would be an appropriate counterpart of necessary further downward correction of the foreign exchange value of the dollar.

A total move of the euro from about $0.90 to about $1.40 implies a real appreciation against the dollar (measured as a logarithmic change) of 44 percent. This means that appreciation of the euro would contribute significantly more than the average amount required to achieve a 30 percent real effective depreciation of the dollar. This is reasonable in view of the excessive depreciation of the euro at a value of $0.90 and the continuing relatively strong external payments position of the euro area.

The timing of further euro appreciation is a more subtle matter. The significant appreciation of the euro in the past two years already makes an important contribution to the needed downward correction of the dollar, while contribution from other (particularly developing-country) exchange rate adjustments has been more modest or nonexistent. Meanwhile, the recovery of the euro area economies since 2001 has been quite sluggish, probably partly as a consequence of the euro's appreciation against virtually all other currencies. Thus, it would not seem untoward if market forces allowed further euro appreciation to take a bit of a breather while other needed exchange rate adjustments catch up.

The exchange rate of the pound sterling has been very strong in recent years, with the pound tending to follow the dollar up against the euro in fiscal 1999–2000 and tending to follow the euro up against the dollar in fiscal 2002–04. In mid-2004 (at the time of this writing), the pound appears somewhat overvalued in real effective terms. (The UK economy has prospered because of strong household consumption and residential investment, but the tradable goods sector has suffered.) This suggests that modest further appreciation of the pound against the dollar (of about 5 percent, to about £1 to $1.90, from just above $1.80) should be more than offset in real effective terms by further moderate depreciation (of about 10 percent) against the euro.

In total, taking the pound-dollar exchange rate from about $1.50 in the base period to about $1.90 amounts to a 24 percent appreciation of the pound against the dollar (measured logarithmically). Thus, with an exchange rate that was already strongly valued in the base period, the pound would reasonably contribute somewhat less than the average to a 30 percent downward correction of the dollar.

The Japanese economy was exceptionally weak from 1997 through 2001. With two recessions, cumulative real GDP growth was negative during this five-year period; and the general price level was falling in the only episode of sustained deflation in an industrial country since the 1930s. Traditional macroeconomic policies were pressed to their expansionary limits, with the government budget in large deficit and monetary authorities pursuing a zero interest rate policy for most of the period.

In this situation, a weak foreign exchange value of the yen was desirable, in comparison with the exchange rate that would have been appropriate for a more normally performing Japanese economy. And it was appropriate for the authorities to encourage a suitably weak yen through foreign exchange market intervention when that was not the outcome of market forces.

As a consequence of these forces, the yen-dollar exchange rate in the base period (mid-2000 to mid-2002) was only about ¥125/$1. Subsequently, the yen has appreciated against the dollar, briefly reaching ¥105/$1, but more recently stabilizing at about ¥110/$1. Thus, the appreciation of the yen against the dollar since the base period has been about 13 percent (measured logarithmically), in comparison with an appreciation of the euro of about 30 percent. (Because inflation in Japan has been slightly negative and meaningfully below inflation in the United States, the real appreciation of the yen against the dollar since the base period has been only about 8 percent.)

During the past two years, aided by a weak yen, the Japanese economy has begun to recover more vigorously and has achieved significantly stronger real GDP growth than the euro area. Through March 2004, the Japanese authorities maintained their policy of resisting rapid appreciation of the yen through official intervention—which reached a massive scale during the first quarter of 2004 (see chapter 8 of the present volume). However, now that the Japanese economy appears to have regained significant forward momentum, a policy of trying to keep the yen exceptionally weak no longer makes sense—especially from a global perspective that recognizes both the longer-term need to reduce key external imbalances and the shorter-term requirements for keeping output close to potential in a number of countries with significant economic slack.

In the short term of the next year or so, continued Japanese recovery might be threatened if the yen were to appreciate suddenly much beyond ¥100/$1; and the authorities might reasonably offer some resistance to market pressures tending to produce such rapid appreciation. However, over the next three to five years, assuming that the Japanese economy continues to recover toward its potential growth path, it is reasonable to expect that the yen will appreciate significantly further against the dollar to a level of ¥85 or ¥90/$1. This implies a total appreciation of the yen-dollar exchange rate of about 35 percent (measured logarithmically) from the base period. Taking account of inflation differentials, the total real appreciation is slightly less than 30 percent.

Moreover, if the currencies of other countries (notably Asian emerging-market countries as well as other industrial countries) also appreciate significantly against the dollar, then the total real effective appreciation of the yen will be substantially less than 30 percent—probably only 15 percent. This is a quite modest adjustment considering that the Japanese yen was (for good but temporary reasons) exceptionally weak in the base period.

Although their economies performed relatively well, the exchange rates of the Australian, Canadian, and New Zealand dollars were very weak in the base period. Subsequently, all these currencies have appreciated against the US dollar and (somewhat less so) in real effective terms—aided by rising world commodity prices.

Focusing on Canada, given its much greater importance as a US trading partner than Australia or New Zealand, the appreciation of the Canadian dollar has been about 14 percent—from about US$0.65 in the base period to about US$0.75 around mid-2004. Further appreciation during the next few years might reasonably take the Canadian dollar above US$0.80, to perhaps as high as US$0.85. This would amount to a total appreciation of the Canadian dollar against the US dollar from the base period of about 25 percent. The real effective appreciation of the Canadian dollar would be only moderately less (about 20 percent), reflecting the dominant position of the United States as Canada's principal trading partner. This fairly large change in Canada's real effective exchange rate makes reasonable sense in view of the large swing from deficit to surplus in the Canadian current account since the mid-1990s—evidence that the Canadian dollar was meaningfully undervalued in much of this period.

Exchange Rate Adjustments Against Developing Countries

Nearly 40 percent of US trade now takes place with developing countries, and a significant fraction of the deterioration of the US external payments position since the mid-1990s corresponds with the improvement in the aggregate current account position of developing counties. From these facts, it is apparent that developing countries as a group must play an important role as counterparts to both the improvement in the US current account and the depreciation of the real effective exchange rate of the dollar.

This does not mean that on a bilateral, country-by-country basis the US trade balance should necessarily be expected to improve against all individual developing countries. Nor, in particular, does it mean that exchange rate and other adjustments by individual developing countries should be targeted on some basis, such as the size of bilateral trade imbalances with the United States.

Nevertheless, developing countries as a group are far too large a fraction of "the rest of the world" for anyone reasonably to believe that a substantial reduction in the US external deficit could occur without a significant movement in the other direction in the aggregate external payments position of developing countries. Similarly, a substantial (30 percent real effective) depreciation of the dollar—which is essential to restoring a sustainable US current account position—must include significant real depreciation of the dollar against the broad range of developing countries.

For developing countries, however, this required exchange rate adjustment poses policy issues that do not arise for most industrial countries. With the notable exception of Japan, industrial countries generally allow the exchange rates of their currencies against the US dollar to fluctuate freely in response to market forces—without resorting to massive official intervention or other policies to influence the exchange rate against the dollar. During the past two years, these floating exchange rate policies have allowed substantial real appreciations against the dollar—real appreciations that will go a considerable distance toward those required to achieve a more sustainable pattern of international payments positions.

In contrast, for most developing countries there has been very little real currency appreciation against the dollar during the past two years. Indeed, on a real effective basis, many developing countries have experienced real depreciations. This is not generally the result of market forces operating on market-determined exchange rates (although it may be so in some cases, e.g., Mexico). Instead, it is primarily the result of the exchange rate policies of many developing countries that either peg the rate against the dollar (de jure or de facto) or that aggressively limit fluctuations in the rate against the dollar through official intervention and other policies.

One important manifestation of these exchange rate policies is the massive buildup since 2001 of official foreign exchange reserves by several key Asian emerging-market economies (and the similar buildup of official reserves by Japan). In this regard, China is the country whose exchange rate policy and reserve accumulation are most often cited as issues of concern; and my colleagues Morris Goldstein and Nicholas Lardy have rightly focused on the need for adjustment in China's exchange rate and related policies (see Goldstein's chapter in the present volume).

However, important as the Chinese case may be, the issues about exchange rate policies and reserve accumulation apply much more broadly than just to China. Indeed, combined official reserve accumulation since 2001 by the main Asian surplus economies other than China has been more than double the reserve accumulation of China, and the combined current account surpluses of these countries are much larger than China's surplus, both in absolute terms (measured in dollars) and relative to GDP.

Because exchange rates are—by definition—exchange values between different national currencies, no country can logically claim exclusive property rights in "its" exchange rate. And especially because present concerns about external imbalances are fundamentally global concerns, the exchange rate adjustments needed to reduce these imbalances should be made from a multilateral and global perspective.

The importance of this multilateral and global perspective on exchange rate issues is well illustrated by the case of China. As convincingly advocated by Goldstein and Lardy, an appreciation of the renminbi by 15 to 25 percent against the dollar—together with repegging to a basket of the dollar, the euro, and the yen and with allowance for a wider band of market-determined exchange rate fluctuation—is a reasonable response to the clear need for a significant modification of the Chinese exchange rate policy.

Yet the Goldstein-Lardy proposal makes much more sense if (as they intend) it is part of a broader modification of exchange rate policies of most Asian emerging-market economies (and Japan). Appreciation of the renminbi against the dollar means much less in terms of effective appreciation against all Chinese trading partners if it is accompanied by significant appreciations of other Asian emerging-market currencies (and the yen). Similarly, for other Asian emerging-market economies, upward adjustments in the foreign exchange values of their currencies will appear much more digestible if they are not pursued in isolation but rather as part of a general upward adjustment in the value of Asian currencies against the dollar.

In view of the general need for downward adjustment in the real effective exchange rate of the dollar, of the strength of the external payments positions of Asian emerging-market economies, and of the evident market pressures for appreciations of these currencies, appreciations of 20 to 25 percent of

Asian currencies (including the yen) appear broadly appropriate over the next few years.

Of course, the situation does differ somewhat across different Asian economies. For example, the difficulties of Hong Kong's economy in recent years suggest that the case for the appreciation of the Hong Kong dollar is weaker than for most Asian currencies, including the Chinese renminbi. Accordingly, the appreciation of the Hong Kong dollar against the US dollar should plausibly be somewhat less than the appreciations of other Asian currencies, implying relatively little real effective appreciation of the Hong Kong dollar. On somewhat different grounds, a case can be made that the appreciations of the Indonesian rupiah, the Thai baht, and the Philippine peso should be somewhat less than the average for Asian currencies. But the details of individual country cases are too complex to get into in detail.

The situation in Latin America is quite different from that in emerging Asia. Argentina, Brazil, and Venezuela, as well as several smaller countries, have experienced significant economic difficulties since 2000; and the exchange rates of their currencies have all come under significant downward pressure. Mexico, which is by far the most important US trading partner in Latin America, has not experienced an economic crisis, but the peso has been under downward pressure and, in response to market forces, has depreciated against the dollar from about 9.5 pesos to $1 in the base period to more than 11 pesos to $1 in mid-2004, implying a real depreciation against the dollar of about 15 percent.

Looking ahead, it seems plausible that as the Mexican economy regains stronger forward momentum and as the currencies of countries that produce competing products for export to the United States appreciate, the peso should recover the ground that it has recently lost against the dollar. But real appreciation of the Mexican peso to 20 or 30 percent above its level in the base period does not seem plausible. Unlike virtually all other currencies, the Mexican peso was probably too strong against the dollar from mid-2000 to mid-2002; and the implication now is that there is not great potential for appreciation above that base-period level.

For other key Latin American countries, the potential for real appreciation against the dollar from the exchange rates prevailing in mid-2004 should be substantial—at least over a time horizon of three to five years. In the context of a series of economic crises since the collapse of the Argentine exchange rate peg in December 2001, the currencies of Argentina, Brazil, the Dominican Republic, Uruguay, and Venezuela have all depreciated substantially (in real terms) against the dollar. Some recovery of these real exchange rates from their crisis lows has already occurred; and following the pattern of many previous crises, more real appreciation should be expected if economic recovery continues.

Moreover, in contrast to Mexico, most of Latin America's trade is not heavily focused on the United States. Accordingly, in a situation where other industrial-country currencies and Asian emerging-market currencies are appreciating against the dollar, the appreciation of most Latin American currencies against the dollar translates into significantly less appreciation in real effective terms. Over a five-year horizon, real appreciation of Latin American currencies (excluding the Mexican peso) of 20 percent or so is not an unreasonable prospect.

The third group of developing countries meriting specific attention (because of their importance for US external payments) is the oil-exporting countries in the Middle East, Africa, Asia, and Latin America (including Russia and, perhaps somewhat bizarrely, Norway). For most of these countries, what matters for an impact on the US balance of payments is not primarily the currency exchange rate but rather the world price of oil. The increase in the world oil price from an average of about $20 per barrel in the 1990s to $30 per barrel in 2003 directly implies an increase in the cost of US energy imports of about 0.4 percent of US GDP. Further increases in the world oil price to about $40 per barrel by mid-2004 (and even higher thereafter) indicate further deterioration of the US current account by a similar magnitude.

Looking ahead, oil futures markets continue to predict that world oil prices will decline during the next few years, but to a level now estimated to be closer to $30 per barrel rather than $20 per barrel. If world oil prices decline as predicted by oil futures markets, this should tend to improve the US external balance, plausibly by about half of a percentage point of US GDP. If world oil prices remain high, the effects on the US external position are more difficult to project. Experience suggests that in the short run, oil exporters will save a significant part of the windfall from higher oil prices, thereby adding to their current account surpluses and to the current account deficits of oil importers such as the United States.

In the longer run, however, oil exporters are likely to spend much of the gain from higher oil prices on increased imports, including imports from the United States. This should mitigate (but probably not eliminate) the long-run negative effect of higher world oil prices on the US external balance. For the exchange rate of the dollar, the implications are murky because other oil-importing countries make up the vast bulk of US trade and are in much the same situation as the United States vis-à-vis world oil prices.

Beyond the other industrial countries, Asian emerging-market economies, Latin America, and the oil exporters, there is not much left that matters in the world economy for the US external payments position. The region of Central and Eastern Europe is closely linked economically to Western Europe and is likely to become even more so with the recent enlargement of the European Union. Even before formal expansion of the euro area, the currencies of most of these countries are likely to move in sympathy (if not lockstep) with the euro against the dollar.

Thus, further appreciation of the euro against the dollar should apply to a wider range of countries than those now inside the euro area. In Africa, South Africa is by far the most important economy (and other economically important countries, including Nigeria, have been covered as oilexporters). South Africa's market-determined floating exchange rate has already appreciated more than 30 percent from its (much depressed) level in the base period. Many other African countries (especially the African franc zone) have exchange rates closely linked to the euro. And for many African countries, linkages to US external payments are both of very minor importance and more influenced by commodity prices than by currency exchange rates.

In sum, adding up the suggested adjustments of real exchange rates of the dollar against other currencies, how do we come out vis-à-vis the notion of a 30 percent real effective depreciation of the dollar from its value in the base period from mid-2000 to mid-2002? The answer is somewhat ambiguous because the suggested adjustments of individual exchange rates have (for good reason) been a little vague, and not all exchange rates have been covered.

Nevertheless, broadly speaking, the suggested individual exchange rate adjustments (from the base of mid-2000 to mid-2002) add up to a real effective depreciation of the dollar of more than 25 percent but a little short of 30 percent. The presumed real appreciation of more than 40 percent by the euro is more than enough to offset the allowance for limited real appreciation of the Mexican peso (and some other developing-country currencies) and push the average above 25 percent. But projected appreciations for the Canadian dollar, the pound sterling, and the average of Asian emerging-market currencies below 30 percent keep the average a little below 30 percent.

So what? The spirit of the exercise has been to suggest plausible orders of magnitude for the adjustments of particular exchange rates and the economic reasoning behind these judgments. Precision concerning the magnitude and (especially) the timing of exchange rate adjustments is neither achievable nor desirable. A complex of macroeconomic forces operating over the next few years will determine the course that exchange rates will actually follow. If the result after four or five years is anywhere close to what has been suggested here, then the exercise will have been a great success.

Policies to Contribute to the Orderly Reduction of External Imbalances

Exchange rate adjustments are not the only important class of macroeconomic adjustments necessary for a more sustainable pattern of international payments. Indeed, as was noted at the outset, the key policy challenges associated with securing an orderly reduction in international payments imbalances, consistent with sustainable economic growth around the world, are related primarily to the other two classes of macroeconomic adjustments:

- Domestic demand growth in the United States must be kept moderately below potential output growth to allow room for improvements in net exports and for corresponding improvements in the US national savings/investment balance and reductions in the needed inflow of foreign capital.

■ Domestic demand growth in the rest of the world must be boosted somewhat above potential output growth to support output and employment in the face of deteriorations in net exports and, correspondingly, to provide the global offset to the improvement in the US savings/investment balance and the decline in capital flows to the United States.

What key policies in the United States, in other industrial countries, and in developing countries would contribute constructively to these necessary macroeconomic adjustments?

Fiscal Consolidation in the United States

For the United States, a gradual and cumulatively substantial tightening of fiscal policy is clearly necessary to achieve medium- and longer-term fiscal sustainability, especially in view of the fiscal strains arising from an aging population. This would be so even if the United States had no external deficit. But the need to reduce a large external deficit means that fiscal consolidation (which is desirable for more basic reasons) can also play a useful role in constraining the growth of domestic demand relative to domestic output in the United States, and, correspondingly, in reducing the current account deficit, improving the national savings/investment balance, and diminishing the need for net foreign capital inflows—all of which are part and parcel of reducing the US external imbalance.

This prescription that US fiscal consolidation should make an important contribution to the orderly reduction of external imbalances does not rely on the simplistic notion that the US fiscal deficit and US current account deficit are closely related "twins" and that a reduction in the fiscal deficit will automatically result in a similar reduction in the current account deficit. Rather, the fiscal deficit and current account deficit are related through a complex of macroeconomic interactions that must be taken into account in assessing the likely effect of fiscal consolidation on the US external deficit.

From this macroeconomic perspective, it is relevant to take account of the following facts: Margins of slack in the US economy are now relatively low. Business investment appears to be taking over from consumer demand as the mainstay of domestic demand growth. Although not yet sufficient for the longer term, there has already been a substantial downward adjustment of the real foreign exchange value of the dollar that should tend to shift world demand toward US goods and services. The strengthening of demand growth now apparently under way in much of the rest of the world should further aid the improvement in US net exports. In this situation, it is reasonable to expect that gradual fiscal consolidation will exert modest restraint on domestic demand growth and will tend to improve the national savings/investment balance and the US current account without posing a critical threat to the sustainable growth of US output.

Of course, it is possible that if financial markets react exuberantly to evidence of gradual fiscal consolidation, pushing up asset values and private investment, the effect may be to keep the dollar unduly strong and to worsen rather than improve the current account. But there is no a priori reason to anticipate such perversity; and should it occur, the perversity will tend to be naturally self-limiting as foreign investors come to recognize the longer-run implications of rapidly rising US net external liabilities.

For US monetary policy, the fundamental objective is to keep inflation low while supporting the sustainable growth of output and employment. Fiscal consolidation implies that monetary policy should be able to achieve these fundamental objectives by pursuing a course for policy interest rates that is lower than it would be in the absence of such fiscal action. Other things being equal, an easier course for monetary policy should normally mean a lower path for the foreign exchange value of the dollar. A cheaper dollar, in turn, should help to bring both an improvement in the US external balance and a positive (or less negative) contribution from net exports to output and employment growth in the United States. The latter effect will help to offset the short-run negative impact of fiscal consolidation on output and employment.

Enhancing Demand Growth in Japan and Europe

In the rest of the world, the main macroeconomic adjustments necessary to achieve a smaller external surplus are essentially the reverse of the adjustments needed in the United States; that is, an increase in domestic demand growth relative to output growth (and a corresponding deterioration in the savings/investment balance and a reduction in net capital outflows) and real currency appreciation to help shift demand away from domestic output and toward US output. Unfortunately, the macroeconomic situation in much of the rest of the world is not the reverse of that in the United States; and the policies that would contribute to reducing the rest of the world's external surplus, while maintaining sustainable noninflationary growth, are difficult to prescribe.

In particular, in Japan and most of Western Europe, margins of slack are generally wider than in the United States, while the medium- and longer-term need for fiscal consolidation is generally no less pressing. This means that fiscal expansion cannot generally be prescribed in these countries as a means for stimulating domestic demand growth to offset the loss of effective demand that is inevitably associated with declining external surpluses. As a consequence, monetary policy faces an increased responsibility for sustaining adequate growth of domestic demand—especially so if fiscal policies are oriented toward consolidation rather than mere neutrality.

Japan's situation in this regard is a vivid case in point. After more than a decade of disappointing growth and five years of outright deflation, facing a large fiscal deficit and a massive buildup of government debt, and with policy interest rates effectively at zero, Japan confronts particularly difficult challenges in designing policies to achieve sustainable growth while contributing appropriately to the reduction of global payments imbalances.

Indeed, as noted above, the challenging experience of Japan in recent years provides a rationale for its highly aggressive policy of resisting rapid appreciation of the yen through massive foreign exchange market intervention. However, now that the Japanese economy appears to have regained substantial forward momentum, massive intervention to resist further orderly appreciation of the yen is not a desirable or defensible policy.

With substantial margins of slack remaining in the Japanese economy and with no signs of a resurgence of inflation, Japanese monetary policy should continue to pursue a course of unusual ease for a considerable period. This, in turn, will tend to imply a somewhat weaker course for the foreign exchange value of the yen than would likely prevail with a more robust Japanese economy, but it is clearly not inconsistent with a significant appreciation of the yen from its recently depressed level. In the longer term, as the Japanese economy recovers its traditional strength, substantial further real appreciation of the yen against the dollar should reasonably be expected as part of the process of gradually reducing global payments imbalances.

For industrial countries other than Japan, exchange rate adjustments since the peak of the dollar in 2000–02 are already quite substantial. In general, these adjustments should be enough to achieve a significant fraction (although not the entire amount) of what is needed to restore a sustainable pattern of international payments. In three key US trading partners—Australia, Canada, and the United Kingdom—demand growth in recent years has also been sufficient to achieve reasonable output growth.

For these three countries, further fiscal expansion cannot generally be recommended as a responsible means to augment demand growth (especially not in the United Kingdom). But longer-term fiscal prospects appear to be sound without the need for substantial consolidation—implying that fiscal contraction will not add to problems of sustaining output growth in the face of some deterioration of net exports. In addition, monetary policies in Australia, Canada, and the United Kingdom have all been tightened somewhat since the end of the global recession of 2001, and this leaves significant room for monetary easing should that seem needed to ward off excessive weakness in output growth.

In the euro area, economic performance since the mid-1990s has been better than in Japan but somewhat worse (especially in domestic demand growth) than in Australia, Canada, and the United Kingdom (as well as in the United States). Fiscal deficits and government debt burdens are generally not as large as in Japan but are more of a concern than in Canada and the United Kingdom. Monetary easing by the European Central Bank (ECB) to combat recent sluggishness has cut policy interest rates down to only 2 percent, compared with zero in Japan (and 1 percent in the United States). But, for good reason, there has not yet been any move by the ECB to begin the cycle of monetary tightening already under way in Australia, Canada, and the United Kingdom (and more recently in the United States).

Thus, it is fair to say that economic policy in the euro area retains greater room for maneuver to address issues arising from the correction of external imbalances than in Japan, but less so than in Australia, Canada, and the United Kingdom. Moreover, it is relevant that, unlike Japan, authorities in the euro area have not intervened at all to resist the substantial appreciation of the euro against the dollar that has occurred since mid-2002.

Looking forward, however, economic policy in the euro area faces critical challenges that will not be made easier to meet by the need to contribute to the reduction in global payments imbalances. Substantial fiscal deficits and government debt burdens and the fiscal demands of aging populations do not allow room for expansionary fiscal policies to prop up domestic demand growth in order to offset declining net exports.

Moreover, monetary policy for the euro area does not provide an easy way out of this conundrum (even if the ECB were willing to recognize this possibility). Facing prospective weakness in domestic demand growth (especially if fiscal consolidation is pursued), as well as weakness in output growth from the deterioration of net exports, monetary policy would normally be expected to follow a somewhat easier course to properly serve its basic objectives. But an easier course for monetary policy should normally be expected to work against the exchange rate adjustments (i.e., further appreciation of the euro against the dollar) that are needed to facilitate the reduction of external imbalances.

Policy Challenges for Developing Countries

For developing countries, the nature and timing of the macroeconomic and policy adjustments necessary to contribute to a successful and orderly reduction of external imbalances differs considerably across regions and specific economies. Indeed, as already discussed in connection with exchange rate adjustments, the contrast between most of emerging Asia and much of Latin America is particularly striking. Aside from the brief setbacks associated with the global recession of 2001 and the SARS scare of the spring of 2003, economic growth in virtually all of emerging Asia has been very strong since recovery from the Asian crisis began in late 1998. Also, Asian emerging-market economies typically have very strong external payments positions. In contrast, several key Latin American countries have experienced considerable economic weakness in recent years, and the external payments position of most Latin American countries is generally less secure than that of Asian emerging-market economies.

Taking account of these differences, it appears that emerging Asia should have relatively little difficulty in absorbing some deterioration in external payments positions as a partial counterpart to the needed improvement in the US external payments position. Real appreciations of Asian currencies against the dollar are essential contributions to this shift in external payments positions. Provided that Asian currencies appreciate together against the dollar, the negative impact on demand and output growth should be moderate and within the capacity of macroeconomic policies to offset. A danger to be avoided is prolonged resistance to nominal exchange rate appreciation, which would lead to excessive domestic credit expansion and an unsustainable economic boom. This is an important part of the story of the buildup to the Asian crisis of 1997–98. These mistakes should not be repeated.

For many developing countries that do not enjoy the same strengths as Asian emerging-market economies, the key policy requirement is to establish and maintain sound macroeconomic policies that will support sustainable economic growth and instill confidence in domestic and foreign investors. Even if this does not imply any short-term contribution to reducing key global payments imbalances, in the longer run it will mean stronger real exchange rates and a capacity to attract reasonable inflows of foreign capital that will finance moderate and sustainable current account deficits.

An important potential threat to this favorable long-term scenario is the risk of another round of emerging-market financial crises. At present, this risk seems relatively low. Global economic recovery is under way, policy interest rates in industrial countries are still quite low, and global financial markets are still taking a relatively benign view of the risks in emerging markets.

During the next several years, however—as interest rates in industrial countries probably rise and as the global expansion probably loses some of its recent robustness—it is not unlikely that one or more of the emerging-market countries will have to face a potential external financing crisis. As occurred in the 1990s (and in earlier episodes of emerging-market financial crises), it is also not unlikely that a financial crisis afflicting one emerging-market economy will spread through a variety of mechanisms to affect others. In contrast to the 1990s, however, a rapidly expanding US current account deficit (supported by particularly rapid growth of domestic demand in the United States) is unlikely to provide the necessary counterpart for emerging-market countries seeking rapid improvements in their current account positions under the pressure of external financing crises.

This concern also applies in reverse. Emerging-market financial crises that generate the need for rapid improvements in the external payments positions of these countries will tend to interfere with the orderly reduction of the US external payments deficit. And the effects of this problem will not be limited to emerging-market countries and the United States. If the expansion of the US external deficit is to be less of a counterpart to crisis-induced improvements in the external payments positions of emerging-market countries, then adjustments in the external positions of other industrial countries will need to shoulder more of the load—and this will be in addition to, not as a substitute for, adjustments that are needed as the counterpart to improvements in the US external position.

Thus, virtually all countries have a self-interest in avoiding or minimizing possible future emerging-market financial crises—as one element of the broader strategy to secure orderly reductions in international payments imbalances. Of course, the primary responsibility for reducing vulnerabilities to a crisis inevitably rests with each emerging-market country itself—and there is much that countries can do in this regard. But the international community also has an important role to play in reducing the risk of crises and in ameliorating the consequences when crises occur.

Conclusion: The Virtues of Some International Policy Cooperation

Dealing with potential emerging-market financial crises is one area where some international policy cooperation is clearly helpful. Important progress has been made in recent years in the decisions of a number of developing countries to adopt more flexible exchange rate policies, in the increased flow of relevant and reliable information to financial markets, and (one hopes) in the awareness of both governments and investors of the factors that contribute to risks of emerging-market financial crises and of the need to contain these risks. However, critical issues still remain to be fully addressed: how the international financial community will react to actual or potential crises (especially concerning the appropriate level and conditionality for support from the International Monetary Fund), and how sovereign defaults will be resolved.

Beyond the particular issues of emerging-market financial crises, international policy coordination can probably play a constructive but limited role with regard to the general problem of reducing global payments imbalances. It is unrealistic to believe that there is or could be a reasonable consensus among industrial countries on the magnitude and time of exchange rate adjustments needed to contribute to a reduction of the US external deficit to sustainable proportions. For this reason and several others, I believe that it is fruitless (and perhaps dangerous) to seek to coordinate on fostering specific adjustments of industrial-country exchange rates or on establishing some form of "target zones" for these rates. Nevertheless, it probably is feasible to agree that some further downward correction of the dollar is likely to be needed and that market developments tending in this direction should not be resisted—unless they threaten to become disruptive.

Concerning other key macroeconomic policies, I see no harm in other countries pressing the United States on the need for a more responsible fiscal policy. Similarly, there is nothing wrong with pressing other industrial countries with the need to do all that is feasible and reasonable to stimulate more rapid and sustainable growth of domestic demand. However, one should not harbor much optimism that such exhortations will dramatically affect either the concerns that govern central bank decisions about monetary policies or the political forces that largely determine key fiscal policy decisions.

Finally, concerning the exchange rates of the Asian emerging-market economies, there clearly is some role for international cooperation among these economies and with the broader international community. As was emphasized above, the general appreciation of Asian currencies (including the yen) needs to be part of the process of reducing unsustainable payments imbalances. For Asian countries, it clearly makes an important difference that they see adjustments of their individual exchange rates as part of a general appreciation against the dollar and not as isolated appreciations by individual Asian countries. The industrial countries also have an interest in fostering the upward adjustment of Asian currencies against the dollar, and they should make this interest clear. However, the key argument is not that the appreciation of Asian currencies is needed by the industrial countries or by the world in general, but rather that it is in the longer-term interest of Asia as a participant in the global economy.

In this regard, industrial countries should insist that they are not asking Asia to do what they themselves are not prepared to do—namely, to allow exchange rates to adjust to take appropriate account of the need to reduce global payments imbalances. If most Asian countries do not want their exchange rates to fluctuate in response to market forces to the same extent as most industrial countries now permit, then they must be prepared to adjust their exchange rate policies with due regard to what market forces suggest is required for the medium and longer terms.

6

The Impact of Trade on US Job Loss, 2000–03

MARTIN NEIL BAILY and ROBERT Z. LAWRENCE

After growing strongly in the 1990s, the US economy entered a period of weakness after 2000. Economic growth and employment growth started to fall off during 2000, and then slower growth became recession. The National Bureau of Economic Research dates the business-cycle peak in March 2001. Total private payroll employment peaked in December 2000 and fell by 3.4 million between then and August of 2003. The employment decline was heavily concentrated in the manufacturing sector, where job loss started as early as October 1998 and continued through January 2004. Job loss is frequently very costly for workers and their families, often involving a spell of unemployment and income loss, and requiring relocation to find a new job. Job losses of the magnitude experienced after 2003 imposed substantial costs on large numbers of Americans.

What caused this job loss? There are two main explanations of the weakness in employment during this period. The first looks at domestic factors, such as the overall business cycle, including the technology, capital investment, and inventory components of that cycle. In addition, there was unusually strong growth of productivity, so that growth in GDP did not translate into growth in employment to the degree that is typical of US recoveries.

Martin Neil Baily is a senior fellow at the Institute for International Economics and a senior adviser at the McKinsey Global Institute. Robert Z. Lawrence is a senior fellow at the Institute for International Economics and the Albert L. Williams Professor of Trade and Investment at Harvard University. They would like to thank Gunilla Pettersson and Katherina Plück for excellent research assistance. Jacob F. Kirkegaard provided invaluable help and comments. The views expressed are those of the authors and do not necessarily reflect the views of the staff or trustees of the Institute for International Economics or Harvard University.

The second explanation is that the decline of US employment reflected a loss of jobs to overseas competitors. The United States ran large trade deficits in the 1980s, and these returned in the 1990s, particularly after 1995 as the dollar strengthened and the US economy grew relatively much faster than the rest of the world. In current-dollar terms, the trade and current account deficits continued to widen even after 2000.

In the minds of many, the reason job losses have been so great is that the United States simply cannot compete against low-wage countries that can gain access to the latest production technology. Some even argue that because China has emerged as a manufacturing power, selling large amounts to the United States, and because India has become an attractive location for service-sector offshoring, virtually all US jobs are now "threatened."

To most economists, this fear is misplaced. Chronic US trade deficits are a macroeconomic issue—inadequate national saving—and are not an inevitable consequence of trade itself. The general view among both economists and policymakers is that trade benefits the United States, although there may well be negative effects on groups of workers who are displaced by imports.

This chapter does not tackle the full complexity of the impact of trade on the economy. Rather, we tackle a much simpler issue: Using simple but reasonable approximations, we estimate two numbers. First, we estimate the extent to which changes in imports and exports during the period 2000 to 2003 could have contributed to the loss of US manufacturing employment. And second, we look at the magnitude of service-sector offshoring to India, both in software and in business processes (business process offshoring includes such activities as call centers and "back office" processing for financial services companies).[1]

A clear conclusion from this analysis is that trade does not account for the bulk of US manufacturing job loss during the period 2000 to 2003. This conclusion emerges even when the assumptions made to make the estimate tend to exaggerate the impact of trade on the number of US jobs. An equally important conclusion is that to the extent that trade has contributed to the decline in the number of manufacturing jobs over this period, this has come entirely from the weakness in US exports. The fact that imports grew rather slowly during the period actually cushioned the extent of job loss.

As for the movement of jobs to India, we understand that it is unsettling for groups of workers who were previously not subject to international competition. This has contributed to the rise of political concern about the issue. However, we find that in practice the magnitude of the loss of US service jobs resulting from offshoring to India is very small compared with the typical growth in overall service-sector employment. In sum, these two pieces of analysis indicate that the view that the decline in employment

---

1. We have benefited from the work of Jacob F. Kirkegaard (2004) and Catherine Mann (2003) in the area of offshoring. We have also benefited from the offshoring study by the McKinsey Global Institute (MGI 2003).

Figure 6.1   US SIC manufacturing employment compared with NAICS manufacturing employment, 1992–2004
(millions of workers, seasonally adjusted)

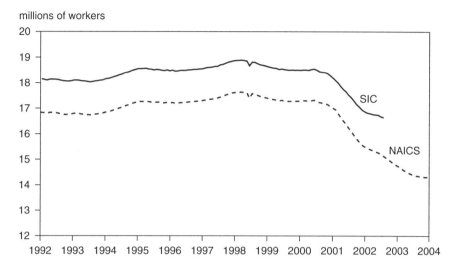

millions of workers

SIC = Standard Industrial Classification System
NAICS = North American Industry Classification System
Source: Bureau of Labor Statistics.

from 2000 to 2003 occurred because US jobs were shipped overseas en masse and replaced by imports is simply not true.

The Decline in Employment in Manufacturing

As a share of total US employment, the number of jobs in the manufacturing sector has been declining for at least half a century. This is not unique to the United States; rather it is typical of developed economies and even of many developing economies. The basic reason is that while the demand for the output of the manufacturing sector is growing, it does not grow fast enough to offset productivity growth in the sector, and so the demand for labor declines. Agriculture is another sector with a similar pattern.

In terms of the absolute level of manufacturing employment, the picture is less severe. As figure 6.1 illustrates, employment in manufacturing remained fairly stable in the 1990s, through 2000. Indeed, the level of employment in manufacturing has been roughly constant since the early 1970s, except for cyclical ups and downs. Figure 6.1 includes two lines showing manufacturing employment based on the Standard Industrial Classification (SIC) definition and the newer North American Industry

Figure 6.2   US manufacturing trade deficit as a share of manufacturing value added and as a share of gross output, 1989–2003

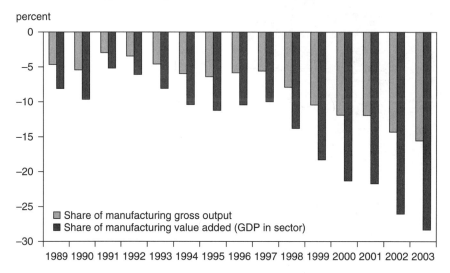

Sources: US International Trade Commission, Bureau of Economic Analysis, Bureau of Labor Statistics.

Classification System (NAICS). The old SIC figures showed a substantially higher level of employment in the sector because they included many workers who were not engaged in actual manufacturing activities. About 1½ million such workers have been excluded from the NAICS figures, which have become the new official numbers. Fortunately, the two series move very closely together over the period for which they overlap, so the extent of job loss for our focal period, 2000 to 2003, is very similar in both data series. Using annual data from the NAICS estimates, the US manufacturing sector lost 2.74 million jobs during this period.

The Trade Deficit in Relation to Manufacturing Output: Gross Output or Value Added?

One reason people point to the role of international trade in the jobs picture is that the United States has run an increasing deficit in its manufacturing trade since 1992 and the magnitudes of the deficits have been large relative to the size of the sector. Figure 6.2 illustrates this point by showing the trade deficit expressed as a percentage of manufacturing output. However, output is measured in two different ways. The first measure is value added in the industry—the GDP that originates in the sector. On this basis, the trade deficit had grown to 28.3 percent of manufacturing output in 2003, up from 21.3 percent in 2000.

The second measure shown in figure 6.2 is the gross output of the sector—how much manufacturing sells outside the sector—whether to US buyers or overseas. This measure is estimated at the Bureau of Labor Statistics (BLS) by adding up the output of all manufacturing establishments and then estimating what fraction of that output consists of sales to other parts of the same sector. These intramanufacturing sales are then netted out, and the remaining output consists of the gross output of the sector. On this basis, the trade deficit does not look like quite such a large factor in the manufacturing picture. The deficit equaled 15.6 percent of gross output in 2003, up from 11.9 percent in 2000.

Together, these measures provide a useful perspective on the likely size of the trade effects on the sector. Those who want to emphasize that trade is hurting the US sector generally focus on the larger number. We argue here that the use of the value-added or sector-GDP measure will result in an overstatement of the impact of trade on manufacturing employment, whereas the use of gross output will likely understate the impact of trade. Hence, we do the calculation of the impact of trade on jobs twice, using both output measures, to give the range of possible outcomes.

Estimating the Employment Impact of the Changes in Manufactured Exports and Imports

A fully rigorous analysis of the impact of trade on manufacturing employment would take a range of factors into account in a full general equilibrium context. This chapter's approach is to make a first-round, partial equilibrium estimate. We ask what was the impact on employment of falling exports and rising imports after 2000, assuming a direct link between employment in the sector and output—a link based on average output per employee. In addition, the appropriate way to measure how trade affects jobs is to estimate separately how many jobs are generated by exports and then how many are displaced by imports.

The specific method used is as follows. In any given year, there was a certain volume of exports. There was employment associated with that volume of exports that is calculated from the level of output per employee in the sector *during the same year*. That calculation is made for 2000 and then again for 2003, taking into account the change in output per employee in manufacturing over the three-year period. Because exports are expressed in current-year dollars, the calculation of output per employee should be made based on how current-dollar output per employee evolved over time.

A similar calculation is then made for imports, with the assumption that if this value of imports had been produced in the United States, then output per employee would have been the same as the average for the manufacturing output that actually was produced in the United States.[2]

There are two main sensitivities to this calculation. The first goes back to the discussion above and is about whether output per employee is taken to be value added per employee in the sector or gross output per employee in the sector. A simple case to analyze occurs if there are no imports of components into the United States. Consider the impact of $1 million in exports under this assumption. Each million dollars in exports generates employment in manufacturing by an amount that depends upon gross output per employee. In addition, there would be employment generated in the non-manufacturing industries in the United States that supply manufacturing.

The same logic applies to imports. By assumption, these displace US manufacturing production dollar-for-dollar and displace US employment by an amount that depends upon gross output per employee. If the assumption of no imported components were correct, then using value added per employee for these calculations would substantially overstate the number of jobs generated by exports and displaced by imports, and would then overstate the estimate of the manufacturing job loss that resulted from trade over the period.

The other simple case is when the US manufacturing sector buys nothing from other US industries and, instead, the difference between value added and gross output consists of the amount of imported components. In this case, imports and exports displace or generate US employment to the extent reflected in value added per employee. Using gross output per employee would understate the employment effect of trade.

Getting the job loss calculation exactly correct requires a detailed knowledge of the import content of US production, and in future work we plan to make that calculation, drawing on input-output tables. For the present, doing the calculation both ways provides the range of values that should bracket the actual number.

The calculation's second sensitivity comes from making an estimate of current dollar productivity in 2003, because there is no actual number available—the latest figure being for 2001. Beyond 2001, the published real manufacturing output figures are based on the Federal Reserve's industrial production index. To estimate real output per employee in 2003, we used actual real output per employee for 2001 and extended that to 2003 using the productivity growth estimates for the sector for 2002 and 2003 reported by BLS. To get the current dollar values of output per employee in 2003, we extrapolated the trend rate of price change based on the experience for 1995 to 2001. Both the value added and the gross output deflators declined over that period, with the value-added deflator declining

---

2. This is one way in which our estimates may understate the job impact of trade. Output per employee would be lower in import-competing industries than in export industries.

Table 6.1   US job loss due to trade based on gross output, 2000 and 2003

Aspect	2000	2003	Change
Exports (billions of dollars)	692	626	−66
Employment generated by exports (thousands)	4,693	3,797	**−896**
Imports (billions of dollars)	1,013	1,027	+14
Employment if produced in the United States (thousands)	6,870	6,230	**+640**
Trade effect on jobs (thousands)			**−256 net**

Sources: US International Trade Commission, Bureau of Labor Statistics, Bureau of Economic Analysis, authors' calculations.

more slowly, reflecting an increase in the relative price of purchased input prices over the period, particularly energy prices.

Table 6.1 shows the results of our estimates of job loss using gross output per employee. We see that in 2000 $692 billion in US exports generated 4.693 million jobs, under that assumption. By 2003, exports had fallen to $626 billion and output per employee had risen, so that only 3.797 million jobs had been created through exports. There was a loss of nearly 900,000 jobs as a result.

On the import side, $1,013 billion in imports in 2000 would have required 6.87 million workers if the imports had been produced in the United States at the average US productivity level. In 2003, imports had risen slightly, to $1,027 billion, but the increase in productivity meant that to produce this much output in the United States would have required only 6.230 million workers. So the job displacement due to imports actually fell by 640,000 over this period. The net effect on manufacturing employment of trade was therefore a net job loss of about 260,000.

If the same calculations are made using value added per employee, the jobs due to imports are much higher in each year and the job loss is greater (table 6.2). The cushioning effect of the slow growth of imports is also greater, but the net job loss figure is substantially higher at nearly 600,000 workers.

To summarize our calculations: *The loss of manufacturing jobs between 2000 and 2003 that can be attributed to trade is between 260,000 and 600,000, representing between 9 percent and 22 percent of the total decline. Even with the high estimate, therefore, only a moderate fraction of the job loss was trade related.*

Table 6.2 US job loss due to trade based on value added per employee, 2000 and 2003

Aspect	2000	2003	Change
Exports (billions of dollars)	692	626	−66
Employment generated by exports (thousands)	8,424	7,023	**−1,401**
Imports (billions of dollars)	1,013	1,027	+14
Employment if produced in the United States (thousands)	12,332	11,521	**+811**
Trade effect on jobs (thousands)			**−590 net**

Sources: US International Trade Commission, Bureau of Labor Statistics, Bureau of Economic Analysis, authors' calculations.

Moreover, the job losses came entirely from the export side and not from a surge in imports. Job loss from any source is costly, but it is a mistake to scapegoat trade, because it was not the main reason for the overall manufacturing job decline.

Two Other Indicators of the Impact of Offshoring on Manufacturing Employment

There are two other indicators of the impact of offshoring on manufacturing employment. *First, the value-added share of production has remained stable.* There are many examples of US manufacturing companies that have retained parts of their value chain in the United States but have moved other portions either to foreign affiliate companies or to subcontractors overseas. These examples have led people to believe that the whole US manufacturing sector has been hollowed out.

If this were the case, we would expect to see a decline over time in the ratio of value added in manufacturing to the gross output of the sector. But in fact this is not the case, according to Bureau of Economic Analysis (BEA) and BLS data. Figure 6.3 shows that value added and gross output moved pretty much in line over the period 1987 to 2001 (the data for 2002 and 2003 are extrapolations)—the ratio of value added to gross output has remained roughly constant. It must have been the case that the offshoring of parts of the manufacturing value chain that took place was offset by the development of new products generating additional value added in the United States.

Figure 6.3 The share of US manufactured output produced within the sector has remained the same, 1987–2003
(index: 1987 = 100)

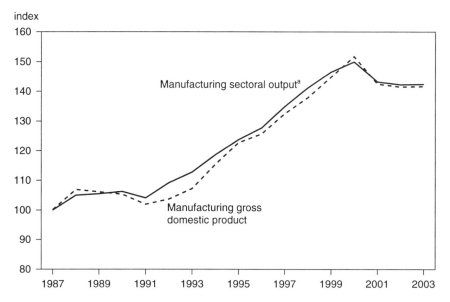

index

a. Gross output excluding intrasector transactions.
Note: Manufacturing equals SIC 20–39, real indexes.
Sources: Bureau of Economic Analysis and Bureau of Labor Statistics.

Second, manufacturing companies report that only a small fraction of mass layoffs is due to overseas relocation. BLS has been collecting information on mass layoffs for many years. A "mass layoff" occurs when 50 or more applications for unemployment insurance benefits are received from former employees of a given establishment over any five-week period. A sample of such establishments is then surveyed and asked for data on the number of layoffs occurring and the reasons for the mass layoff. These survey figures specifically for the manufacturing sector are not published by BLS, but they are available on request.

Table 6.3 shows data on mass layoffs in manufacturing for the five years 1996 to 2000 and the three years 2001 to 2003. The annual average number of workers subject to mass layoffs is shown for the two periods. It is a rather high number both in good times (1996–2000) and in times of labor market weakness (2001–03)—somewhat higher in the latter period, as would be expected. The annual average decline in manufacturing jobs over the corresponding periods is also shown in the table, and it is vastly different between the two periods. Clearly, during the period of job loss in manufacturing, the problem was a lack of job creation much more than the increase in mass layoffs.

Table 6.3   US mass layoffs in manufacturing, selected periods

	Number of workers subject to mass layoffs	Layoffs due to import competition (percent)	Layoffs due to overseas relocation (percent)
Annual averages (percentages of total shown in brackets)			
1996–2000	373,113	15,131 (4.1)	7,036 (1.9)
2001–03	483,236	20,960 (4.3)	14,575 (3.0)
Annual average decline in manufacturing jobs			
January 1996–January 2001		22,600	
January 2001–January 2004		742,500	

Note: Reasons for the extended mass layoffs are reported by the establishments. The sample is drawn from establishments generating 50 or more unemployment claims in any 5-week period. Workers must be separated from their jobs for at least 31 days. Based on NAICS scheme.

Source: Bureau of Labor Statistics.

Also shown in table 6.3 are two of the reasons given for mass layoffs—the two associated with trade and offshoring. Only a little over 4 percent of the mass layoffs resulted from import competition, and 2 to 3 percent were due to overseas relocation. Overseas relocation did become more important in the latter period. In summary: While responses to this BLS survey may not always be accurate, these results do show that employers do not report that either trade or offshoring are major reasons for mass layoffs, either before or after 2000.[3]

The Offshoring of Service Jobs to India

According to data from BEA, the United States runs a service trade surplus with India, and there is no record of substantial increases in service imports from India in recent years—indeed, the level of imports is very small indeed. Thus if one were to rely on this standard US data source, the phenomenon of service-sector offshoring would be seen as virtually nonexistent. Data from India suggest otherwise. Nasscom, an Indian trade association, reports large exports of services to the United States both in the software category and in business processes.

There are several reasons why the discrepancy in data sources may occur. BEA admits that its company surveys may miss a lot of the recent offshoring, because it may be destined to sectors not traditionally cov-

---

3. Bureau of Labor Statistics, "Extended Mass Layoffs Associated with Domestic and Overseas Relocations, First Quarter 2004 Summary," June 2004, also points to the limited extent of overseas relocation of US workers.

**Table 6.4   US software jobs lost to India, fiscal 2000–01
            to 2003–04**

	Number
Increase in software employment in India	200,000
Involved in exports to the United States	134,000
US employment loss, assuming one-for-one job transfer	**134,000**

Source: Nasscom (an Indian trade association), authors' calculations.

ered in detail.[4] It may also classify some service imports as goods imports (e.g., if the software is to be used in a packaged software product).[5] There may be reasons that the data from Nasscom exaggerate India's exports— for example, programmers on assignment to and located in the United States may be counted as Indian exports if they are working under a contract to a company based in India. On balance, therefore, the numbers from Nasscom on the offshoring of services from the United States probably provide an upper bound on the actual value of US service imports.

Nasscom reports its data on a fiscal-year basis, ending in the first quarter of the year. Table 6.4 shows that over the period from fiscal 2000–01 to fiscal 2003–04 (ending, respectively, in the first quarters of 2001 and 2004), there was an increase in software employment in India of 200,000. Of this total, 134,000 employees were involved in activities whose end products or services were exported to the United States. On the assumption that this work would have required the same number of employees in the United States—that is, that the productivity levels of the US and Indian industries are the same for these activities—then this involves a loss of 134,000 US jobs.

Table 6.5 shows a comparable computation for business process offshoring. There was an increase in India of 175,500 jobs, and 140,400 of these were in activities whose products or services were exported to the United States. With the same assumption of one-for-one job transfer, this means that there was a loss of 140,400 US jobs in this service activity.

The assumption of comparable productivity is a strong one. On the basis of the evidence of persons who have studied and visited the industry, the productivity differences are mixed. For instance, there is some evidence that call centers are more productive in India because they can attract higher-quality employees (college graduates in India vs. high school graduates in

---

4. Inherently, it is easier for Indian statisticians to cover a limited number of information technology service exporters via surveys than it is for BEA to cover the entire spectrum of potential information technology service importers in the US economy, especially at a time when such imports may be going to new sectors.

5. This problem is not large, however, as the US imports less than $10 million worth of "Records, Tapes and Discs SITC End-Use Category 41220" a year.

Table 6.5 The impact of business process offshoring of US jobs to India, fiscal 2000–01 to 2003–04

	Number
Increase in business process offshoring employment in India	175,500
Involved in exports to the United States	140,400
US employment loss, assuming one-for-one job transfer	**140,400**

Sources: Nasscom (an Indian trade association), authors' calculations.

the United States). Also, these jobs are not well liked by US workers, and turnover is very high in call centers (e.g., see case study of offshoring in MGI 2003). On balance, however, it is likely that productivity would be higher in the United States for the same activity, especially for higher-end programming that needs intensive research and development. Thus the job loss estimates are probably above the actual job losses experienced.

This conclusion is reinforced by two additional and related factors. First, some of the tasks that were moved to India would have been performed by automated information technology hardware in the United States and not by workers—for example, voice response units replacing call center workers. Second, because the services being provided from India are cheaper than they would be when provided by the United States, it is likely that the amount of services purchased by US customers is greater than if Indian offshoring were not available.

Table 6.6 assesses the overall magnitude of service-sector offshoring to India in relation to overall US service-sector employment. Adding the software and business process employment together suggests that at most about 274,000 jobs moved to India over the three-year period fiscal 2000–01 to 2003–04. This equals an annual average change of about 91,500. For the workers who were displaced, the costs of this increase in trade were substantial. But a job shift of this size is very small compared with the typical 2.1 million service jobs created every year during the 1990s and is even small compared with the net annual job increase of about 327,000 from 2000 to 2003.

Implications of the Analysis

Cyclical recovery is the main cure for US job loss. To the extent that trade adversely affected manufacturing jobs after 2000, it did so because of weakness on the export side. The best bet for increasing US exports in the future is for the economic recovery to continue and become stronger in the rest of the world—something that is amenable to demand management policies by foreign governments. In addition, US exports would be helped by a further decline in the dollar. The value of the dollar is not under the direct control

Table 6.6 Offshoring to India in relation to total US service-sector employment

	Number
Total service-sector jobs offshored to India, fiscal 2001/02–2003/04	274,400
Average annual change	91,467
Average annual change in US service-sector employment	
1990–2000	2,137,200
2000–03	327,100

Sources: Previous calculations; Bureau of Labor Statistics.

of policymakers here and abroad, but there are policies that can facilitate a dollar decline, including a gradual reduction of the US fiscal deficit, as well as greater exchange rate flexibility in Asia.

A factor that is not directly in the control of policymakers is the magnitude of private capital flows to the United States. These flows triggered the rise of the dollar after 1995 but have since fallen off. The pattern of future flows is hard to predict, but most likely foreign residents will not be willing to finance a US current account deficit of 5 percent of GDP (and growing) indefinitely. That means that the prospects for a lower dollar and stronger US exports are good—albeit with a cost to the United States from the resulting adverse terms of trade movement.

Good policies here and abroad will contribute to economic growth and job growth. But policymakers should not exaggerate the impact of trade on US employment and resort to trade protectionism. Today, the US economy is growing fast enough to create jobs again, even in manufacturing. Both the number of manufacturing and service-sector jobs created in the United States and the nature of those jobs are determined primarily by domestic US forces, including technology, productivity, and the strength of overall US domestic demand.

References

Kirkegaard, Jacob F. 2004. Outsourcing—Stains on the White Collar? Washington: Institute for International Economics. http://www.iie.com/publications/papers/kirkegaard0204.pdf.

Mann, Catherine L. 2003. *Globalization of IT Services and White-Collar Jobs: The Next Wave of Productivity Growth*. International Economics Policy Brief PB03-11. Washington: Institute for International Economics.

MGI (McKinsey Global Institute). 2003. *New Horizons: Foreign Direct Investment in Emerging Markets*. San Francisco: McKinsey Global Institute.

7

Locked in a Close Embrace? Canada's Current Account Adjustment Vis-à-vis the United States

PAUL MASSON

In 2003, Canada's currency appreciated by 20 percent against the US dollar. Given the lags in the adjustment of trade to relative price changes, what are the prospects for Canada's current account position? Will Canada, as the United States' largest trading partner, contribute substantially to reestablishing equilibrium in the US external accounts, currently in a large deficit? Or on the contrary, is Canada so closely integrated with the US economy that exchange rate changes will have little impact, for instance, because Canadian prices and wages adjust fully, or because Canadian industry, which exhibits substantial US ownership and is well integrated with the US economy, produces inputs that are closely linked to US activity?

These issues are addressed here by considering the effects of movements of the exchange rate on Canada's economic activity, prices, and overall current account position.[1] After first reviewing recent macroeconomic performance in Canada, I then describe a simple framework of analysis and attempt to quantify the effects on the current account in the context of this framework.

Another important issue is whether the adjustment of the Canadian dollar is likely to continue. From Canada's perspective, the answer to this

Paul Masson is adjunct professor and research fellow at the Rotman School of Management of the University of Toronto. He is grateful to Peter Dungan for access to the University of Toronto's Focus model and data, and to John Murray, Bill Robson, and Larry Schembri for comments; they should not be held responsible for the views expressed here, however.

1. Though data for the bilateral position with the United States exist, they are less complete than for the overall position. Given the importance of the United States for Canada's international trade and investment, in practice the overall position is a good proxy for the bilateral one.

question will be strongly influenced by the path for Canadian interest rates relative to US ones, and the prospects for commodity prices. The Bank of Canada's inflation-targeting framework keys interest rates to the forecast for inflation, which, in turn, is dependent on both the output gap and the extent to which appreciation is passed through into domestic prices. Movements in commodity prices have historically been linked to movements of the Canadian dollar, given the importance for the Canadian economy of agriculture, metals and minerals, and forest products.

Whether the Canadian dollar will continue to appreciate is also related to developments in the United States. The contrasting trends in net foreign asset positions in the United States and Canada are detailed here, and they are anecdotally related to trends in fiscal policies. If the current expansionary stance of US fiscal policy continues—combined with Canada's fiscal prudence—it is argued that the Canadian dollar's real appreciation against the US dollar is unlikely to be permanent. Indeed, a reversal is already occurring.

Canada's Recent Macroeconomic Performance

Canada in 2003 suffered from the global slowdown, and in particular from slow growth in its major trading partner, the United States. Earlier in the year, growth prospects in Canada seemed better than in its neighbor to the south, leading the Bank of Canada to raise its target for the overnight rate in the context of upward price pressures and a positive output gap (i.e., output above potential).

However, a subsequent slowdown in activity, fueled in part by special factors such as SARS and mad cow disease, but also by the rise in the Canadian dollar, led to a reversal of those interest rate increases. For the year as a whole, real GDP grew by 2.1 percent relative to the average for 2002, well below US growth of 3.1 percent.[2] By the end of the year, core inflation was under the midpoint of the Bank of Canada's target range, 2 percent, while the output gap had returned to negative territory.

Roughly paralleling the adjustment of other major currencies against the US dollar, the Canadian dollar experienced a sharp bilateral appreciation, and during 2003 gained about 22 percent—more than the euro (20 percent), but less than the Australian or New Zealand dollars (34 and 25 percent, respectively). As detailed in a report by the TD Bank Financial Group (2004), the upward adjustment in the value of the Canadian dollar was not unexpected—various measures had suggested that the currency had been undervalued since the mid-1990s, but the appreciation

---

2. These figures reflect revisions to US and Canadian national accounts data announced at the end of May 2004. The new data were not, however, used in estimating the equations described below.

Figure 7.1   Real and nominal bilateral exchange rate, Canada, 1980–2003

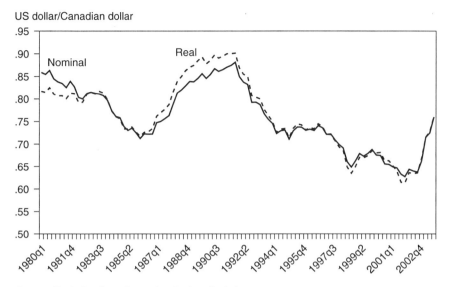

US dollar/Canadian dollar

Source: Statistics Canada, and author's calculations.

was surprising in its sharpness. Despite the longest history of floating among global currencies (the Canadian dollar was already floating in the 1950s, and has floated continuously since 1970), never had the currency appreciated by 20 percent in such a short time span (figure 7.1).

The reason for expecting some upward adjustment of the value of the currency included several years of Canada's strong external balance of payments position and favorable movements in relative prices, and, more recently, a short-term interest differential in favor of Canada. Historically, Canada has run large current account deficits, but these had been reduced dramatically by the mid-1990s. Starting in 2000, Canada was running current account surpluses of 2 to 3 percent of GDP (figure 7.2).

During the 1990s, the Canadian dollar depreciated in nominal terms against the US dollar, though Canadian inflation was consistently below that in the United States. At the end of 2002, the loonie[3] was worth about 63 US cents, not far from its record low, and the real bilateral exchange rate was about 25 percent below its level of a decade earlier. Measures of the equilibrium exchange rate based on purchasing power parity or the pro-

---

3. The term "loonie" comes from the image of the loon on the dollar coin (unlike the United States, Canada no longer has a one-dollar bill). The replacement of the two-dollar bill also stimulated a search for a nickname, with "toonie" winning out over "doubloon."

Figure 7.2 Canada's current account, 1980–2003

percent of GDP

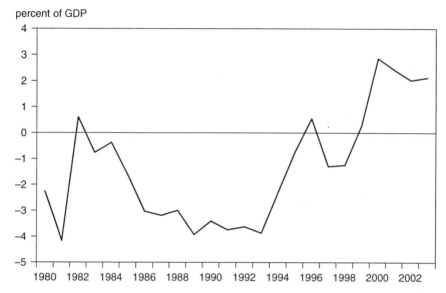

Source: Statistics Canada and author's calculations.

ductivity gap between the two countries all suggested some appreciation, but the range of estimates was wide, from 72 to 89 US cents (TD Bank Financial Group 2004). Thus, the appreciation that occurred was well within that range of equilibrium estimates.

The timing and size of the appreciation were no doubt affected by movements in US and Canadian interest rates. While weakness in activity and an absence of inflationary pressures led the US Federal Reserve to lower interest rates throughout the period 2001–03, the strength of the recovery in activity led the Bank of Canada to raise interest rates twice early in 2003. After the Canadian dollar's sharp appreciation and in the light of subsequent negative shocks to economic activity, Canada's central bank lowered rates once again by a total of 50 basis points in July and September 2003, and by a further 75 basis points in January, March, and April 2004. The Canadian dollar—after peaking at 78.86 US cents in January—had declined back to 72 US cents by mid-May 2004, as the strength of the US recovery stimulated speculation about an imminent increase in US interest rates by the Fed.

Various reasons have been advanced to explain the weakness of the loonie in the decade preceding its recent appreciation. Canada underwent a period of fiscal retrenchment during the 1990s, contributing to weak aggregate demand; and the North American Free Trade Agreement (NAFTA) led to a restructuring of Canadian industry and disruption to aggregate supply. The early 1990s were a period of constitutional crisis

Figure 7.3   Share of United States in Canada's exports and imports, 1980–2002

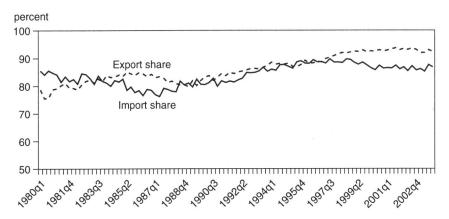

Source: Statistics Canada and author's calculations.

and until 1995, when Quebec voted "no" in a referendum on sovereignty, uncertainty about the future of the country. Given Canada's poor growth performance, high government indebtedness, and political problems, foreign observers did not view the country as an attractive place for foreign investment. And finally, the Canadian dollar seems to have been strongly influenced by developments in commodity prices, which were weak for much of the period and have strengthened only recently, at roughly the same time as the appreciation of the currency. Indeed, an equation developed at the Bank of Canada explains the bilateral exchange rate, using as main explanatory variables nonenergy commodity prices and the Canada–United States interest differential (Djoudad et al. 2001).

Of course, the Canadian dollar's appreciation has to be understood in the context of the downward adjustment of the US dollar against most other currencies as well. But in Canada, that dimension is usually ignored—due to the overwhelming importance of the US economy for Canada. Indeed, the United States has become a more and more important trading partner, reflecting the effects of NAFTA, and now accounts for more than 85 percent of Canada's total imports and more than 90 percent of exports (figure 7.3). Thus, Canada's effective exchange rate largely mirrors movements in its bilateral rate with the United States.

A Model of Canadian Current Account Adjustment

In the next section, we consider the effects of the appreciation that took place in 2003 for economic activity, inflation, and the current account in the following two years. To do so, I use an estimated aggregate demand and supply framework, accompanied by conventional equations for export and import prices and volumes, which together allow inference to be made on the path for the current account. The econometric framework is described in this section. After using it for forecasting 2004–05, I then go on to consider whether the current account would be at its equilibrium level (somehow defined), or alternatively whether the appreciation of the Canadian dollar is likely to go further, and, if so, what might be its effect in future years.

The equations used in the assessment were estimated using quarterly data for the period 1980–2003. They are conventional in that they assume, given the stickiness of prices, that GDP is determined by demand in the short run. The rate of change of prices depends on the pressures of excess demand and, in addition, on long-run tendencies to reestablish purchasing power parity. Finally, Canada's net exports depend on economic activity in Canada and abroad, and the real exchange rate. The notation is as follows: lowercase letters indicate logarithms of the relevant variable, and D is the first-difference operator. Unstarred variables refer to Canada, and starred variables refer to the United States. Thus, $p(p^*)$ refers to the log of the Canadian (US) GDP deflator, and $y(y^*)$ to the log of Canadian (US) real GDP. The exchange rate e in logs is defined as US dollars per Canadian dollar, so that an increase in e is an appreciation, as is an increase in the real exchange rate, rer (defined in terms of GDP deflators): $rer = p + e - p^*$.

The change in the log of real GDP (Dy) depends on lagged values for the real interest rate (RR, defined as the 90-day finance company paper rate, minus the four-quarter rate of inflation, as a percent), which influences domestic demand, the log of the real exchange rate, and foreign activity (explaining the demand for Canadian goods from abroad). Given the importance of the United States, foreign activity can be well approximated by the log of US GDP (y^*). When the latter is included, there is no significant role for non-US, foreign GDP. I have also constrained the long-run coefficient for US GDP to be unity. The log of the real exchange rate is strong and significant, while the real interest rate is less important. A time trend, t, which increases by one each quarter (first quarter of 1960 = 0) is also included to account for different trend growth rates in the two countries (absolute t-ratios are given in parentheses):

$$Dy = \underset{(5.10)}{0.448Dy^*} + \underset{(4.97)}{0.396Dy^*_{-1}} - \underset{(3.46)}{0.0253rer_{-1}}$$

$$\underset{(1.46)}{-0.000470RR_{-1}} - \underset{(2.36)}{0.0651\left(y_{-1} - y^*_{-1}\right)} - \underset{(3.05)}{0.000133t} + 0.320.$$

$$\text{Adjusted } R^2 = .5791 \qquad (7.1)$$

The estimated equation can be interpreted as an error-correction model, where the long-run cointegrating vector is given by

$$y = y^* - 0.388rer - 0.00722RR - 0.00205t + const. \qquad (7.2)$$

Thus, after accounting for lags in adjustment, a 1 percent real appreciation produces a roughly three-eighths of 1 percent decrease in GDP, while a 1-percentage-point increase in the real interest rate reduces output by about three-quarters of 1 percent. Their short-run effects, evident from equation 7.1, are considerably smaller, however—only 0.03 and 0.05 percentage points, respectively, in the quarter following. A 1-percentage-point increase in US output growth increases Canadian GDP growth by 0.45 percentage points in the same quarter, a cumulative 0.85 percentage points after two quarters, and a full 1 percent in the long run.[4] However, the coefficient for the time trend reflects the slower trend growth of Canadian GDP in the sample period we have used; it implies that in steady state, Canada's quarterly growth of GDP would be lower by 0.2 percent, or 0.8 percent on an annual basis.

In explaining the rate of change of the GDP deflator, I began with a conventional Phillips curve, where inflation depended on expected inflation, plus the output gap, that is, the extent that GDP differs from full-employment (or nonaccelerating-inflation) output. Due no doubt in part to the problems of estimating the unobserved expectations and output gap variables, this specification gave relatively little role to domestic excess demand pressures. Instead, therefore, I departed from the conventional Phillips curve and estimated an equation where the price adjustment is viewed as an error-correction model with a long-run relationship linking prices in Canada to those in the United States, corrected for the exchange rate. This can be viewed as adjustment toward purchasing power parity, that is, to an equilibrium level for Canada's real exchange rate, defined in terms of relative GDP deflators with the United States:

$$Dp = 0.972 Dp^* + 0.0375 (Dp_{-1} + De_{-1}) - 0.0127 rer_{-1}$$
$$ (6.09) (1.42) \phantom{(Dp_{-1} + De_{-1})} (2.21)$$
$$+ 0.0580 \left(y_{-1} - y^*_{-1} \right) - 0.278.$$
$$ (2.64)$$

$$\text{Adjusted } R^2 = 0.5793 \qquad (7.3)$$

Interestingly, this specification gave a more satisfactory estimated equation than the conventional Phillips curve, which did not produce a significant coefficient on the output gap variable. The estimates reflect the strong pull from the United States, in which both the real exchange rate and the difference in the logs of Canadian and US GDPs explain pressures on Canadian inflation. Though it does not rely on an estimate of trend or capacity output, this specification nevertheless gives a role for demand pressures

---

4. The unit coefficient is imposed in estimation; not doing so gives a coefficient for US GDP in the cointegrating vector of 2.0, but also a much more negative time trend. So the unconstrained equation gives an even greater role for the United States, and the coefficient on lagged US output is significant at the 1 percent level.

(and hence Canadian monetary policy) in affecting Canada's inflation (as does a conventional Phillips curve). In addition, it enforces a long-run error correction of deviations from purchasing power parity. The estimated equation implies that increases in US inflation affect Canada's inflation rate almost one-for-one in the same quarter, while a 1 percent increase in the lagged difference in GDP levels in favor of Canada produces a 0.06-percentage-point acceleration in Canada's inflation. The lagged change in the nominal exchange rate has a small, and not very significant, effect, which is consistent with a very low short-run pass-through of exchange rate changes into prices.[5] Thus, the recent exchange rate appreciation (according to this equation) should have only a modest effect on the GDP deflator in the short run.

There is also an effect of the lagged real exchange rate, which can be interpreted as an error-correction term tending to reverse deviations from purchasing power parity, albeit with a long lag: The error-correction term implies that prices adjust over time to bring about a normal level of competitiveness relative to the United States. Thus, the equation does not imply that Canada's inflation is "made in the United States": Canadian monetary policy affects inflation through changes in the exchange rate as well as in aggregate demand. Given the importance of the United States for the Canadian economy, it is not surprising that such US variables turn out to be strongly significant, however. It would be interesting to do further tests of this specification against others that included only Canadian variables.

Error-correction models explain Canada's export and import volumes and prices. Export prices (px) depend on commodity prices ($pcom$) and the US GDP deflator, both denominated in Canadian dollars:

$$Dpx = \underset{(2.34)}{.0787 Dpcom} + \underset{(4.87)}{.3181(Dp^* + De)} - \underset{(3.73)}{.2087 px_{-1}}$$
$$+ \underset{(3.46)}{.0613 pcom_{-1}} + \underset{(3.14)}{.0730(p^*_{-1} + e_{-1})} - .0525$$

$$\text{Adjusted } R^2 = .3713 \qquad (7.4)$$

Export volumes (x) depend on US output and export prices relative to the US GDP deflator, with the change in US output being the main driving force:

$$Dx = \underset{(4.27)}{1.400 y^*} - \underset{(1.55)}{.2132(Dpx - Dp^*)} - \underset{(2.00)}{.0893 x_{-1}}$$
$$+ \underset{(1.51)}{.1321 y_{-1}} - \underset{(1.38)}{.0717\left(px_{-1} - p^*_{-1}\right)} - .0770$$

$$\text{Adjusted } R^2 = .2048 \qquad (7.5)$$

---

5. When entered by itself (either contemporaneously or lagged), the change in the nominal exchange rate did not have a significant effect.

Import prices (*pm*) similarly depend strongly on US prices, converted to Canadian currency, as well as on Canadian output prices (though only the first difference of the latter, and not their lagged level, came in significantly):

$$Dpm = .2889Dp + .7261(Dp^* + De) - .1530pm_{-1}$$
$$\quad\ \ (2.41) \qquad (18.31) \qquad\qquad\ (3.48)$$

$$\quad + .0824\left(p^*_{-1} + e_{-1}\right) - .0333$$
$$\quad\ \ (3.50)$$

$$\text{Adjusted } R^2 = .8062 \qquad (7.6)$$

Import volumes depend conventionally on import prices relative to the Canadian GDP deflator and Canadian activity, with the latter variable constrained to have a unit elasticity in the long run:

$$Dm = 1.231Dy + .4169(Dp - Dpm) + .5735Dx$$
$$\quad\ \ (3.67) \qquad (2.85) \qquad\qquad\quad (5.69)$$

$$\quad - .1041(m_{-1} - y_{-1}) + .0951(p_{-1} - pm_{-1}) + .0431x_{-1} - .6649$$
$$\quad\ \ (2.14) \qquad\qquad\quad (2.60) \qquad\qquad\qquad (1.75)$$

$$\text{Adjusted } R^2 = .4973 \qquad (7.7)$$

In addition to the usual determinants, exports are also included and enter significantly, reflecting the large imported input component of Canada's exports (due, for instance, to the integrated North American automobile production and assembly industry).[6]

Finally, I include an equation explaining Canada's consumer price index (CPI) on the basis of Canadian and US output prices. Here, neither the national accounts import price (*pm*) nor the exchange rate came in significantly; instead, US prices in domestic currency dominate any other foreign price variables:

$$Dcpi = .4760Dp + .4426Dp^* - .1579cpi_{-1} + .1483p_{-1} + .0305p^*_{-1} + .0131$$
$$\qquad\ \ (6.02) \qquad (2.78) \qquad\ (3.30) \qquad\ (2.88) \qquad (1.42)$$

$$\text{Adjusted } R^2 = .7806 \qquad (7.8)$$

An interesting and important conclusion that emerges from estimating this model is the strength of linkages with the United States. Canadian GDP depends strongly on economic activity in the United States. Similarly, movements in Canada's GDP deflator mirror one-for-one inflation in the United States, provided Canada's output and real exchange rate are at equilibrium levels. Canada's exports are strongly influenced by activity in the United States, but the trade balance less so, because higher exports are associated

---

6. A dummy variable for either the free trade agreement with the United States or its successor, NAFTA, did not enter significantly.

with higher imports. There is an important independent effect on exports and imports of Canadian prices relative to US prices, but because US prices strongly influence those in Canada, the scope for divergent movements is limited. No doubt further testing of specifications that contain other foreign influences in addition to that of the United States, and other Canadian variables, is warranted. However, it is clear from these results that US influences on the Canadian economy are strong—a fact that needs to be taken into account when considering how Canada may contribute to US external adjustment.

What does this conclusion of a tight linkage with the United States imply for the possibility of adjusting the United States' current account position relative to Canada? It is important to understand that this does not mean that the trade balance cannot be changed by policy measures or exchange rate changes. On the contrary, aggregate demand and relative price effects are strong. If one simulates the equations for trade prices and volumes together (taking real GDP and its deflator as exogenous), then in the long run, a 10 percent real appreciation relative to the United States can be expected to reduce Canada's overall net exports by about 2 percent of GDP (with 1.2 percent of GDP occurring by the end of the second year), whereas 1 percent higher Canadian activity would reduce the net export ratio by 0.4 percent of GDP (0.5 percent by the end of the second year, declining back subsequently as lower exports reduced imports).

However, output and price developments in the United States will have a big impact on activity and prices in Canada, and these adjustments to Canadian variables will have the effect of muting the impact on the current account of US policy changes—unless the exchange rate adjusts in the desired direction. Instead, we take movements in the exchange rate as exogenous for the purpose of this exercise. Though there is some evidence of long-run mean reversion toward a purchasing power parity level of the exchange rate and of short-run effects of interest rate differentials, structural models of the exchange rate are not very successful in the short run, as has been well documented.

The Effect of Dollar Appreciation on Prospects for 2004–05

We now turn to the forecasts of the model for 2004–05 assuming that the exchange rate takes on the value of 75 US cents for those two years, under different assumptions concerning US growth and inflation. Commodity prices are assumed to remain unchanged in Canadian dollar terms at their fourth-quarter 2003 levels. The simulated values are presented in table 7.1.

In the base case, we assume that US real GDP grows at a 3 percent annual rate for each quarter of 2004–05, and that the US GDP deflator increases at a 2 percent annual rate. It can be seen (table 7.1) that such a scenario for the United States produces a less positive outcome for Canada, which experi-

162 DOLLAR ADJUSTMENT: HOW FAR? AGAINST WHAT?

Table 7.1 Constant exchange rate, various scenarios for Canada, 2003–05 (growth in percent; or ratio to GDP, in percent)

| Scenario | Fourth quarter/fourth quarter | | | Annual average | | |
	Actual 2003	Forecast 2004	Forecast 2005	Actual 2003	Forecast 2004	Forecast 2005
Base case						
GDP	2.4	1.4	1.6	2.1	2.0	1.5
GDP deflator	2.4	1.8	1.4	3.2	1.7	1.5
Ratio of current balance to GDP	2.3	1.7	1.0	2.4	2.2	1.2
Consumer price index	1.7	2.2	1.9	2.7	1.7	2.0
Memorandum: US GDP	4.3	3.0	3.0	3.1	3.9	3.0
Memorandum: US GDP deflator	1.6	2.0	2.0	1.7	1.8	2.0
Stronger US growth						
GDP	2.4	2.7	1.7	2.1	2.8	2.1
GDP deflator	2.4	1.8	1.3	3.2	1.7	1.4
Ratio of current balance to GDP	2.3	1.6	0.8	2.4	2.2	1.1
Consumer price index	1.7	2.2	1.8	2.7	1.7	1.9
Memorandum: US GDP	4.3	4.6	3.0	3.1	5.0	3.5
Memorandum: US GDP deflator	1.6	2.0	2.0	1.7	1.8	2.0
Higher US inflation						
GDP	2.4	1.4	1.6	2.1	2.0	1.5
GDP deflator	2.4	3.9	3.4	3.2	3.0	3.5
Ratio of current balance to GDP	2.3	1.4	0.3	2.4	2.0	0.7
Consumer price index	1.7	4.2	4.0	2.7	2.9	4.1
Memorandum: US GDP	4.3	3.0	3.0	3.1	3.9	3.0
Memorandum: US GDP deflator	1.6	4.1	4.1	1.7	3.0	4.1

Source: Author's calculations.

ences slower growth than the United States in both 2004 and 2005, due in part to the lower growth trend as well as the lagged effects of 2003's exchange rate appreciation. The latter also helps keep inflation low, and the midpoint of the Bank of Canada's target for the core rate of change of the CPI seems likely to be achieved, because inflation stays below 2 percent for most of the period. Canada's current account surplus[7] declines, and it runs at about 1 percent of GDP at the end of 2005. This scenario for Canada suggests that Canada's central bank might have the scope to lower interest rates further, which could help to cushion any short-run weakness in activity.

We also consider alternative US scenarios in table 7.1. First, in line with some forecasters who expect a sharper rebound in US activity from the recent recession (preliminary 2004 data are consistent with this view), we assume growth in real GDP at a 5 percent rate in the first half of 2004, declining to 4 percent in the second half, and 3 percent in 2005. We keep the

---

7. The current account ratio is linked to net exports, which are forecast using the equations above. The current account balance was lower than net exports by 0.466 percent of GDP in 2003. That difference is mainly accounted for by factor services (i.e., net payments abroad to labor and capital), and it is assumed to remain constant at its average 2003 level in 2004–05.

other assumptions unchanged. Second, we return to the base case's growth assumption but assume higher US inflation, 4 percent instead of 2 percent.

In the first alternative scenario, Canadian GDP growth is substantially higher, at more than 2 percent in both years, but still below most measures of its potential. Inflation is little affected, nor is the current account. It is notable that Canada's current account surplus does not widen in response to higher US growth, because Canada's growth also responds. Thus, the integration of the two economies suggests that "expenditure-reducing" policies in the United States—that is, policies that affect US aggregate demand (to use the old dichotomy)—are not effective in adjusting current account imbalances between the two countries, in the absence of changes in the exchange rate. Of course, in the other direction, a reduction of Canadian demand would not have much of an effect on US GDP, so it would likely have a bigger impact on their bilateral current account. In the next section, we consider "expenditure-switching," that is, adjustment through altering relative prices.

The final scenario in table 7.1 considers higher inflation in the United States. In this scenario, Canadian growth is not much affected, but Canadian inflation rises sharply. As a result, Canada's real exchange rate does not depreciate, and the current account does not improve—indeed, it worsens because of a terms of trade deterioration as input prices rise. Canada's CPI increases by about 4 percent (fourth quarter/fourth quarter) in 2004 and in 2005. Such a scenario would probably lead to a tightening of monetary policy in Canada to avoid breaching the Bank of Canada's 2 percent inflation target. Given the weakness in Canadian activity, this would be a "worst-case" scenario; like the oil price shock of the early 1970s, it would involve stagflation, in which the need to resist inflationary pressures added to the dampening effects on activity of a negative supply shock.

Continued Exchange Rate Appreciation?

In the base-case scenario, Canada's current account position has declined substantially but remains in surplus. We therefore consider a scenario with further Canadian dollar appreciation. Here it is simply assumed that the loonie appreciates by a further 10 percent (from 75 US cents), to 82.5 US cents. This is given in the first panel of table 7.2, where it is assumed that US growth and inflation take the values of the base case in table 7.1. Whether that appreciation occurs will likely be influenced by the path of US and Canadian interest rates, which we consider below.

Such a scenario of further appreciation implies still slower economic activity in Canada, and GDP grows by less than 1 percent in 2005. Despite the weakness of Canadian activity, Canada's current account surplus decreases further relative to the base case of table 7.1 as a result of the real appreciation, moving to a surplus of only 0.6 percent of GDP at the end of 2005. Consistent with the weakness of activity and the downward pressure on import prices, inflation remains low.

Table 7.2 Further appreciation of the loonie by 10 percent, various scenarios for Canada (growth in percent; or ratio to GDP, in percent)

Scenario	Fourth quarter/ fourth quarter			Annual average		
	Actual	Forecast		Actual	Forecast	
	2003	2004	2005	2003	2004	2005
Base case						
GDP	2.4	0.7	0.9	2.1	1.6	0.7
GDP deflator	2.4	1.8	0.6	3.2	1.8	0.9
Ratio of current balance to GDP	2.3	1.2	0.6	2.4	1.8	0.8
Consumer price index	1.7	2.2	1.4	2.7	1.7	1.7
Memorandum: US GDP	4.3	3.0	3.0	3.1	3.9	3.0
Memorandum: US GDP deflator	1.6	2.0	2.0	1.7	1.8	2.0
Real rate reduced by 1 percentage point						
GDP	2.4	0.9	1.0	2.1	1.7	0.8
GDP deflator	2.4	1.8	0.7	3.2	1.8	0.9
Ratio of current balance to GDP	2.3	1.2	0.4	2.4	1.8	0.7
Consumer price index	1.7	2.2	1.5	2.7	1.7	1.7
Memorandum: US GDP	4.3	3.0	3.0	3.1	3.9	3.0
Memorandum: US GDP deflator	1.6	2.0	2.0	1.7	1.8	2.0
Commodity prices stronger by 10 percent						
GDP	2.4	0.7	0.9	2.1	1.6	0.7
GDP deflator	2.4	1.8	0.6	3.2	1.8	0.9
Ratio of current balance to GDP	2.3	1.8	1.3	2.4	2.2	1.5
Consumer price index	1.7	2.2	1.4	2.7	1.7	1.7
Memorandum: US GDP	4.3	3.0	3.0	3.1	3.9	3.0
Memorandum: US GDP deflator	1.6	2.0	2.0	1.7	1.7	2.0

Source: Author's calculations.

Thus, a further appreciation of that magnitude would bring the Canadian economy close to recession. In those circumstances, the Bank of Canada would almost certainly be induced to react by lowering interest rates (unless this were combined with the third scenario of table 7.1, with higher US inflation). The second scenario of table 7.2 thus assumes that the real short-term interest rate would decline to zero from its fourth-quarter 2003 level of about 1 percent (which was assumed to remain unchanged in the scenarios of table 7.1). Such a policy reaction would produce little extra GDP growth, but applying more monetary stimulus might be constrained by the fact that nominal interest rates, already low, cannot go below zero. As it is, the 90-day finance company paper rate, at 3 percent, is at record low levels.[8] In this scenario, it is assumed to decline to 2 percent at the end of 2005. The current account position is not very different from the base case, given

---

8. The overnight rate, the Bank of Canada's operating target, was 2 percent in May 2004, a four-decade low.

that the real exchange rate is very similar in the two scenarios of table 7.2. The second scenario could of course be questioned for having assumed the same nominal exchange rate as in the base case, and criticized for being internally inconsistent. Lower Canadian interest rates could be expected to limit the extent of further Canadian dollar appreciation, to an extent that would depend on the length of time the differential vis-à-vis the United States could be expected to last, and through this channel provide greater stimulus to economic activity in Canada.

A final scenario suggests that if commodity prices strengthen further— by 10 percent (in Canadian dollar terms) throughout 2004–05 relative to their level in the fourth quarter of 2003, then Canada's current account could continue to show a surplus well in excess of 1 percent of GDP. Nevertheless, given that economic activity and inflation are projected to remain weak, appreciation beyond the level of 80 US cents would still seem unlikely, in the light of the downward pressures they would impose on Canadian interest rates.

Canada's Equilibrium Current Account Position

The previous section did not consider what the equilibrium current account balance might be. There is an extensive literature on this issue; for instance, macroeconomic balance in the short to medium run may require an excess of domestic saving over investment (Isard et al. 2001). Here we explore a longer-run anchor for the current account, namely, a country's desired net foreign asset position.

If Canada reaches a steady-state equilibrium, then its net international investment position vis-à-vis the rest of the world, converted to Canadian dollars, must grow in line with Canadian nominal GDP. If we use upper-case letters to indicate dollar figures and lowercase letters to indicate ratios to Canadian GDP, and if we let F equal the net foreign asset position, DF the first difference in F, CA the current account balance, TB the trade balance (actually, the balance on goods and services excluding investment income), and r the return on net foreign assets, then

$$DF = CA = TB + rF \tag{7.9}$$

In a steady state, F grows at the same rate (call it γ) as GDP, so

$$DF = \gamma F = TB + rF \tag{7.10}$$

or, assuming that $r > \gamma$,

$$TB = -F/(r - \gamma) \tag{7.11}$$

And as ratios to GDP,

$$tb = -f/(r - \gamma) \tag{7.12}$$

Thus, if we can derive an equilibrium value for the net foreign asset ratio, f, then we can infer the equilibrium trade balance that is consistent with it: a surplus if the net foreign asset position is negative (so that Canada needs to export more than it imports, to service its debts), or a deficit if the net foreign asset position is positive (so that Canada can afford to spend some of its investment earnings abroad). Once we know the equilibrium trade balance, we can calculate the equilibrium real exchange rate from equations linking it to exports and imports.

During the past two decades, the United States and Canada have had dramatically different trends in their net foreign asset positions. The United States was a net international creditor until the early 1980s, but it had a net debtor position that was the equivalent of 7 percent of its GDP in 1994 (valuing direct investment at market prices) and 25 percent of GDP at the end of 2002, the latest year for which there were data available from the US Bureau of Economic Analysis at the time of this writing. In contrast to the United States, Canada ran down its net international indebtedness considerably, from 45 percent of GDP in the mid-1990s to 15 percent in 2002 (figure 7.4).

Does economic theory have anything to say about the long-run international investment position? There are two candidates: the literature on "stages of economic growth" and classical saving theory. The literature on stages of economic growth suggests that countries in the course of their development should move through various phases (Crowther 1957; Fischer and Frenkel 1972). First, being little developed initially they should exhibit a high rate of return on foreign capital and attract foreign investment; they become debtors as well as running trade and current account deficits. As they develop export capacity, they may start to run trade surpluses even though the current account is in deficit, as they are still servicing large foreign indebtedness. Eventually, they pay off debt and accumulate foreign assets. The final stage, that of a "mature creditor," should see a current account surplus that is consistent with a constant positive ratio of net foreign assets to GDP, with the current account surplus corresponding to a small trade deficit that is more than offset by a surplus on net investment earnings from abroad.

Unfortunately, the literature on stages of economic growth has proven of little use in explaining the evolution of external balances of either poor or rich countries. On the one hand, the poorest countries do not seem to have profitable investment opportunities (for reasons that are much debated but no doubt include poor governance, lack of contract enforcement, and inadequate infrastructure). On the other hand, some rich countries, like the United States and Canada, have large net debtor positions. Moreover, the United States, surely a mature and developed country, has dramatically moved from creditor to debtor in the past two decades, as was mentioned

Figure 7.4 Canada's net foreign assets, 1980–2002

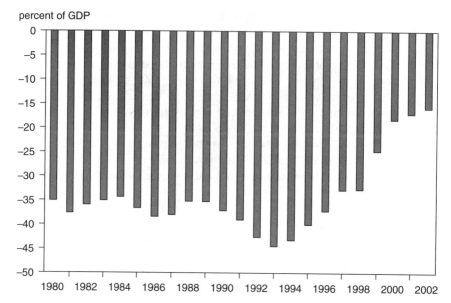

percent of GDP

Source: Statistics Canada and author's calculations.

above. The notion of growth stages has also been challenged on theoretical grounds, with Michael Bazdarich (1978) showing that they would not occur in an optimal growth model.

The second theory, related to classical saving theory, suggests that in the long run the country with the higher rate of time preference should be a borrower from abroad, while countries with less impatience should be creditors (see Buiter 1981). At first glance, this does not give us much guidance, for it is hard to marshal evidence that the rate of time preference is an unchanging structural parameter that differs systematically across countries. However, one component of "impatience" is the willingness to run fiscal deficits.

In fact, the path of fiscal policy (relative to other countries) provides a broad-brush explanation of the postwar trends in net foreign asset positions (and in current accounts).[9] The effect of the Ronald Reagan administration's spending spree on the US external balance has been much studied, and the George W. Bush administration seems bent on emulating it, completely squandering a brief accumulation of surpluses achieved by Bill Clinton's administration. In the short to medium run, US fiscal policy

---

9. Masson, Kremers, and Horne (1994) found that the net foreign asset positions of the Group of Three countries were cointegrated with public debt and demographic variables.

seems likely to involve continuing deficits. Canada also had a period of fiscal profligacy in the 1980s and early 1990s, but this was followed by a determined and successful attempt to eliminate public deficits. It seems likely, in the light of the February 2004 federal budget and trends in provincial finances, that Canada's general government fiscal position will remain in surplus, or close to it—though the June 2004 Canadian federal election campaign gave some grounds to doubt this.

Conclusions

What do these trends portend for the two countries' current account positions in the medium to long run? It seems likely that fiscal influences point to a continuation of US current account deficits and Canadian surpluses. Canada has learned the hard way that a small open economy with considerable foreign investment is very vulnerable to a crisis of confidence, because foreign investors withdraw capital at signs of unsustainable fiscal policies. As a result of their experience of the 1980s and 1990s, Canadians require their politicians to act with a high degree of fiscal prudence. Indeed, the latest federal budget brought forth some protests that the projected surplus did not provide as large a cushion as would be desirable.

In contrast, the United States has benefited from its unique position in the world economy; exporting to the US market is a key element of other countries' development strategies, and the US dollar is the preeminent reserve currency. Foreign central banks and private investors have shown themselves willing to accumulate US dollar claims seemingly without limit, even at very low rates of interest and in the face of dollar overvaluation (Dooley, Garber, and Folkerts-Landau 2003, 2004). As a result, there has been little pressure to adjust US policy toward fiscal and external sustainability.

If these trends continue, and foreigners do not put pressure on the United States, it seems unlikely that we will see the types of adjustment of Canada's current account that are illustrated by the scenarios described above. Instead, the United States will, as its economy picks up, raise interest rates, thus providing additional incentives for foreign capital inflows. The combination of loose fiscal policy and tight monetary policy—the Reagan administration's policy mix—will also produce a strong US dollar and continued US current account deficits. As a result, the appreciation of the Canadian dollar may not go further but instead may be at least partially reversed. By mid-May 2004, the exchange rate was back to 72 US cents, having reversed about half of the 20 percent appreciation that occurred in 2003.[10]

---

10. The exchange rate is clearly subject to much volatility; by August, it had returned to 76 US cents.

References

Bazdarich, Michael. 1978. Optimal Growth and Stages in the Balance of Payments. *Journal of International Economics* 8 (August): 425–43.

Buiter, Willem. 1981. Time Preference and International Lending and Borrowing in an Overlapping Generations Model. *Journal of Political Economy* 89 (August): 769–97.

Crowther, G. 1957. *Balances and Imbalances of Payments.* Cambridge, MA: Harvard University Press.

Djoudad, Ramdane, John Murray, Tracy Chan, and Jason Daw. 2001. The Role of Chartists and Fundamentalists in Currency Markets: The Experience of Australia, Canada, and New Zealand. In *Revisiting the Case for Flexible Exchange Rates.* Ottawa: Bank of Canada.

Dooley, Michael, David Folkerts-Landau, and Peter Garber. 2003. *An Essay on the Revived Bretton Woods System.* NBER Working Paper 9971. Cambridge, MA: National Bureau of Economic Research.

Dooley, Michael, David Folkerts-Landau, and Peter Garber. 2004. *The Revived Bretton Woods System: The Effects of Periphery Intervention and Reserve Management on Interest Rates and Exchange Rates in Center Countries.* NBER Working Paper 10332. Cambridge, MA: National Bureau of Economic Research.

Fischer, Stanley, and Jacob Frenkel. 1972. Investment, the Two-Sector Model and Trade in Debt and Capital Goods. In *Trade, Stability and Macroeconomics,* ed. G. Horwich and P. Samuelson. New York: Academic Press.

Isard, Peter, Hamid Faruqee, G. Russell Kincaid, and Martin Fetherston. 2001. *Methodology for Current Account and Exchange Rate Assessments.* IMF Occasional Paper 209. Washington: International Monetary Fund.

Masson, Paul, Jeroen Kremers, and Jocelyn Horne. 1994. Net Foreign Assets and International Adjustment: The United States, Japan, and Germany. *Journal of International Money and Finance* 13 (February): 27–40.

TD Bank Financial Group. 2004. *Loonie Tunes: Understanding the Rally in the Canadian Dollar and Its Consequences.* TD Economics Special Report. Toronto: TD Bank Financial Group.

8

The Yen and the Japanese Economy, 2004

TAKATOSHI ITO

This chapter presents an overview of the Japanese macroeconomy and its exchange rate policy and monetary policy in the period 2003–04. It also examines the effects of the exchange rate changes on Japanese trade balances. The monetary authorities of Japan—namely, the Ministry of Finance and the Bank of Japan (MOF-BOJ)—intervened in the foreign exchange market frequently heavily in 2003–04. The authorities sold ¥35 trillion (or $320 billion), 7 percent of the Japanese GDP, between January 2003 and March 2004. This chapter examines the presumed objectives of the large interventions and their effectiveness. Why the Japanese authorities intervened to this unprecedented extent is explained here in the context of the macroeconomic conditions and developments in the foreign exchange, spot, and futures markets.

To summarize the chapter's conclusions, interventions were conducted for several reasons—including to prevent "premature" appreciation in the midst of a weak economy, to help monetary policy by providing opportunities for unsterilized interventions, and to defuse excessive speculative pressure. These hypotheses on the motivations for intervention are supported by data, but it is more difficult to judge whether the intended effects of the MOF-BOJ's actions were achieved.

Japan's macroeconomic conditions are described in the chapter's second section. The third section examines the relationship between the exchange rate and net exports of Japan. The next sections explains the reasons for heavy interventions from January 2003 to March 2004 and section provide data to back up these explanations. The last section offers conclusions.

Takatoshi Ito is a professor at the Graduate School of Economics, University of Tokyo.

171

Figure 8.1 Growth rates of Japan, 1973–2003 (percent)

percent

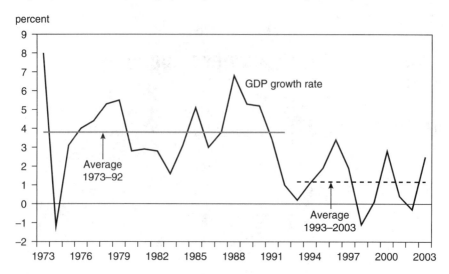

Source: Cabinet office, government of Japan.

Macroeconomic Conditions: The End of Japan's Lost Decade

Japan has been underperforming for the past 14 years. Since 1992, its average growth rate has barely been above 1 percent. This contrasts with an approximate 4 percent average growth rate from the mid-1970s to 1992. Figure 8.1 shows trend and time series changes of the country's growth rates. This period of slow growth—what is often dubbed the "lost decade" of Japan—has also been accompanied by deteriorating financial and capital market conditions: deflating asset prices, mounting problems of nonperforming loan, a series of bank failures, and a downgrading of government bonds. Since the mid-1990s, prices have declined.[1] The inflation rate, measured by the consumer price index (CPI), reached about negative 1 percent in 2000–01, while the inflation rate measured by the GDP deflator reached between negative 2 and 3 percent in 2002–03. The combination of a declining GDP deflator and weak real growth implied declining nominal GDP from 1997 to 2002. The Japanese economy from the mid-1990s to 2003 was probably the first example, since the United States in the 1930s, of a major economy that suffered from deflation and associated problems.

---

1. See, e.g., Bayoumi and Collyns (2000) and Callen and Ostry (2003) for the views of the International Monetary Fund staff on Japanese stagnation. See also Ito (2003b, 2004). See Cargill, Ito, and Hutchison (1997, 2000) and Hoshi and Patrick (2000) for analyses of financial sector problems in Japan.

In the period 2001–02, the Japanese economy, along with that of the United States, experienced very low growth. By the end of 2002, the Japanese economy was considered to be in a crisis stage, or a repeat of the financial crisis of 1997–98. Japan's negative growth in 2002 had placed it in this crisis mode. At the beginning of 2003, the prospects for the country's economy looked very bleak. The economy was coming out of the negative growth of 2002, yet all indicators seemed to worsen. The unemployment rate reached 5.5 percent in January, and it seemed to be rising further (but did not). The stock price index, the Nikkei 225, dropped below 8,000, one-fifth of the peak achieved at the end of 1989. The major banks had to report huge losses from unrealized capital losses in stock portfolios as well as writing off nonperforming loans. Prices were declining; monetary policy, at the zero interest rate, lacked conventional tools; and fiscal policy, already facing high fiscal deficits and high debts, seemed to be limited in its room for deficit financing. The Resona Bank failed in May; its capital ratio was found to have sunk below 4 percent. Because the Financial Services Agency decided to nationalize the bank and inject ¥2 trillion—raising the capital ratio well above 8 percent, without writing down existing shareholders' equity—the stock prices of banks started to rise in the summer, and business activity picked up the pace. Exports to China and other Asian countries started to increase sharply, and companies started to invest and expand capacity in Japan. In the second half of 2003, the rate of economic growth began to increase.

In 2004, there were growing signs that Japan is finally getting out of a long tunnel of depressing events and macroeconomic underperformance. The Japanese economy grew at 2.5 percent in 2003, and 6.1 percent in the first quarter of 2004 (annualized quarter-to-quarter growth).[2] According to the International Monetary Fund (*World Economic Outlook,* April 2004), Japan was expected to grow at 3.4 percent in 2004, compared with 4.6 percent for the United States and 1.7 percent for the euro area, as is shown in table 8.1.[3] Growth would only accelerate, compared with 2003, in Japan as the well as the other Group of Seven (G-7) countries.

Japan's current recovery is the third time that its economy has grown by more than 2.5 percent in the past 14 years—and the country's third attempt to get out of stagnation. The first recovery attempt was during the period 1995–96, with a sudden end in 1997, mainly due to the tax rate hike in April 1997, which was followed by the Asian currency crisis and the Japanese banking crisis. The second recovery attempt was in 2000–01, with a sudden

---

2. The number is based on the announcement by the Cabinet Office, May 18, 2004. The new number became available since the first draft of this chapter was written. Growth slowed down in the second quarter of 2004 to 1.7 percent (as announced on August 13, 2004).

3. The IMF number was calculated before the first-quarter number became known on May 18, and it was later revised upward. The IMF assessment of the Japanese economy, made public on August 11, has a projection of 4.5 percent growth in 2004.

Table 8.1 Economic growth rates of major economies, 2001–04

Country or region	2001	2002	2003	2004
Canada	1.9	3.3	1.7	2.6
China	7.5	8.0	9.1	8.5
France	2.1	1.2	0.2	1.8
Germany	0.8	0.2	–0.1	1.6
Italy	1.8	0.4	0.3	1.2
Japan	0.4	–0.3	2.5	3.4
United Kingdom	2.1	1.7	2.3	3.5
United States	0.5	2.2	3.1	4.6
Euro area	1.6	0.9	0.4	1.7

Sources: International Monetary Fund, *World Economic Outlook*, April 2004, except for Japan in 2003, which was updated by the Cabinet Office announcement on May 18, 2004.

end in 2001 due to the collapse of the information technology stock bubble and the mistaken monetary policy initiated in August 2000—a policy of tightening during deflation.

Two engines for the current Japanese recovery are exports and corporate investment. The former increased by 3.9 percent (quarter-to-quarter change), and the latter by 2.4 percent in the first quarter of 2004. Exports to the United States and to China have shown significant increases since about 2002. Corporate investment has increased due to high levels of profits among large manufacturing companies.

Stock prices have risen by 50 percent since the trough in April 2003. This has given breathing room to financial institutions that hold equities as portfolios as well as to individuals with stock portfolios. The increase in stock prices, fueled by foreigners in 2003, is contributing to an increase in demand for consumption and investment. The unemployment rate is also showing encouraging signs; after it peaked at 5.5 percent in January 2003, it fell to 4.7 percent in March 2003 and to 4.6 percent in May 2004.

Deflation has accompanied low growth in the past several years. In fact, low growth has been both a cause and result of deflation. An output gap has put downward pressure on prices, but deflation has discouraged corporate and housing investment. Nonperforming loans will continue to emerge as deflation continues, because borrowers suffer from an increasing real burden of nominally contracted debt. On the basis of the CPI, price levels have been declining since 1998. The worst decline was in the period 2001–02, when the CPI was decreasing at a rate of about 1 percent. Recently, the rate has narrowed to about zero. However, the GDP deflator is still showing deflation of about 2.5 percent. Deflation has not ended in Japan.

Economic growth may accelerate beyond that forecast, if several pieces fall into place in 2004. First, stock price increases may generate a virtuous cycle: Wealth effects due to stock price increases generate more spending among individuals and corporations, leading to higher profits, higher stock prices, and further wealth effects. Higher stock prices would also help strengthen financial institutions' balance sheets.

If sufficient progress is made in economic growth, prices in Japan may finally start rising instead of falling. The Bank of Japan is sending the right signal: that it will not increase the interest rate until the CPI inflation rate becomes positive for several consecutive months with no prospect of falling back to deflation.[4] Therefore, ending deflation may not automatically trigger an interest rate hike. In fact, the Bank of Japan should be extra patient before even thinking of an interest rate hike, to make up for the drop in the price levels since 1998.

The most encouraging sign suggesting an increase in domestic demand is a rise in corporate investment. But this may also be linked to export demand. For the Japanese economy to begin to grow autonomously with increases in domestic demand rather than export demand, household expenditures will have to rise beyond the current level (1.0 percent quarter-to-quarter growth). For this, both employment and wages will have to increase. When restructured corporations start to report profits and wages start to increase, the scenario of rising household expenditures will become a reality. This may happen soon, because higher profits are now trickling down to the household sector.

Most banks are now reporting healthier balance sheets. Although several weak banks, including the UFJ Bank, are still showing large nonperforming loans and undercapitalization, there is no financial panic. The episode of nationalizing the Resona Bank and Ashikaga Bank in 2003 shows that the Financial Services Agency can handle weak banks swiftly without raising concern about systemic risk.

However, there are also downside risks. The first risk is of a sharp appreciation of the yen, or of a depreciation of the dollar vis-à-vis the yen. Recall that exports are still one of the most powerful engines for Japan's recovery. The United States and China—the dollar-linked country—are the favorite destinations for Japanese exports. However, the volume of exports to the United States is declining, though their value is being maintained. The dollar's collapse would adversely hit the Japanese economy and bring the Japanese recovery to a sudden stop.

---

4. The necessary condition to stop providing current extra liquidity with a zero interest rate had changed from "until the deflation fear is dispelled" (February 1999) to "until the CPI inflation rate (excluding fresh food) becomes stably above zero" (March 2001) and then to the current statements put out in October 2003: First, the tendency of an inflation rate measured by CPI excluding fresh food being zero or above should be "confirmed over a few months," and second, the tendency should be forecasted by many Policy Board members. These are the necessary conditions.

Similarly, any substantial deceleration of the US and Chinese economies would slow down Japanese exports. An interest rate hike in the United States and credit restraints in China also would slow down the two economies, which some regard as on the verge of overheating.

The scenario of a virtuous cycle of stock price increases and a rise in real expenditures depends totally on the movement of stock prices, which in turn depends on foreign investors' behavior. As soon as foreigners turned to net selling in the second quarter of 2004, stock prices started to slump.

Another financial crisis would have substantial adverse effects on Japan's economy. The UFJ Bank—along with its stockholding umbrella, the UFJ Financial Group—was placed under special examination by the Financial Services Agency from March to May 2004, and it was ordered to increase provisioning for problematic loans. As a result, the UFJ Bank reported large losses for the fiscal year ending in March 2004, and the bank's capital ratio was reduced to just above 8 percent. Another shock to the UFJ Bank would push its capital below the critical 8 percent level, triggering the Bank to be forced to withdraw from international business, and in the worst case, nationalization like the Resona Bank.[5]

In April 2005, the blanket guarantee of bank deposits will be almost completely lifted, and that may trigger deposit shifts from weaker institutions to stronger ones. Some smaller regional banks may have difficulty keeping deposits. However, at that point, the probability of another systemic risk to the financial system will be low because the safety net will be well established.

Higher social security contributions are projected because the pension system is facing deficits in the medium run. As the proposed "reform" plan has passed the Diet, households will face a continuous increase in social security contributions in the next several years. This will have an effect similar to a scheduled tax rate hike. However, many young to middle-age workers are skeptical about how much they would receive in return for paying into the pension system. Household expenditures are not forecast to increase sharply.

Other kinds of downside risk, originating abroad, also would affect the Japanese economy. Higher oil prices are an obvious downside risk for oil-importing Japan. However, the oil-import expenditures are small relative to Japanese exports, so moderately higher oil prices would hardly make a dent in the country's macroeconomic trade balance. More than half of the

---

5. The UFJ Bank executives will have to take responsibility if the plan for rehabilitation, which was specified at the time of the capital injection in 1998–99, is not achieved (i.e., profits are below the target by more than 30 percent) for two fiscal years in a row. Since the first draft of this chapter was written, the Mitsubishi Tokyo Financial Group and UFJ Holding agreed to merge. This will be essentially a rescue merger, a financially healthy Mitsubishi Tokyo Financial Group, including the Bank of Tokyo-Mitsubishi, injecting capital to UFJ Holding, including the UFJ Bank.

retail gasoline price is accounted for by the gasoline tax, so crude oil price increases would not cause a sharp retail price increase in percentage terms, unlike in the United States. The political impact on household perception of oil price increases would be much less in Japan, although it is still a downside risk to the economy.

In addition to oil prices, commodity prices in general have risen since 2003, partly due to the demand from China. Further rises in commodity prices—including coal, iron ore, and grain—would have an adverse impact on the Japanese manufacturing sector. Conversely, however, the growth of the Chinese economy is beneficial to Japanese corporations, including steel and shipbuilding companies.

The Yen-Dollar Exchange Rate and Japanese Exports and Imports

The yen-dollar exchange rate has been fluctuating most of the time from 1992 to 2004 at between 100 and 135 (as of this writing)—with the notable exceptions of a brief period of appreciation to 80 in the spring and summer of 1995, and a brief period of depreciation to 145 in June–August 1998. Although the short-run (e.g., daily) movement of the yen is hard to explain, the medium-term (e.g., quarterly) movement can be associated with various factors, such as growth potentials, interest rate differentials, and other macroeconomic factors. But here I do not attempt to explain the movement of the exchange rate. Instead, the exchange rate is taken as given, and I try to explain exports by, among other things, movements of exchange rates.

It can be argued that the Japanese external (trade or current account) balances have become less sensitive to the yen-dollar rate but maintained a relationship, with a lag, to the real effective exchange rate (REER). It is important to differentiate the REER (the multilateral, real rate) of Japan from the yen-dollar rate (the bilateral, nominal rate). Figure 8.2 shows the time series of the two exchange rates. Most of the time, they move in parallel. However, since 2001, the REER has remained stable, while the yen-dollar rate has appreciated by 20 percent. The difference is partly due to a widening price gap between Japan (under deflation) and the United States (under moderate inflation) and partly due to stable exchange rate movement vis-à-vis Japan's other trading partners (mainly Asian countries).

Figure 8.3 shows changes in net Japanese exports and the REER (the inverse of the REER as defined by the IMF). It shows that sharp appreciations, like those in the periods 1985–88 and 1991–95, produced a corresponding decline in net exports, with a one-year lag in the peak of net exports. Depreciation episodes, like those in 1995–98 and 2000–03, are also accompanied by an increase in net exports. Thus, net exports are indeed sensitive to yen movements, with a time lag.

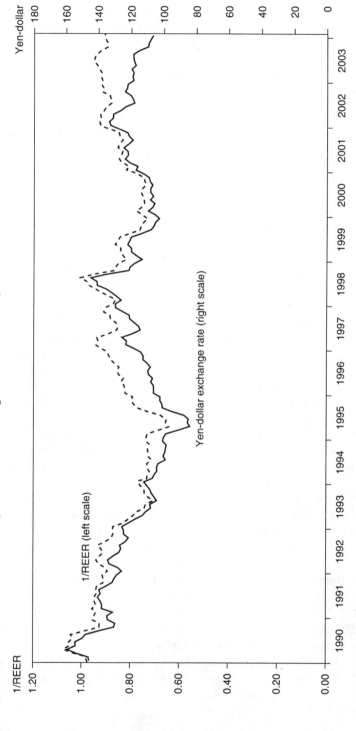

Figure 8.2   Time series for the yen-dollar exchange rate and REER, 1990–2003

REER = real effective exchange rate

Note: REER, defined by IMF, 1995 = 100.

Source: IMF, *International Financial Statistics,* May 2004.

178

Figure 8.3 Real effective exchange rate and trade balances, 1976–2003

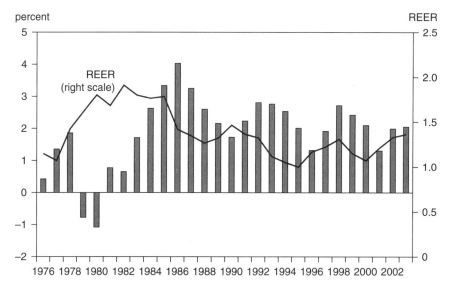

Note: Bars represent the trade balance as a percent of GDP (left scale).
      REER, (right scale) defined by IMF, 1995 = 100.

Source: IMF, *International Financial Statistics*, May 2004.

If the correlation between the REER and trade balances can be taken seriously, then the following back-of-the-envelope calculation is possible: If the REER appreciates by 30 percent from the level of 2003 to make the yen's REER value close to the level in 1995–96 and 2000, then net exports of the following year would be 35 percent less. This spells a recession (like the ones in 1997 and 2001–02), unless domestic demand increases sharply.

The point of this exercise of comparing the REER and the yen-dollar exchange rate is that looking at the yen-dollar rate is misleading on two fronts: It is bilateral and it is nominal. The weight of the United States in Japan's trade has decreased over time, so the bilateral exchange rate may be misleading in predicting export competitiveness. In addition, Japanese deflation has caused real exchange rate stability, despite the fact that the nominal exchange rate appreciated in the period 1998–2003. A comparison of 1998 and 2003 proves the point. The yearly average of the nominal yen-dollar exchange rate was 131 for 1998 and 116 for 2003, but the REER (1995 = 1.00) was 1.31 for 1998 and 1.36 for 2003. Thus, the yen did not appreciate at all in 2003 compared with 1998, the trough of the financial crisis for Japan and Asia.

To evaluate a claim that to keep the yen from appreciating would help the export industry of Japan, a standard export function can be estimated. The export/GDP ratio, $EXY(t)$, is explained by the lagged variable $EXY(t-1)$; the log of the real effective exchange rate (an increase being appreciation),

Table 8.2   The export function for Japan
(dependent variable: Gross export/GDP ratio, *EXY*)

Variable	Coefficient (standard error)	*t*-statistic	Significance
Constant	0.0879 (0.0231)	3.81	0.000
EXY(*t* – 1)	0.6412 (0.0735)	8.73	0.000
LREER(*t*)	–0.0087 (0.0037)	–2.34	0.019
LREER(*t* – 1)	0.0042 (0.0038)	1.11	0.267
LJPY(*t*)	–0.0073 (0.0022)	–3.31	0.001
LUSY(*t* – 1)	0.0041 (0.0010)	3.80	0.000

Notes: *R* bar squared = 0.856. Linear regression: estimation using a Gaussian mixture model, with 4 lags. Quarterly data were used, from the fourth quarter of 1976 to the first quarter of 2004.

Source: International Monetary Fund, *International Financial Statistics*, June 2004.

$LREER(t)$ and $LREER(t - 1)$; the Japanese output level, $LJPY(t)$; and the US output level, $LUSY(t - 1)$. The US output level is used as a proxy for global demand for Japanese exports. It is lagged because it may take time for higher US income to generate exports from Japan.[6] The export function equation takes this form:

$$EXY(t) = Y\alpha + \beta_1 EXY(t - 1) + \beta_2 LREER(t)$$
$$+ \beta_3 LREER(t - 1) + \beta_4 LJPY(t)$$
$$+ \beta_4 LUSY(t - 1) + \varepsilon(t) \tag{8.1}$$

The equation is estimated using a Generalized Method of Moments (GMM), and table 8.2 shows the result. The Japanese export/GDP ratio will indeed increase if the exchange rate depreciates, if Japanese growth slows, and if US growth accelerates. This result is broadly consistent with conventional expected signs of coefficients. The estimated coefficients imply not so large effects from the change in the real effective exchange rate to the export/GDP ratio—a 10 percent change in REER in the medium run will cause a decline of 0.1 point in the export/GDP ratio.[7] It needs to be noted that this result pertains not to net exports but to gross exports, so one should be careful in interpreting the result in a macro-economic context.

In sum, Japanese exporters have much more robustness against the yen's appreciation in terms of the nominal yen-dollar rate than in the period 1998–2000, because the Japanese economy has experienced deflation (real depreciation) and exports to non-dollar-linked Asia have risen.

---

6. I acknowledge the excellent research assistance of Kentaro Kawasaki.

7. The medium-term effect of a permanent change in *LREER* (a percent change) on *EXY* would be $d(EXY)/d(LREER) = (\beta_2 + \beta_3)/(1 - \alpha) \approx -0.01$.

Table 8.3 Summary of interventions by the Japanese authorities, January 2003–March 2004

Intervention	In trillions of yen	Yen-dollar average for the period	In billions of dollars
January–March 2003	2.3867	118.66	20.1
April–June 2003	4.6116	119.30	38.7
July–September 2003	7.5512	115.90	65.2
October–December 2003	5.8755	108.43	54.2
January–March 2004	14.8314	106.30	139.5
Total	**35.2564**		**317.7**

Sources: Intervention: Ministry of Finance; yen-dollar rate: Bank of Japan.

Japanese Interventions

The magnitude of interventions conducted by the Ministry of Finance–Bank of Japan from January 2003 to March 2004 was particularly large, in Japan's intervention history and in comparison with other countries. Table 8.3 shows the quarterly aggregate of intervention amounts in yen from the first quarter of 2003 to the first quarter of 2004. The MOF-BOJ sold a total of ¥35 trillion, or purchased about $317 billion, of which 42 percent was concentrated in the first quarter of 2004. The Japanese authorities' total intervention amount from April 1991 to December 2002 was less than ¥34 trillion.[8] So the interventions in the 15 months from January 2003 to March 2004 exceeded those of the 11 years and 9 months preceding that period.

The interventions of this period started on January 15, 2003—the first since June 28, 2002—just a day after Zembei Mizoguchi became Vice Minister for International Affairs. The amount of the intervention on January 15, 2003, was ¥8.3 billion, or $70 million, and it was rather a modest one. (The average size of the intervention from June 1995 to June 2002 was ¥520 billion per intervention day.) However, interventions were conducted in eight days in January, five days in February, and four days in March. This was a higher frequency of interventions than between June 1995 and December 2002.

But day-to-day interventions were not confirmed on the day by the MOF-BOJ during the heavy intervention episode. Mizoguchi, when asked about them, did not confirm or deny the interventions—so they were later dubbed "stealth interventions." This was a contrast to previous interventions from 1995 to 2002 under Eisuke Sakakibara and Haruhiko Kuroda, both of whom were known for their vocal interventions as well as for playing up actual interventions with announcements.

---

8. The daily intervention data on and after April 1, 1991 have been disclosed.

Rumors of interventions were increasingly abundant from January to March 2003. Since monthly aggregates of interventions were fairly accurately guessed from Bank of Japan statistics released at the end of each month, the fact that stealth interventions had been conducted became known at the end of January 2003. In addition, the Ministry of Finance itself confirmed the monthly aggregate number of interventions at the end of January, February, and March. However, the detailed day-by-day statistics were not available until the first week of June. When the daily intervention records of January to March 2003 were then disclosed, many in the market were surprised by the frequency and size of the interventions. For transparency, disclosure of the monthly aggregate of interventions started in June 2003, along with conventional daily intervention disclosure four times a year. But the market participants were left to guess whether there had been an intervention on a particular day until the quarterly disclosure of the daily figures.[9]

Factors That Influence Intervention Decisions

Below I give a rather detailed description of interventions from January 2003 to March 2004, with some conjectures as to the reasons for them. From previous studies (e.g., Ito and Yabu 2004), it appears that two of the most common reasons for interventions are a sharp appreciation (or depreciation) and a deviation from the long-run trend. So-called smoothing operations are aimed at slowing down the pace of appreciation or depreciation, when movements (of preceding days) are regarded as too fast. On many occasions, the Minister of Finance or the Vice Minister for Inter-national Affairs, Ministry of Finance, mentioned that the too-rapid movements were the reason for an intervention. Even when the exchange rates move quickly, the MOF-BOJ may not intervene if the level is near long-run equilibrium, or if the movement is toward equilibrium rather than away from it. It has been shown (Ito 2003a) that the Japanese authorities, since 1991, never sold dollars below ¥125/$1 and never bought dollars above ¥125/$1. The level as well as the speed of change influences the decision to intervene.

However, these two traditional reasons for interventions do not seem to adequately explain why the Japanese authorities intervened so much after January 2003. Three more reasons are considered below: to prevent "premature" appreciation; to purchase foreign bonds as a means of expanding the monetary base (i.e., unsterilized intervention); and to prevent speculative forces from moving the yen-dollar exchange rate.

---

9. See Ito (2003a) and Ito and Yabu (2004) for a description and analysis of interventions before the Mizoguchi regime.

Preventing Premature Appreciation

First, interventions seemed to have been conducted to prevent "premature" appreciation—that is, appreciation when macroeconomic conditions were deteriorating. This explanation may apply to interventions in the first 6 to 8 months of 2003. The economy was still considered to be very weak, and stock prices declined sharply from January to March. The *Monthly Report of Recent Economic and Financial Developments* of the Bank of Japan showed its assessment of the stagnant economy until August 2003.[10] Stock prices according to the Nikkei index had been declining from 14,000 in April 2002 to 10,000 in July 2002, 8,700 in December 2002, and 7,600 at the end of April 2003. This decline in stock prices by more than 40 percent in 12 months set off alarms in the MOF-BOJ. The declining stock prices also hit bank balance sheets, and the mood was quite bad.

Against these deteriorating conditions, the yen was on an appreciating trend. One reason was the bearish assessment of the dollar against the background of the war in Iraq. Another factor was that foreign investors thought that the Japanese stock markets were near the bottom and that the timing was right to purchase stocks. But the yen's appreciation in the first half of 2003 was considered to be inconsistent with macroeconomic fundamentals. Sharp appreciation would cause further deterioration of macroeconomic conditions. Even when macroeconomic fundamentals and stock prices showed recovery in the second half of 2003, the recovery was considered to be very weak, so any sharp appreciation was then considered to be "premature." It is not surprising that the Japanese authorities thought that it would be prudent to prevent sharp appreciation at the stage of deteriorating macroeconomic conditions, or at the stage of weak recovery. In sum, a concern to prevent "premature" appreciation can broadly explain interventions from January 2003 to August 2003.

Second, interventions might be conducted to help monetary policy to stimulate the economy. The short-term interest rate (call rate) had been zero since February 1999 (except for temporary tightening to 0.25 percent from August 2000 to March 2001; quantitative easing was used after March 2001). For the BOJ to expand the monetary base (i.e., quantitative easing), it must purchase assets. Buying short-term treasury bills—the usual instrument—is not very effective, because at a zero interest rate, cash and treasury bills are perfectly substitutable for the public. If the BOJ purchases different kinds of assets—such as long-term bonds, foreign bonds, equities,

---

10. The Bank of Japan's views were that "economic activity remains virtually flat" in July and August 2003; then "economic activity still continues to be virtually flat as a whole, although signs of improvement have been observed in such areas as the environment for exports" in September 2003; "the foundation for a gradual recovery in Japan's economy is being laid, as the environment for exports and business sentiment have improved" in October 2003; and "Japan's economy is starting to recover gradually" in November.

and real assets—then unconventional channels of monetary policy may open up. Unsterilized intervention is one such instrument. Because interventions are conducted by the MOF, unsterilized intervention can be achieved only by cooperation between the BOJ and MOF. A combination of large interventions and a large increase in the monetary base can be regarded as a method of unsterilized intervention.

Third, the MOF-BOJ was determined that the yen-dollar exchange rate would not fluctuate due to speculative forces. In the minds of officials in Japan, the yen-dollar movement between the spring of 1995 and October 1998 seems to be still vividly remembered. From April to August 1995, the yen-dollar rate moved from 100 to 80 and then back to 100. The rate's appreciation from 100 to 80 in a matter of several weeks is considered to have been driven by speculative buying of the yen, knock-out options, loss cuts, and other technical forces that were unrelated to the macroeconomic conditions at the time. The level of ¥80/$1 was considered to be unsustainable and harmful to exporters. Several interventions from June to September 1995, in particular forceful ones in August and September, made it possible to reverse the trend and pushed the yen-dollar rate back to the 100 level.

From October 5 to 9, 1998, the yen appreciated from ¥135/$1 to ¥116/$1. This very rapid movement was caused by the unwinding of the yen carry trades that had been popular among hedge funds before that week. Unwinding became necessary when sensitivity to risk suddenly changed after disclosure of the failure of Long-Term Capital Management, a large hedge fund. All other hedge funds liquidated positions to fatten cash reserves. As a result, the yen was bought to square the short position. These episodes are remembered as examples that speculative positions and technical factors could move the yen-dollar market easily. Japanese officials may think that interventions can be more easily justified when they are used against the speculative buying and selling of the yen.[11] The next sections analyze the timing of these interventions and the underlying factors that are considered to have prompted them.

Unsterilized Intervention

Another justification for a large intervention is that it was helpful to achieve monetary easing. The Bank of Japan, under its new governor, Toshihiko Fukui, was increasing excess reserves in several steps from April to December 2003. Unsterilized intervention in the usual circum-

---

11. There is a fundamental difference between fighting against the pressure of a depreciating currency (e.g., the United Kingdom's in 1992) and fighting against the pressure of an appreciating currency (e.g., Japan's in 1995 and in 2003–04). The former has a limitation of foreign reserves as ammunition and the latter has unlimited resources for intervention by printing money.

Figure 8.4   Intervention and the monetary base, Japan, 2003–04

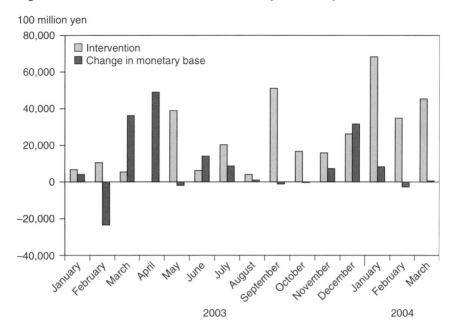

Sources: Intervention, Ministry of Finance, Japan; monetary base, Bank of Japan.

stance (the interest rate being positive) would be effective in depreciating the currency by relaxing the monetary condition (lowering the interest rate). According to the view that monetary policy works only through the interest rate, unsterilized interventions simply increase excess reserves, with no effect through the interest rate channel, under a zero interest rate regime, like that in Japan in 2003.

However, monetary policy may work through channels other than the interest rate. First, because more liquidity in the system will make corporations and households shift their portfolio toward risky assets, like stocks and foreign bonds, unsterilized interventions even at a zero interest rate will likely cause depreciation and have real effects. Second, if market participants are convinced that the BOJ, by making unsterilized interventions, is signaling a future monetary policy of maintaining the zero interest rate for a long period—longer than previously believed—after the economy starts to recover, then unsterilized intervention will have real effects.

Figure 8.4 shows the monthly aggregate of interventions and monthly changes of the monetary base. It appears to be the case that the two series have very little correlation. Figure 8.5 shows the same two series, but with the past three-month moving average of the monetary base. Now the movement seems to be more correlated, although the correlation coefficient is not perfect. From January to December 2003, cumulative interventions amounted to ¥20.2 trillion, while the cumulative increase in the monetary

Figure 8.5   Interventions and the monetary base, Japan, 2003–04
(3-month moving average)

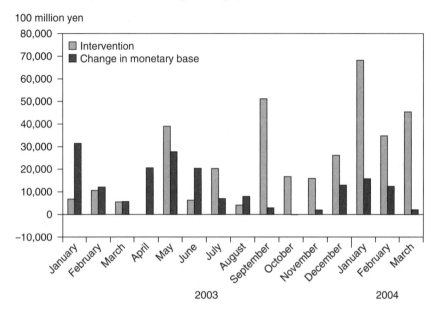

Sources: Intervention, Ministry of Finance, Japan; monetary base, Bank of Japan.

base was ¥12.5 trillion. In 2003, it was not inconsistent to say that more than half of the interventions were unsterilized. When the time span is made a little bit longer, as since March 2001, when quantitative easing was initiated, then the cumulative intervention amount and the cumulative increase in the monetary base match at the end of March 2004, as is shown in figure 8.6.[12] It is not immediately clear to observers whether the MOF, which again is in charge of intervention, and the BOJ, which is in charge of monetary policy, were consciously coordinating so that unsterilized intervention could be realized. It could have been just a coincidence of two independent decisions.[13]

---

12. I owe this insight to James Harrigan.

13. Deputy Governor Kazumasa Iwata, when asked about this on October 1, 2003, replied that "the amounts of interventions amounted to ¥13.5 trillion so far this year, and the additional liquidity supplied by the Bank of Japan amounted to ¥10 trillion—¥2 trillion in March, ¥5 trillion in April, and ¥3 trillion in May—so far. The two amounts have been about the same, although it must be a coincidence. Thus, the simultaneous interventions and liquidity provision, ex post, have the same effect as unsterilized intervention. Also, ex post, they had the same effect as the case where the Bank of Japan purchases US government securities" (press interview, Deputy Governor Iwata, October 1, 2003, at Sendai; printed in Japanese, translated by the author. Available at http://www.boj.or.jp/press/03/kk0310a.htm).

Figure 8.6　The monetary base and cumulative intervention, Japan, 2001–2004

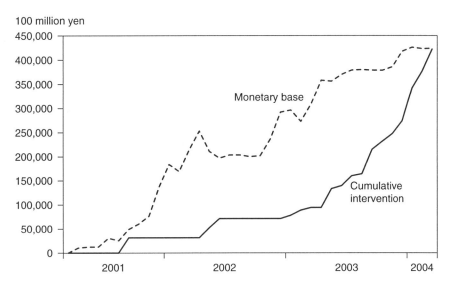

100 million yen

Sources: Intervention, Ministry of Finance, Japan; monetary base, Bank of Japan.

An important point is that intervention was helping to broaden the menu of quantitative easing. In other words, intervention policy and monetary policy were pointing in the same direction. As Lars Svensson (2001) pointed out, many economists approved of unsterilized intervention because it would help Japan get out of deflation at zero interest rate by raising the expected inflation rate in the future.

The Fight Against Speculators

Another possible reason that the MOF-BOJ intervened so much was to prevent the exchange rate from becoming misaligned by speculative positions. Although speculators may not cause permanent damage, short- to medium-run volatility would be greatly increased if there were massive capital flows in and out of the yen asset markets. One indicator of such a futures position is represented in the weekly figure for the International Monetary Market (IMM) position on the Chicago Mercantile Exchange.[14] The data on long and short positions on Tuesday are disclosed on the following Friday. The net long position (i.e., long minus short) is frequently regarded as potential (downward or upward) pressure in the market for the currency.

---

14. Available at http://www.cme.com/prd/overview_JY2466.html.

Figure 8.7   The International Monetary Market net long position of yen futures, 2000–04

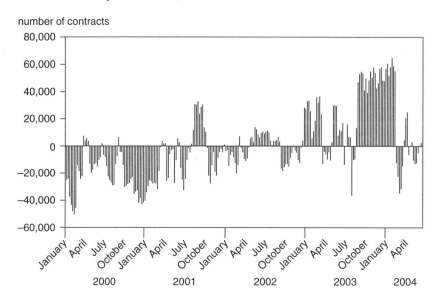

number of contracts

Note: The International Monetary Market is part of the Chicago Mercantile Exchange. Data are for the 11th of January, April, July, and October of the year represented.

Source: Chicago Mercantile Exchange, International Monetary Market.

Figure 8.7 shows the net long position of IMM yen futures on the Chicago Mercantile Exchange. In the period from 2000 to 2004, the positions from January 2003 to February 2004 were very large. Figure 8.8 shows the magnified picture for the period from January 2003 to June 2004, with weekly intervention amounts (the positive number of interventions here means yen sales or dollar purchases). It is striking that when yen net long positions were large, it is more likely that interventions were conducted to offset that pressure. The timing seems to be very close, except for the period from mid-February to mid-March 2004.

There were three waves of high net long positions and interventions. The first wave of long positions coincided with the beginning of the stealth interventions. The position jumped from basically zero to the high 20,000s (the number of contracts, and one of which is for ¥12.5 million) on December 31, 2002. The strong appreciation pressure must have been felt in the market. It is quite likely that the MOF-BOJ also noticed the change in the wind in the market. The large net long position continued a week later (January 7, 2003), and even increased to more than 30,000 on January 14, 2003, the day before intervention started. The high long position continued until mid-March. These on-and-off interventions continued from January 15 to March 10, and then the interventions stopped—until May 8. The duration of the interven-

Figure 8.8 The International Monetary Market yen net long positions and interventions, 2003–04

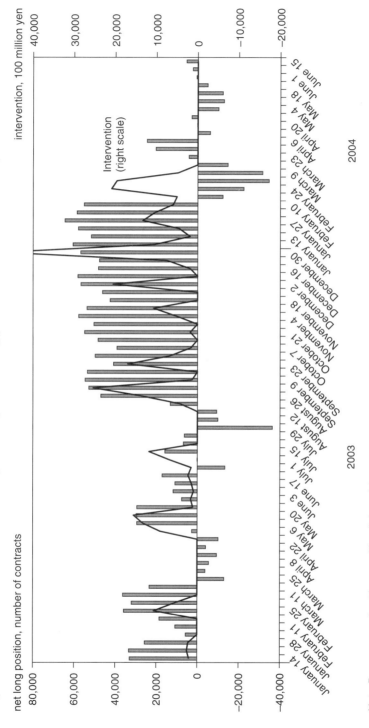

net long position, number of contracts

intervention, 100 million yen

Note: Bars represent net long position (left scale).

Sources: Net long position, Chicago Mercantile Exchange, International Monetary Market; intervention, Ministry of Finance, Japan.

tions and the duration of the high net long positions in the first wave match almost exactly.

The second wave of high long positions started on May 13, with almost 30,000. The high long positions continued until July 15, with a few dips in the number. Interventions started on May 8 and continued on and off until July 16 (before resuming on August 29). Again, the stretch of high net long positions and that of interventions match in the second wave.

After a hiatus of a month and a half, interventions resumed on August 29, followed by interventions almost every day in the first half of September. The resumption of high long positions started on August 26, with 13,000, and then quickly rose to more than 46,000 on September 2, and to more than 52,000 on September 9. At this time, the market started to focus on criticism from the United States and Europe of Japanese intervention and the Chinese dollar peg. The coming G-7 finance ministers' meeting was on the radar screen. Many financial institutions started to bet on yen appreciation.

As was explained above, the Japanese intervention stopped between September 16 and 30, and the yen appreciated from ¥116/$1 to ¥112/$1. This must have encouraged speculators to keep high long positions on the yen. In fact, the IMM net long positions on the yen remained quite high, in the range of 40,000 to 60,000, from October 2003 to February 17, 2004. This extended stretch of high long positions also matched a stretch of heavy interventions by the MOF-BOJ.

The net long positions in the IMM almost exactly match the period of heavy interventions, except for two periods: one from September 16 to 30, 2003, at about the time of the Dubai G-7 meeting, and one from mid-February to March 16, 2004, when interventions continued even while the net long positions fell dramatically. The latter period is puzzling in the sense that the interventions continued until one month after the end of the high net long positions.

Why Stealth Interventions?

Because these were "stealth interventions," there was no explicitly stated goal as to when they were to be conducted. It was never clear whether the Japanese monetary authorities wanted to check the speed of appreciation (smoothing operation) or to keep the floor of the exchange rate (target zone). As is explained below, the immediate goal seems to have shifted from smoothing operations to a target zone, and then the floor yen-dollar exchange rate seems to have been revised several times.

Why there had to be stealth interventions—that is, not confirming the fact of interventions on the day—during this period is harder to explain. If the above logic was recognized clearly by the authorities, the announcement of determination might have had more impact on the market. The amount of intervention, and certainly the frequency of interventions, might have been much less if the interventions had been announced.

Exit Policy

The frequency and size of interventions increased sharply during the 3 months from January to March 2004 compared with the preceding 12 months. The fundamentals of the Japanese economy became much stronger and more robust, compared with the 12 preceding months, when interventions started, and Japanese exporters were reporting higher profits. In early February, a very high GDP growth rate for the fourth quarter of 2003 was announced. The only reason for heavy interventions in the first quarter of 2004 was to counter the speculative pressure that was shown in the IMM long positions.

There was no intervention after March 16, 2004, a fact which became public knowledge in the first week of May, the yen drifted to depreciate somewhat, and the yen-dollar rate moved toward ¥113 by mid-May. One interpretation that is kind to the Japanese authorities is that with heavy intervention from January to mid-March 2004, the Japanese authorities finally convinced the market that even with the improved fundamentals, the current yen-dollar rate at the time was an appropriate level, and there was no more room for speculative movements. This view is supported by the analysis of IMM positions above. The authorities quit interventions a month after the net long positions disappeared.

A more critical view of the exit policy is that the authorities exited due to criticism from US policymakers—or at least, as was reported in the press. It was just "luck" that a soft landing was possible. This "luck" included a stronger hint of a coming US interest rate hike and capital flows shifting out of the Japanese market and reverting to the US market. One bit of supporting evidence for this view is that despite the yen's depreciation, stock prices came down in April to May 2004, due to foreigners selling Japanese stocks in preference to overseas assets.

At the time of this writing (July 2004), no intervention seems to be imminent because the yen-dollar rate is hovering at about ¥110. A real test of the authorities' resolve would come if the yen appreciates again toward 100.[15] However, the hurdle for restarting intervention may be much higher now, when the economy is projected to grow by more than 3 percent in 2004.

Were the Interventions Effective?

The MOF-BOJ may claim that the economy's recovery from −0.1 percent in 2002 to 2.5 percent in 2003, and the stock price increase of 50 percent from

---

15. Hiroshi Watanabe assumed the position of vice minister for international affairs at the Ministry of Finance from Zenbei Mizoguchi on July 2, 2004. Watanabe's method and philosophy of interventions may be different from those of Mizoguchi, according to analysts of the market.

April 2003 to April 2004, would not have been possible without massive interventions. Objectives were achieved, and now the exit from heavy intervention is appropriate, is possible, and has been made, for the economy is solidly on the recovery path (as of the end of the first quarter of 2004). The last intervention was March 16, 2004. This is probably the most sympathetic view of the intervention episode from January 2003 to March 2004.

Using the econometric model of measuring effectiveness for the earlier period, we can compare the effectiveness of the Mizoguchi interventions. I have proposed (Ito 2003a) to measure the effectiveness of interventions by regressing the change in the exchange rate (the New York close of day $t-1$ to the New York close of day t) on the past exchange rate movements and interventions (Japanese intervention, US intervention, and Japanese first-of-the-week intervention).[16] The model equation takes this form:

$$\Delta s(t) = \beta_0 + \beta_1 \Delta s(t-1) + \beta_2[s(t) - s^T(t-1)]$$
$$+ \beta_3 Int(t) + \beta_4 IntUS(t)$$
$$+ \beta_5 IntIN(t) + \varepsilon(t) \qquad (8.2)$$

where $\Delta s(t) = s(t) - s(t-1)$, $s(t)$ is the New York close of the yen-dollar exchange rate, and s^T is the long-run backward moving average (here 180 days). The first three terms on the equation's right-hand side capture the movement of the yen-dollar rate in the absence of interventions. If one strongly believes that the exchange rate follows a random walk, then a condition, $\beta_0 = \beta_1 = \beta_2 = 0$, should be imposed. However, in general, a short-run bandwagon effect ($0 < \beta_1 < 1$) and a medium-run mean reversion ($\beta_2 < 0$) may be allowed. $Int(t)$ is the Japanese intervention amount; $IntUS(t)$ is the US intervention amount (in yen). $IntIN$ denotes the first-in-the-week interventions; it takes the value of intervention when the intervention of the day was not preceded by any intervention for five days:

$$IntIN(t) = Int(t) \text{ if } Int(t) \neq 0$$

and

$$Int(t-1) = Int(t-2) = \cdots = Int(t-5) = 0,$$

or, otherwise, $IntIN(t) = 0$. This term captures the power of infrequent, "surprise" interventions, as opposed to continuous interventions. Interventions often are done in a cluster. Namely, one intervention tends to be followed by others. Therefore, an intervention, when done for the first time in a certain span of days, signals that the authorities are not happy with the level

---

16. See Dominguez and Frankel (1993), Dominguez (2003), and Sarno and Taylor (2001) for general references on the effectiveness of interventions. See Truman (2003) for a skeptical view of the effectiveness of interventions.

Table 8.4   Estimates of the effectiveness of interventions by the
Japanese authorities, 1991–95, 1995–2003, and 2003–04

Variable or parameter	April 1, 1991– June 20, 1995	June 21, 1995– January 13, 2003	January 14, 2003– March 31, 2004
β_0	−0.0008 (0.0002)**	0.0001 (0.0002)	−0.001 (0.0005)*
β_1	−0.028 (0.031)	−0.0022 (0.026)	−0.033 (0.053)
β_2	−0.0158 (0.0053)**	0.0019 (0.002)	−0.0038 (0.0089)
β_3	0.0000047 (0.0000008)**	−0.0000007 (0.0000002)**	−0.00000038 (0.00000016)*
β_4	−0.000012 (0.000005)**	−0.000054 (0.000008)**	n.a.
β_5	0.0000008 (0.0000057)	−0.0000014 (0.0000005)**	−0.00000007 (0.0000003)
R^2	0.0031	0.0068	0.0037
Number of observations	1,101	1,962	308

** = statistically significant at the 1 percent level
 * = statistically significant at the 5 percent level
n.a. = not available

Note: Estimated with a Garch model. Numbers in parentheses are standard errors. See Ito (2003a) for details.

or the change of the exchange rate and will be ready to intervene again. It is natural to allow for the possibility that the first intervention of the bunch has a special effect compared with the others.

The equation is now estimated for the three subperiods (pre-Sakakibara, Sakakibara-Kuroda, and Mizoguchi), and the estimated coefficients are compared.[17] The results are shown in table 8.4.

The table shows that interventions were effective in the sense that the yen-selling interventions depreciated the yen, and the yen-buying interventions appreciated the yen in the second and third subperiods. For example, a ¥1 trillion first-time-in-a-week intervention (i.e., the effects of $\beta_3 + \beta_5$) caused a 2.1 percent depreciation in the yen-dollar exchange rate in the second subperiod (1995–2003), while the rate depreciated 0.45 percent in the third period (2003–04). The Mizoguchi stealth interventions were effective, but the degree of impact declined to the level of ⅕. In the case of continuous/subsequent (β_3 only) interventions, the ¥1 trillion interventions depreciated only 0.7 percent in the second period and 0.38 percent in the third period. Taking this estimate and multiplying by 35, we get an estimate of 13 percent depreciation (from the level otherwise) from the massive ¥35 trillion intervention from the level without intervention. However, this is quite

---

17. I am grateful to Tomoyoshi Yabu for his excellent research assistance.

a rough estimate, in the sense that effectiveness is measured only by the immediate impact. My preliminary research shows that the effects of interventions on the yen-dollar rate tend to wear off within several days of interventions. Therefore, 13 percent depreciation should be taken as a maximum estimate, on the assumption that the immediate impact (within a day) tends to stick in the medium run.

Examining Criticism

There are two kinds of criticism of Japanese interventions, from different directions. First, some observers are skeptical of the effectiveness of interventions.[18] They argue that although an intervention has short-term effects, as measured by myself above, the effects on the exchange rate may not last long, as a long-run effect is not tested in my equation. They regard interventions as futile efforts in resisting market forces.

Second, others criticize Japan for "manipulating the exchange rate." If interventions are not effective, then there is no way to manipulate the exchange rate by interventions. Therefore, those who believe in the manipulation story think that the level or the speed of the change in the exchange rate can be altered by interventions. Then, the answer to a question of whether interventions are manipulative depends on what the rate would have been without intervention, and whether the rate without intervention could be consistent with the fundamentals. If the exchange rate would reach a level that is not justifiable from the economic fundamentals, then interventions can be justified, instead of being branded as manipulation.[19]

Several factors can be viewed as supporting the massive amount of interventions in Japan in the period 2003–04. First, the Japanese economy was extremely vulnerable in 2002–03, especially in the banking sector, and the monetary policy instrument was limited after having driven the interest rate down to zero. Massive interventions along with massive additional liquidity in excess reserves meant that the Japanese monetary authorities bought foreign bonds by issuing domestic currencies.

Some European officials reportedly complained, at about the time of the G-7 meeting in September 2003, that the Japanese interventions distorted the euro-dollar exchange rate. Their argument went as follows. The dollar has to fall to make the current account deficits manageable, with the estimate of the necessary fall ranging from 10 to 30 percent, on a REER basis. Given this objective, if the yen does not appreciate by interventions, then the euro has to shoulder an unfairly large adjustment (i.e., appreciation) vis-à-vis the dollar. The European countries that were worried about the relatively high level of the euro demanded that Japan stop its interventions. In short, the target

---

18. See Sarno and Taylor (2001) and Truman (2003) for a good survey of the literature.

19. Preeg (2003) makes the case that Japan and China had "manipulated" the exchange rate by interventions.

REER is the given, and if some currencies refuse to join the concerted appreciation vis-à-vis the dollar, other currencies have to appreciate more.

However, the very assumption of a given REER depreciation of the dollar may be questioned. This may be a theoretical calculation, but it may not be a calculation of market participants of the exchange rate market. Investors in the foreign exchange market often consider the yen and the euro to be close substitutes as nondollar assets. If investors diversify assets between the dollar and nondollar assets, but also among nondollar assets, investors consider the euro and the yen to be perfect substitutes. Then those who would purchase nondollar assets would buy the euro (as it appreciates vis-à-vis the dollar) or the yen, whichever is cheaper (compared with the benchmark). If the yen refuses to appreciate due to interventions, then those who would normally purchase the euro would purchase the yen. The interventions to ease the yen-buying pressure by selling the yen would have to absorb the euro-buying pressure. Those who arbitrage between the yen and the euro would take advantage of interventions by the Japanese authorities by selling the euro and buying the yen. Therefore interventions by the Japanese authorities lessen the appreciation pressure on the euro as well as the yen. Thus, whether the Japanese interventions aggravated or mitigated the euro's appreciation depends on the substitutability between the yen and the euro among major international investors in currencies.

Conclusions

This chapter has analyzed the reasons for Japanese interventions in the foreign exchange market from January 2003 to March 2004. Preventing premature appreciation and preventing market pressures from appreciating the yen—these are the most likely explanations. The timing of IMM net long positions building up and the timing of heavy interventions roughly match each other.

A negative impact of potential dollar depreciation (yen appreciation) on the Japanese economy is much less evident in 2004, compared with 2003. Automobile and high-technology exporters would be able to endure a yen-dollar exchange rate of 100. The deflation since 1998 means that the real bilateral exchange rate is now depreciated compared with five years ago. Approximately ¥100/$1 this year is like ¥110/$1 five years ago, reflecting at least the 2-percentage-point inflation rate differential between Japan and the United States.

Moreover, Japan is becoming less and less dependent on the United States as a destination for exports. Asian markets, especially the Chinese market, have become increasingly important for Japan. The real effective (multi-lateral) exchange rate of the yen has been virtually flat in the past five years. Suppose that the dollar depreciated by 20 percent vis-à-vis the yen and the euro, but that the Chinese renminbi broke the link to the dollar and appreciated with the yen. This might not be such a disaster for Japan and the rest of Asia.

A typical intraregional trade ratio for Asian countries (East and Southeast Asian countries, including Japan) has risen to 50–60 percent. The threat of the dollar's instability (e.g., a loud voice forecasting the dollar's imminent collapse) would make Asian countries realize that it would be in their interest to pay attention to the intraregional stability of their exchange rates, rather than trying to soft peg to the dollar by heavy interventions. With the possibility of a floating Chinese renminbi, it makes sense for the Association of Southeast Asian Nations–plus–Three countries to strengthen their cooperation in exchange rate management.

References

Bayoumi, Tamim, and Charles Collyns. 2000. *Post-Bubble Blues: How Japan Responded to Asset Price Collapse.* Washington: International Monetary Fund.

Callen, Tim, and Jonathan D. Ostry. 2003. *Japan's Lost Decade: Policies for Economic Revival.* Washington: International Monetary Fund.

Cargill, Thomas F., Takatoshi Ito, and Michael M. Hutchison. 1997. *The Political Economy of Japanese Monetary Policy.* Cambridge, MA: MIT Press.

Cargill, Thomas F., Takatoshi Ito, and Michael M. Hutchison. 2000. *Financial Policy and Central Banking in Japan.* Cambridge, MA: MIT Press.

Dominguez, Kathryn M. 2003. Foreign Exchange Intervention: Did It Work in the 1990s? In *Dollar Overvaluation and the World Economy,* ed. C. Fred Bergsten and John Williamson. Washington: Institute for International Economics.

Dominguez, Kathryn M., and Jeffrey Frankel. 1993. *Does Foreign Exchange Intervention Work?* Washington: Institute for International Economics.

Hoshi, Takeo, and Hugh Patrick. 2000. *Crisis and Change in the Japanese Financial System.* Boston: Kluwer Academic Publishers.

Ito, Takatoshi, 2003a. Is Foreign Exchange Intervention Effective? The Japanese Experiences in the 1990s. In *Monetary History, Exchange Rates and Financial Markets: Essays in Honour of Charles Goodhart,* vol. 2, ed. Paul Mizen. Cheltenham, UK: Edward Elgar. (An earlier draft is available as NBER Working Paper 8914. Cambridge, MA: National Bureau of Economic Research, 2002.)

Ito, Takatoshi. 2003b. Retrospective on the Bubble Period and Its Relationship to Developments in the 1990s. *The World Economy* 26, no. 3 (March): 283–300.

Ito, Takatoshi. 2004. Debt, Deflation, and Declining Growth: New Challenges of the Japanese Economy. In *Structural Reform and Economic Policy,* ed. M. Krasner and Robert Solow. New York: Palgrave Macmillan.

Ito, Takatoshi, and Tomoyoshi Yabu. 2004. *What Prompts Japan to Intervene in the Forex Market? A New Approach to a Reaction Function.* NBER Working Paper 10456. Cambridge, MA: National Bureau of Economic Research; http://www.nber.org/papers/w10456.

Preeg, Ernest H. 2003. Exchange Rate Manipulation to Gain an Unfair Competitive Advantage: The Case Against Japan and China. In *Dollar Overvaluation and the World Economy,* ed. C. Fred Bergsten and John Williamson. Washington: Institute for International Economics.

Sarno, Lucio, and Mark P. Taylor. 2001. Official Intervention in the Foreign Exchange Market: Is It Effective and, If So, How Does It Work? *Journal of Economic Literature* 39 (September): 839–68.

Svensson, Lars. 2001. The Zero Bound in an Open Economy: A Foolproof Way of Escaping from a Liquidity Trap. *Bank of Japan, Monetary and Economic Studies* 19, no. S-1: 277–312.

Truman, Edwin M. 2003. The Limits of Exchange Market Intervention. In *Dollar Overvaluation and the World Economy,* ed. C. Fred Bergsten and John Williamson. Washington: Institute for International Economics.

9

China and the Renminbi Exchange Rate

MORRIS GOLDSTEIN

During 2003 and 2004, there has been considerable debate about, and much international criticism of, China's exchange rate and its currency regime. It is a theme of this chapter that criticism of China's exchange rate policy is *not* simply a reflection of scapegoating, policy failures, and a lack of strategic planning outside China. China's exchange rate policy itself is seriously flawed, given its current macroeconomic circumstances and its longer-term policy objectives. On the basis of ongoing research with my colleague at the Institute for International Economics, Nicholas Lardy (Goldstein and Lardy forthcoming), I argue here that (1) the renminbi (RMB) is currently significantly undervalued—on the order of 15 to 25 percent; (2) that China has been "manipulating" its currency, contrary to IMF rules of the game; (3) that it is in China's own interest, as well as in the interest of the international community, for China to initiate soon an appreciation of the RMB; and (4) that China should neither stand pat with its existing currency regime nor opt for a freely floating RMB and completely open capital markets. Instead, China should undertake a "two-step" currency reform. Step one, to be implemented immediately, would have three elements. It would involve simultaneously a switch from a unitary peg to the US dollar to a basket peg,

Morris Goldstein is the Dennis Weatherstone Senior Fellow at the Institute for International Economics. This chapter includes ongoing work (Goldstein and Lardy, forthcoming) with my Institute colleague, Nicholas Lardy. I am indebted to Nick for helpful comments and advice and for allowing me to borrow from his substantial inventory of charts on the Chinese economy. I am grateful for Dean DeRosa's help in calculating the trade balance effects of a change in the renminbi exchange rate. Thanks are also due to C. Fred Bergsten, Pieter Bottelier, Michael Mussa, Ted Truman, and John Williamson for useful suggestions on an earlier draft. Thomas Flynn and Gunilla Pettersson provided excellent research assistance.

a 15 to 25 percent appreciation of the RMB, and wider margins (say, 5 to 7 percent on either side) around the new peg. Existing controls on China's capital outflows would be either maintained or liberalized only marginally, at least in the short run. Step two, to be implemented later when China's banking system is considerably stronger than it is today, would involve a transition to a "managed float," along with a significant liberalization of China's capital outflows.

The rest of the chapter is organized as follows. The second section examines two complementary approaches to evaluating the misalignment of the RMB and summarizes the main conclusions. The third section takes up the thorny issue of what does and does not constitute "currency manipulation" and relates those principles to China's exchange market intervention. The fourth section considers how China's exchange rate policy affects its longer-term objectives for strengthening the domestic banking system, for maintaining low and stable inflation, for securing stable market access for its exports, and for achieving a high and sustainable rate of economic growth. The fifth section then discusses what kind of reform of the currency regime would be most suitable for China. The sixth section offers brief conclusions.

Is the Renminbi Out of Line?

There are many approaches to estimating "equilibrium" real exchange rates. Here, I report two back-of-the-envelope estimates—the first solely from the perspective of China's balance of payments, and the second from the perspective of global payments imbalances. In both cases, a working assumption is that there is no large change in China's capital account regime over the next few years.

The Underlying Balance Approach

The underlying balance approach views the equilibrium exchange rate as the rate that produces equilibrium in the country's balance of payments, where the latter is defined as a situation where "normal" net capital flows equal the "underlying" current account. What happens if we apply this underlying balance approach to the recent behavior of the RMB?

Figure 9.1 shows China's overall capital account balance over the past decade. Except for 1998 and 2003, it has shown a moderate surplus relative to GDP. Suppose we take the average for the 1999–2002 period—a surplus of 1½ percent of GDP—and call that "normal" net capital flows. Note that the capital account surplus for 2003 was much larger—just under 4 percent (3.7 percent) of GDP according to the official figures and closer to 7 to 8 percent of GDP if $45 billion of reserve accumulation (subsequently used for bank recapitalization) and capital inflows recorded as errors and omissions

Figure 9.1 China's capital account, 1994–2003

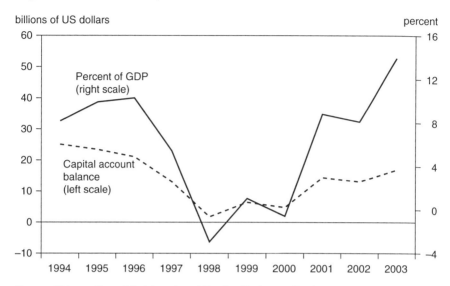

Source: Chinese State Administration of Foreign Exchange (SAFE).

were included in the totals. I have not included 2003 data in normal capital flows because that year's large capital inflow was likely motivated by strong speculation on an expected appreciation of the RMB and hence was not normal.

Figure 9.2 gives the parallel evolution of China's current account balance during the 1994–2003 period. This also shows a moderate surplus relative to GDP. According to the latest official figures, China's current account surplus in 2003 was about $46 billion, or just over 3 percent of GDP. But this is the actual current account surplus. The "underlying" current account surplus in 2003 was certainly larger than that because the Chinese economy was overheating (pushing up both the volume and price of imports) and because the real effective depreciation of the RMB since the beginning of 2002 suggests that some positive trade-balance effects are still in the pipeline.

China's economy grew by 9.1 percent in 2003, the highest growth rate in six years. Investment increased in 2003 by 27 percent, bringing investment's share of GDP to a peak of 43 percent. Bottlenecks have been widely reported for coal, electric power, oil, and transport. Imports were up by 40 percent. By the end of 2003, consumer prices were increasing at an annual rate of more than 3 percent. Recent figures suggest that the overheating of the economy continued in the first-quarter of 2004—with first-quarter GDP growth estimated at almost 10 percent (9.7 percent), with fixed investment and imports both up over 40 percent in March, and with indices of inflation (consumer, producer, raw materials) all increasing at a higher rate than in 2003.

Figure 9.2 China's current account, 1994–2003

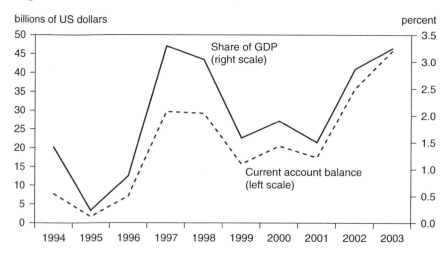

Source: Chinese State Administration of Foreign Exchange (SAFE).

On the exchange rate side, China's trade-weighted real effective exchange rate declined by roughly 6 percent in 2003; it has declined by 7 percent since the beginning of 2002. The lagged trade effects in the pipeline are thus expected to be positive. Putting together the overheating effect and the lagged trade effects of earlier exchange rate changes, a conservative estimate of China's "underlying" current account surplus in 2003 is 4½ to 5 percent of GDP.

Because China's trade account swung into deficit during the first four months of 2004, some might argue that a lower estimate of China's underlying current account surplus would be more appropriate. Perhaps; but the magnitude of the adjustment is far from clear. During the first quarter of 2003, China's trade balance was also in deficit, only to move into surplus for the remainder of the year. Recent private-sector forecasts for China's current account balance for 2004 tend to be 1 to 2 percent of GDP lower than for 2003.[1] Suppose we assumed that China's actual current account surplus for 2004 would amount to, say, 1 percent of GDP. This would still place the 2004 underlying current account surplus in the neighborhood of 2½ percent of GDP.

If overall balance of payments equilibrium requires that the underlying current account offset normal net capital inflows, then China's current

---

1. E.g., Deutsche Bank (*Emerging Markets Monthly*, April 2004) projects China's 2004 current account surplus to be 1.2 percent of GDP lower than the 2003 outcome, whereas Goldman Sachs (*Charting China*, April 2004) projects a 2004 current account surplus at 1.8 percent of GDP lower than last year.

account would have to deteriorate by roughly 4 percent of GDP (or approximately $65 billion, at market exchange rates) to yield that outcome. This 4 percent swing is the difference between today's underlying current account *surplus* of 2½ percent (of GDP) and the underlying current account *deficit* (1½ percent) that would just balance out the assumed 1½ percent of GDP surplus for normal capital flows.

The operative issue then becomes what size real appreciation of the RMB would generate this 4 percent of GDP deterioration in China's current account balance? When we asked that question of a small, barebones, elasticity-based trade model, we found that the answers congregated in the upper half of the 15 to 30 percent range[2]—and this using elasticity values that easily satisfied the Marshall-Lerner conditions.[3]

An important reason why it takes a sizable exchange rate appreciation to move China's trade balance is related to China's important role as a regional processing center. The import content of China's exports is quite high—on the order of 35 to 40 percent. This means that a revaluation of the RMB reduces the local-currency price of China's imports and operates to limit the production cost of exporting more, thereby yielding a lower rise in the foreign-currency price of exports than would occur if revaluation took place in an economy with a very low import content of exports.[4] Put in other words, with a high import content of exports, it takes a bigger exchange rate "pop" to move the trade balance. To sum up, the underlying balance approach suggests that the RMB is undervalued by somewhere between 15 and 30 percent.[5]

The Approach Based on Adjustment of Global Payments Imbalances

Instead of evaluating the RMB exchange rate solely from the perspective of China's balance of payments situation, a complementary approach is

---

2. We first reported this finding in Goldstein and Lardy (2003a).

3. Anderson (2003, 2004b) substitutes the "basic balance" (i.e., current account plus net movements of foreign direct investment) for normal capital flows and the underlying current account and concludes similarly that the RMB is undervalued by roughly 25 percent.

4. Another way to look at the role of imported inputs in the trade-balance effects of an exchange rate change is that an RMB revaluation reduces the volume of exports, which, in turn, leads to a lower demand for imported inputs. We experimented with different ways of modeling China's imported inputs.

5. An advantage of presenting the estimate of RMB misalignment as a range is that it provides some leeway in case the current account turns out to be somewhat different from the baseline estimate, or in case Chinese inflation turns out be somewhat higher this year, or in case subsequent empirical research reveals somewhat different elasticities than employed above. Frankel (2004), using a modified purchasing power parity approach, concludes that the RMB was undervalued by approximately 35 percent in 2000 and is undervalued by at least that much today. In contrast, Wang (2004) finds that it is difficult to arrive at any firm and robust conclusion about the equilibrium level of the RMB using a variety of existing techniques.

to look at the role that the RMB might play as part of the broader adjustment of global payments imbalances—particularly the US current account deficit.

According to IMF (2004) projections, the US current account deficit in 2004 will be about $495 billion, just over 4 percent of GDP;[6] I regard a US current account deficit of that size as "unsustainable." A sustainable one would be, say, half as large.[7]

To reduce the US current account deficit to, say, 2 to 2½ percent of GDP at reasonable cost, it would be helpful to have a real depreciation of the dollar of about 25 percent from its peak (in February 2002). This uses the rule of thumb that each 1 percent fall in the real trade-weighted dollar improves the US current account position by roughly $10 billion; if anything, that is a low estimate of the needed dollar decline, because some analysts find much smaller (closer to $5 billion improvement for each 1 percent dollar depreciation) exchange rate effects. Since February 2002, the dollar has fallen by approximately 15 percent. This means there is something like 10 to 15 percent still to go. The question then is how should this US current account improvement and implicit appreciation in nondollar currencies be shared internationally?

A good adjustment guideline should distinguish between surplus and deficit countries, take account of cross-country differences in the ability to shift demand from external to domestic sources, and consider other relevant factors, including the extent of recent exchange rate adjustments and cross-country differences in reserve holdings. When this is done, China emerges as an economy that ought to be in the lead in accommodating the second wave of dollar depreciation; see table 9.1.

Since the dollar peak in February 2002, the RMB (which has a weight of just under 10 percent in the US Federal Reserve's broad index for the dollar) has fallen in real trade-weighted terms by 7 percent. China is currently growing at nearly 10 percent, with rising inflationary pressure. Its reserves have increased by more than $160 billion in the 12-month period ending March 2004 and now stand at more than $400 billion. It has a moderate surplus on current account and a large one on capital account. It has an external debt ratio of 14 percent of GDP. As James Meade (1951) emphasized more than 50 years ago, the classical remedy for an economy experiencing *both* domestic overheating and external surpluses is exchange rate

---

6. This is quite a conservative estimate; some other analysts forecast a higher US current account deficit for 2004 and for the next few years.

7. A current account deficit of about 2 to 2½ percent of GDP would be sufficient to stabilize the ratio of net foreign liabilities to GDP (at about 42 percent, assuming a 6 percent annual growth of nominal income) and to prevent a further rise in the share of dollars in the foreign portion of non-US investors' portfolios; see Truman (2004) and Mann (2003).

Table 9.1 Sharing the adjustment of payments imbalances, selected economies and Euroland compared with emerging Asia, 2001–04

Economy	Weight in FRB real broad dollar index, 2002–04	Percent change in real effective exchange rate index since the dollar peak,[a] February 2002–April 2004	Current account as share of GDP, 2003	Change in international reserves, 2003 (millions of US dollars)	Change in international reserves, 2003 (percent of GDP)	Growth rate of real total domestic demand, 2001–02 (annual percent)	Growth rate of real total domestic demand, 2003 (annual percent)	Growth rate of real GDP, 2001–02	Growth rate of real GDP, 2003	Projected growth rate of real GDP, 2004	Ratio of external debt to GDP, 2002	Estimated exchange rate undervaluation, 2004 (percent)[d]
Selected countries and Euroland												
Australia	1.3	+27.5	-6.0	11,592	2.3	3.7	5.3	3.2	3.0	3.5	33.6	n.a.
Canada	16.5	+9.9	2.1	-700	-0.1	2.6	4.2	2.6	1.7	2.6	n.a.	n.a.
China	9.8	-7.0	3.3	116,952[b]	8.3	9.3	11.4	7.7	9.1	8.3	14.4	26
Euroland[c]	18.5	+16.6	0.6	-22,233	-0.3	1.8	1.0	1.3	0.4	1.7	n.a.	n.a.
Japan	11.1	+3.0	3.2	203,852	4.7	0.1	2.0	0.1	2.7	3.4	n.a.	37
Mexico	11.0	-10.3	-1.5	8,501	1.4	0.7	2.5	0.3	1.3	3.3	23.7	n.a.
United Kingdom	5.2	+2.7	-2.4	2,635	0.1	2.3	2.7	1.9	2.3	3.5	n.a.	n.a.
Emerging Asia	15.8											
Hong Kong	2.0	-13.0	11.0	6,745	4.3	0.05	0.6	1.4	3.3	6.0	31.8	5
Indonesia	1.0	+9.1	3.7	4,091	2.0	3.7	3.6	3.6	4.1	4.5	75.7	12
South Korea	3.9	+4.3	2.0	34,320	5.7	5.2	0.1	5.4	3.1	4.8	28.9	10
Malaysia	2.3	-11.2	13.0	10,408	10.1	3.1	3.6	2.2	5.2	5.8	52.2	14
Singapore	2.2	+1.4	30.9	13,956	15.3	-4.0	-9.6	0.2	1.1	5.6	23.0	14
Taiwan	3.0	-3.6	10.0	45,545	15.4	-2.1	1.2	0.7	3.2	5.4	12.1	22
Thailand	1.4	-0.7	5.6	3,145	2.2	4.3	7.1	3.8	6.7	7.2	48.1	(2004)

FRB = Federal Reserve Board
n.a. = not available

a. (+) equals appreciation, (–) equals depreciation.
b. The change in international reserves is net of $45 billion transferred for bank recapitalization.
c. Euroland includes Austria, Belgium, Finland, France, Germany, Greece, Ireland, Italy, Luxembourg, the Netherlands, Portugal, and Spain.
d. Anderson (2003).

Sources: FRB real broad dollar index, Federal Reserve Board real effective exchange rate, JPMorgan Effective Exchange Rate Index; China's current account data, Chinese State Administration of Foreign Exchange; current account data on other countries, IMF's *International Financial Statistics;* change in international reserves. IMF's *International Financial Statistics;* real domestic demand: International Monetary Fund; GDP data, *World Economic Outlook;* ratio of external debt to GDP, Deutsche Bank; and exchange rate undervaluation, Anderson (2003).

appreciation, and neither reserve nor debt considerations appear to constrain such exchange rate action.

In contrast, the euro area (with a weight of more than 18 percent) has a small current account surplus (projected at less than 1 percent of GDP for 2004). It is expected to grow by less than 2 percent this year—just below its average rate over the past decade. Real domestic demand is projected to increase by only 1 percent in 2004. The euro has appreciated in real trade-weighted terms by 17 percent since the dollar peak.

China is not the only Asian country for which one could make a case for currency appreciation; indeed, there is a wider Asian problem of exchange rate undervaluation (Bergsten 2003). But what is striking from our cross-country comparison is that no other region or country on the list presents itself as a stronger candidate than China for currency appreciation in the necessary second wave of dollar depreciation.[8]

In thinking about the adjustment of global payments imbalances, let me emphasize what I am *not* saying. I am not saying that currency appreciation by China *alone* would solve the US current account problem.[9] After all, because China's weight in the dollar index is less than 10 percent, a 25 percent appreciation of the RMB would lower the aggregate value of the dollar by only 2½ percent; using the rule of thumb alluded to above, this would translate into only a $25 billion improvement in the (2003) $540 billion US current account deficit.[10] Clearly, a *broad-based* depreciation of the dollar is necessary to reduce the US current account deficit by $250 billion or so.

I am also not saying that the preferred approach to bringing global payments imbalances into a better and more sustainable alignment is by exchange rate actions alone. Adjustments in fiscal and monetary policies would also be most helpful. To sum up, the global payments approach also suggests that the RMB is undervalued and that an appreciation—on the order of 15 to 25 percent—should be a key element of the needed second wave of dollar depreciation.

---

8. Looking at 11 Asian economies, Anderson (2004a) concludes that China has the second largest exchange rate misalignment (undervaluation), behind Japan.

9. Nor would a 20 percent revaluation of the RMB reverse the fall in US manufacturing employment—a problem that has its roots in weak US economic growth over the past few years, slow growth in many US trading-partner countries, rapid productivity growth in US manufacturing, and the high US dollar. Baily (2004) has estimated that the increase in the (overall) US trade deficit over the 2000–03 period accounted for no more than 14 percent of the payroll job decline in the nonfarm sector of the US economy.

10. In Goldstein (2003), I also argue that China's exports to the United States compete mainly with exports from other developing countries and only to a limited extent with US industries; the empirical support for this conclusion can be found in Noland (1998).

The Potential Role of Capital Outflow Liberalization in Misalignment Calculations

Thus far, I have assumed that, over the next few years, China will make no significant changes to its existing restrictions on capital outflows.[11] If that assumption were dropped, then the above conclusions about the undervaluation of the RMB could well be erased.

A quick calculation illustrates the point. Household savings deposits in China are presently equal to approximately 100 percent of GDP. Suppose Chinese savers decided for diversification reasons to put 5 percent of their savings into foreign assets abroad and that China liberalized its restrictions on capital outflows to permit that diversification to take place. A 5 percent of GDP swing in China's capital account would be sufficient to wipe out the assumed $4\frac{1}{2}$ percent of GDP disequilibrium in China's balance of payments.[12]

The crucial issue is one of timing. If China does not liberalize significantly its restrictions on capital outflows for, say, six years, then it is asking a lot—I would say too much—to request the international community that live during the interim with an undervalued RMB just because things may be different down the road.

Conclusion on Misalignment of the Renminbi

Given the dynamic character of the Chinese economy and the margin of uncertainty surrounding underlying parameters, it would be naive to pretend that estimates of the misalignment of the RMB can be made with great precision. That said, as long as China continues to run surpluses on its current and capital accounts (while its economy is overheating) and maintains binding restrictions on capital outflows, and as long as there are serious global payments imbalances afoot, there is a compelling case that the RMB is presently undervalued—on the order of 15 to 25 percent.[13]

---

11. In discussing the current status of China's capital account liberalization, Li (2004) reports that the IMF divides China's capital account into 43 parts: in 8 of those (with a 19 percent weight), capital transfers can be made freely; in 11 (with a weight of 26 percent), transfers can be made with rare limitations; in 18 (with a 41 percent weight), transfers can be made with many limitations; and in 6 (with a 14 percent weight), transfers are subject to strict limitation.

12. If one assumes that such international diversification was largely a one-time event, then it would not offset continuing disequilibria in the balance of payments.

13. In assessing (in November 2003) the Fund's 2003 Article IV Consultation with China, the IMF's Executive Board took a different view. The Public Information Notice (PIN) of that discussion stated: "Most Directors noted that there is no clear evidence that the renminbi is substantially undervalued at this juncture. Directors also felt that a currency revaluation would not by itself have a major impact on global current account balances, particularly given China's relatively small share in world trade."

Is China "Manipulating" the Renminbi?

The Meaning of Manipulation

The troublesome experience with competitive depreciations in the 1920s and 1930s convinced the international community that international rules were needed to discourage "beggar thy neighbor" exchange rate policies. Indeed, that was one of the main motivations for establishing the International Monetary Fund. This concern with antisocial exchange rate policies is reflected both in the Fund's charter and in decisions of the Fund's Executive Board on exchange rate surveillance.

Article IV, Section 1 (paragraph iii) of the Fund's *Articles of Agreement* stipulates, inter alia, that each member shall

> avoid manipulating exchange rates or the international monetary system in order to prevent effective balance-of-payments adjustment or to gain unfair competitive advantage over other members.

Section 3 of Article IV symmetrically delineates the Fund's obligations on exchange rate policies, including the injunctions that the Fund shall

> oversee the compliance of each member with its obligations under section I of this article . . . [and]

> exercise firm surveillance over the exchange rate policies of members, and shall adopt specific principles for the guidance of all members with respect to those policies.

In 1977, the Fund's Executive Board discussed a paper that laid out principles and procedures for its surveillance over exchange rate policies.[14] In the section on principles, the document discusses a number of developments that might indicate the need for discussion with a member. The first development listed was "protracted, large-scale intervention in one direction in the exchange market." Figure 9.3 shows the behavior of China's official foreign exchange reserves over the 1991–2003 period (and the first quarter of 2004); figure 9.4 draws on monthly data to focus on the huge buildup of China's international reserves from 2002 through 2004. Suffice it to say that these reserve developments suggest that, during this period, there has indeed been "large-scale, protracted intervention in the exchange market in one direction."

Two fallacious arguments are often put forward to refute charges of currency manipulation. The first argument is that because the IMF's charter allows countries to adopt the currency regime of their choice and because the maintenance of a fixed exchange rate involves exchange market inter-

---

14. See "1977 Decision on Principles and Procedures of Surveillance over Exchange Rate Policies," reprinted in Boughton (2001).

Figure 9.3 China's official foreign exchange reserves, 1991–2004

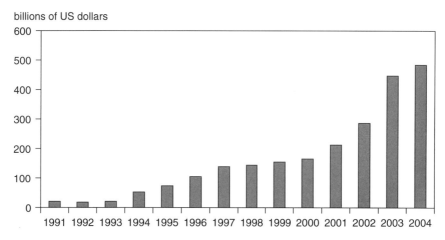

billions of US dollars

Source: Chinese State Administration of Foreign Exchange (SAFE).

vention, there can be no manipulation for countries that opt for a fixed exchange rate regime.[15]

IMF member countries are free to pick fixed rates, floating rates, or practically any currency regime in between.[16] Also, it is true that member countries are permitted to intervene in exchange markets and, indeed, are expected to do so to counter disorderly market conditions. But what member countries should not do (regardless of their currency regime) is seek to maintain the "wrong" exchange rate by relying, inter alia, on large-scale, prolonged exchange market intervention in one direction. Put in other words, countries maintaining fixed rates can intervene if it is of relatively short duration, or if it is on a small scale, or if it is sometimes in one direction and sometimes in the other—but they cannot violate all three conditions simultaneously.

The second argument is that a country cannot be "manipulating" if it has maintained the same fixed parity over an extended period, as China has left untouched since 1995 its fixed parity of RMB 8.28 to $1. This argument fails to recognize that what counts most is the real effective exchange rate, that the real exchange rate has to be evaluated against the changing backdrop of the balance of payments, and that misalignment of the real exchange rate can come about just as easily from "nonmovement" of the nominal exchange rate as it can from excessive movement of the nominal rate.

---

15. Although China describes its currency regime as a "managed float," the behavior of the RMB suggests that it is maintaining (de facto) a fixed exchange rate (pegged to the dollar).

16. The only prohibition on currency regime choice is that the member cannot seek to maintain a fixed value for its currency in terms of gold.

Figure 9.4 China's foreign exchange reserves, January 2002– March 2004

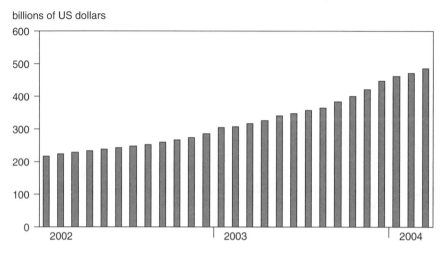

billions of US dollars

Source: Chinese State Administration of Foreign Exchange (SAFE).

China's real exchange rate has been depreciating during the period 2002–04 at the same time that its balance of payments has been moving into a strong underlying surplus. What would be desirable in this context is for China's real exchange rate to be appreciating—not depreciating. If China is preventing the real exchange rate from appreciating because of its intervention behavior, then it is thwarting the international adjustment process by keeping its nominal (bilateral) exchange rate fixed at RMB 8.3 to $1.

Conclusion on Manipulation of the Renminbi Exchange Rate

As the weight of emerging economies in the global economy has increased, the interest of the international community in how these countries conduct their exchange rate policies has increased along with it.[17] This is particularly the case with China's exchange rate policy, because the country is now the world's third largest importer and fourth largest exporter.

The exchange rate system cannot be concerned only with overvalued exchange rates; undervalued exchange rates must also be subject to surveillance and corrective action. International codes of conduct for exchange rate policy are no less necessary than those for trade policy; without them,

---

17. To cite but one reflection of this increased weight for emerging economies, Asian emerging economies alone now hold over 40 percent of global foreign exchange reserves.

there can be a free-for-all that is in no one's interest, least of all the emerging economies that depend so heavily on access to international markets.

The IMF is the institution uniquely charged with the responsibility for overseeing the international monetary system and for exercising firm surveillance over its members' exchange rate policies. It is regrettable that it has not acted with more "firmness" to investigate, discuss, and rule on allegations of currency manipulation. It is striking that at a time when, for example, the Japanese Ministry of Finance has requested financing authorization for 2004 to use (if needed) as much as $575 billion in exchange market intervention (and has already intervened to the tune of nearly $150 billion in the first quarter of 2004), both the IMF and the United States have been practically silent on the currency manipulation issue.

When there is a growing perception that "no one is minding the store" at the international level, then the likelihood increases that responses to alleged exchange rate policy abuses will occur at the bilateral level. There are now at least a half-dozen bills before the US Congress that threaten to impose a unilateral surcharge on China's exports to the United States if negotiation does not produce an end to China's alleged currency manipulation. Far better for such currency issues to be handled multilaterally in the IMF and, over time, for a body of case law to develop that would spell out more fully what is and what is not acceptable behavior on exchange rate policy.

Although it is far from the only country doing it, from 2002 to 2004 China has been engaging in protracted, large-scale intervention in one direction in exchange markets. This is currency manipulation. China should stop doing it and deal instead with the root causes of the problem.

Would a 15 to 25 Percent Appreciation of the Renminbi Be in China's Interest and That of the Rest of the World?

What Would Be in China's Interest?

Would a significant appreciation of the RMB be in China's own interest? My short answer is yes.

The currency regime is not an end in itself. In China's case, the question to ask is how does attempting to maintain an undervalued RMB affect its pursuit of banking reform, of price stability, of continued secure market access for its exports, and of a high and sustainable rate of economic growth? Let me comment on each.

Banking Reform

By now, it is well accepted that banking reform is vital for improving the efficiency of resource use in China (Lardy 1998). Although banking

Figure 9.5 Increase in the stock of loans outstanding, 1998–2003
(domestic currency)

trillions of renminbi

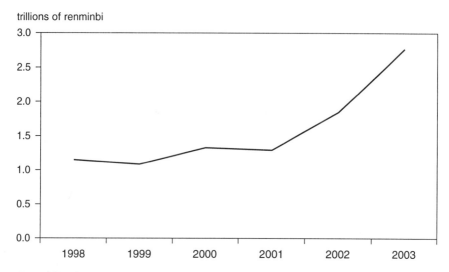

Source: The People's Bank of China, *Quarterly Statistical Bulletin.*

reform contains many elements, a sine qua non is a good credit allocation process, based on a forward-looking, objective assessment of the borrower's creditworthiness (Goldstein 1997). Experience suggests that credit allocation decisions suffer when bank credit expands at very rapid rates, say, 20 percent or more per year.[18] The enormous increase in bank loans that took place in 2003 in the Chinese economy is therefore cause for serious concern—raising the specter of a reversal of the progress recently made in bringing down the ratio of nonperforming loans. As figure 9.5 shows, after rising by an annual average of 1.1 trillion to 1.3 trillion renminbi during the 1998–2001 period, the stock of loans outstanding increased by 1.9 trillion renminbi in 2002 and then mushroomed to an unprecedented 3 trillion renminbi in 2003. Relative to GDP, the 2003 increase in loans outstanding hit 24 percent—an all-time high; see figure 9.6. The last time (in the early 1990s) there was a bank lending boom in China, approximately 40 percent of the loans extended eventually wound up as nonperforming. The People's Bank of China (PBC), in its *Monetary Policy Report for 2003* (PBC 2004), issued in March 2004, acknowledges that there was "excessively fast growth" of commercial bank loans in 2003, and cites concerns about that growth as contributing to its decisions to

---

18. Rapid bank credit expansion was a prominent feature of the Asian financial crisis (see Goldstein 1998), as well as of many earlier banking crises (see Gavin and Hausmann 1996).

Figure 9.6 China's M2 growth, 1998–2003

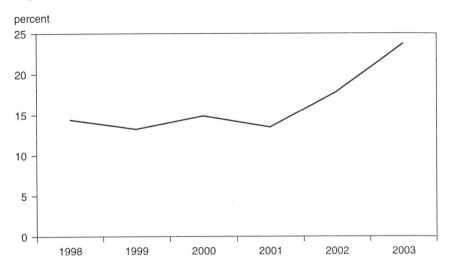

Source: The People's Bank of China.

raise the deposit reserve requirement, to signal risks on real estate loans, to strengthen window guidance on commercial bank loans, and to conduct wide-ranging sterilization operations to control the growth rate of base money.[19]

The average monthly increase of RMB loans outstanding fell from 296 billion renminbi in the first half of 2003, to 230 billion renminbi in the third quarter, to 98 billion renminbi in the fourth quarter.[20] As shown in figure 9.7, however, the increase in bank lending accelerated sharply again in the first quarter of 2004—rising to an average monthly increase of 304 billion renminbi. The increase in bank lending was thus a whopping 20 percent in the first quarter of 2004 (vis-à-vis the first quarter of 2003). We will thus have to wait (at the time of this writing) until at least the third quarter of 2004 to see whether the restrictive measures already taken are having much of a slowing effect.

---

19. In addition to these measures, the State Council raised capital requirements for fixed investment projects (in steel, cement, real estate, and aluminum) and required line ministries and regional governments to evaluate ongoing and planned fixed investment projects in certain sectors; also, the China Bank Regulatory Commission recently advised commercial banks not to front-load loans to projects or to continue lending to overheated sectors.

20. It may be that the low fourth-quarter figure for the increase in bank lending reflected a concentration of bad-loan write-offs in the fourth quarter—not a decline in the rate of new lending.

Figure 9.7 Increase in RMB loans and total loans, 1999–2004

billions of renminbi

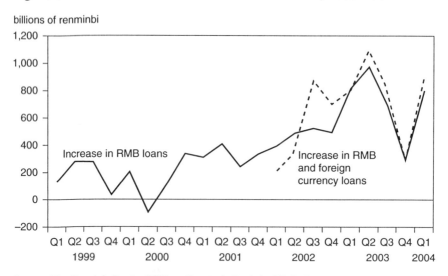

Source: The People's Bank of China, Quarterly Statistical Bulletin.

The link of credit growth to the exchange rate comes about via the impact of an undervalued exchange rate on accumulation of international reserves and, in turn, the effect of reserve accumulation on the expansion of bank reserves and on bank-lending behavior.[21] As was noted above, China's reserve accumulation in 2003—driven mostly by portfolio capital inflows seeking to profit from an expected appreciation of the RMB—amounted to an unprecedented 11 percent of GDP.[22] When reserves increase, banks sell them to the central bank and receive in exchange an RMB account at the central bank. If the funds in that account are larger than the required minimum, banks can use this larger reserve base to increase bank lending. The central bank can "sterilize" some or all of this potential increase in liquidity by undertaking a number of offsetting operations.

As is shown in figure 9.8, both international reserves and RMB loans outstanding have been on strong upward trends during the period 2002–04. Base money grew by almost 17 percent in 2003, and broad money (M2) grew by almost 20 percent; as is shown in figures 9.9 and 9.10, these money growth rates were considerably higher than the average over the past several years.

---

21. In contrast, Mundell (2004) argues that RMB appreciation would aggravate the banking problem by raising the real value of debts to the banking system.

22. This figure for reserve increases does not subtract from reserves the $45 billion subsequently used for bank recapitalization.

Figure 9.8 China's foreign exchange reserves and total RMB loans outstanding, January 2001–March 2004

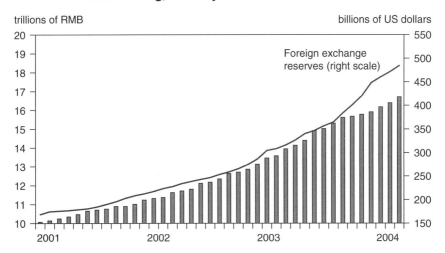

trillions of RMB   billions of US dollars

Notes: Bars represent RMB loans (left scale). From December 2003 on, foreign exchange figures are adjusted to reflect $45 billion transfer to state-owned commercial banks.

Source: Loans, The People's Bank of China, *Quarterly Statistical Bulletin;* foreign exchange, Chinese State Administration of Foreign Exchange (SAFE).

According to our estimates, the PBC last year sterilized almost half (46 percent) of the increase in reserves on base money. Sterilization operations in the first quarter of 2004 appear to have been even more aggressive. Still, broad money growth in the first quarter of 2004 was more than 19 percent (vis-à-vis the first quarter of 2003), and base money growth was more than 14 percent.

Making good estimates of sterilization cost is harder for China than for some other countries. We do not know the maturity composition of China's reserve holdings; because the term structure of US interest rates is significantly upward-sloping, it makes a difference whether we use the 10-year bond rate or the six-month Treasury bill rate in estimating the return on China's reserves. Estimates of sterilization cost could also be significantly affected by future changes in the exchange rate between the RMB and the US dollar. Most problematic—because the involvement of the government in the banking system in China is still considerable and because interest rate deregulation is not complete—there is considerable uncertainty about the true cost of borrowing from the banks.

Whether one calls it "window guidance," "moral suasion," or making bank managers "an offer they can't refuse," it is clear that the Chinese

Figure 9.9 China's base money growth, 1998–2003

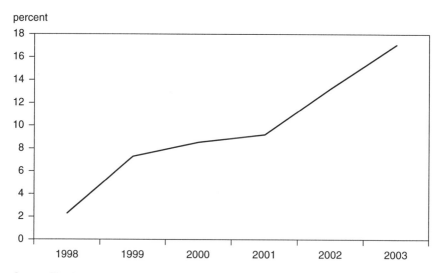

Source: The People's Bank of China.

authorities have leverage with banks that is not captured in posted or observed interest rates.

The incentives for strong loan demand also continue to be impressive. As is shown in figure 9.11, the real interest rate on one-year bank loans—defined as the posted one-year interest rate less the change in the overall corporate goods price index—has been on a steadily declining trend in the period 2002–04; indeed, with the recent increase in the corporate goods price inflation to more than 8 percent in March 2004, the real interest on these loans is now negative.

The fact that the Chinese authorities have been unwilling so far to increase interest rates (by other than a minor amount) in the face of the credit boom also suggests that short-term economic growth considerations and worries about the potential effect of higher interest on further capital inflows are weighing against more aggressive monetary tightening.[23] This increases the risk that they may remain "behind the curve."

To sum up, the Chinese banking system is still faced with a serious non-performing loan (NPL) problem. The good news was that the NPL ratio appeared to be declining in recent years. But the blowout in bank lending in 2003 threatens to erase that progress and send the NPL ratio back

---

23. The PBC raised the rates at which it lends to financial institutions by between 27 and 63 basis points in March 2004.

Figure 9.10   China's M2 (broad money) growth, 1999–2003

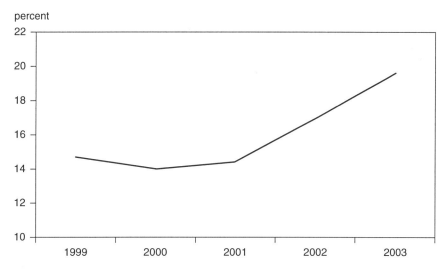

Source: The People's Bank of China.

upward.[24] Even if one believes that the credit boom has been driven primarily by the domestic component of the monetary base, it is undeniable that an increase in international reserves by 11 percent of GDP makes more difficult the reining-in of bank lending to a more prudent and sustainable pace.

The Pursuit of Price Stability

China has good reasons to pursue low and stable inflation. With an average annual per capita income just above $1,000 and with some sectors and regions considerably below that, sizable groups in the population would begin to feel the pinch of lower purchasing power before inflation rates hit double digits;[25] in this sense, control of inflation, like keeping a reasonable cap on unemployment, is seen as an element of social stability.

---

24. Although the PBC (2004) argues that the NPL ratio declined in 2003 (vis-à-vis its level in 2002), one has to be careful about interpreting NPL ratios in a period of very rapid credit expansion; this is because the denominator (total bank loans) is increasing rapidly and because the effects of current lending decisions may show up only in later years.

25. Of course, the pinch of higher inflation on particular groups in the population depends on how inflation affects their terms of trade.

Figure 9.11   China's real lending rates, 2002–04

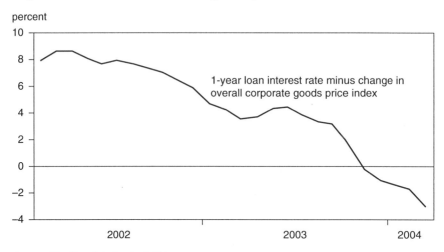

Source: The People's Bank of China.

Inflationary pressures increased during 2003, and those pressures intensi-fied during the final quarter of 2003 and first quarter of 2004. In 2002, the con-sumer price index (CPI) actually fell (year over year) by 0.8 percent. In 2003, the CPI rose by just over 1 percent and the GDP deflator by 2 percent. The most revealing statistics, however, are those that capture both the recent upward trend in inflation and the higher inflation rates for producer goods and raw materials. By December of 2003, CPI inflation had increased to more than 3 percent—a rate that was maintained through the first quarter of 2004. The PBC's monthly index of corporate goods prices showed a rise of 8.3 per-cent in March 2004 (see figure 9.12). No wonder then that official concern has shifted from ending mild deflation (in 2002) to controlling rising inflationary pressures before the latter gets up too much of a head of steam.

Here, too, the exchange rate matters. As was argued above, an under-valued exchange rate spurs speculative capital inflows, reserve accumula-tion, and expansion of the monetary aggregates. All this makes it harder to keep inflation under control; see figure 9.13, which shows the similar time series behavior of M2 money growth and (CPI) inflation in China during the 1990–2003 period.[26] M2 money growth increased by 19 percent in the first quarter of 2004 (relative to the first quarter of 2003). Sterilization of reserve increases permits the authorities to limit the increase in the mone-tary aggregates but has the disadvantage of keeping interest rates higher than would be the case if there were no sterilization; the higher interest rates, in turn, provide an incentive for continuing capital inflows.

---

26. Adjusting for the downward trend in velocity growth and assuming economic growth at potential, several studies have suggested that price stability in China is consistent with a growth of M2 of 13 to 16 percent.

Figure 9.12 People's Bank of China corporate goods price index, percent changes, 1999–2004

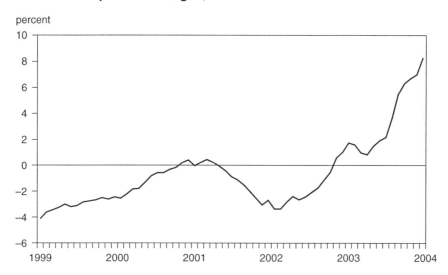

percent

Source: The People's Bank of China.

China's capital account is more open to inflows than to outflows. Indeed, the country has been suffering of late from the classical incompatibility among a fixed exchange rate, open capital markets, and a desire for a more independent monetary policy. The least costly way to overcome that dilemma would be to revalue the RMB. If China persists in sticking to an undervalued parity for the RMB and keeps accumulating reserves at recent rates, the real undervaluation of the RMB will ultimately be undone by a further increase in the country's inflation rate.

A recent Goldman Sachs study by Sun-Bae Kim, Liang Hong, and Enoch Fung (2004) addresses the issue of whether the policy adjustments to date are sufficient to reduce China's GDP growth to a more sustainable level (assumed to be 7 to 8 percent). To answer that question, Kim and colleagues construct a financial conditions index (FCI) for China that incorporates M2 growth, the real interest rate, and the real effective exchange rate. According to the FCI, there has been very little monetary tightening since the third quarter of 2003. Kim and colleagues (2004, 1) find that "policy tightening to date represents only about one-fifth of the total FCI tightening required to bring growth to a more sustainable level." They also find that an exchange rate move would reduce substantially the degree of monetary tightening necessary. In the end, Kim and colleagues conclude that reliance on administrative controls and delays in FCI tightening raise the risk of a more powerful boom in 2004 and a sharper retrenchment in 2005.

To sum up, the question for China is which form of adjustment of its real exchange rate is preferable. Surely, it is the one that relies on the adjustment

Figure 9.13 M2 money growth and CPI inflation, 1990–2003

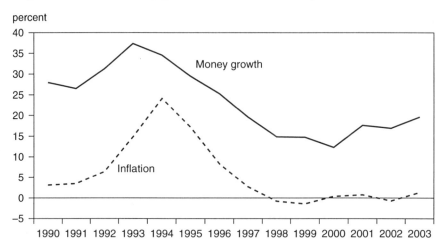

percent

Source: The People's Bank of China.

of nominal exchange rates. The alternative adjustment path, early signs of which are already in evidence, involves an excessive increase in monetary aggregates and a potentially large rise in the inflation rate; these, in turn, could bring with them a weakening of the banking sector, longer-term damage to China's hard-won gains in anti-inflationary credibility, and a higher risk of a hard landing of the real economy later this year or in 2005.[27]

Continued Secure Market Access for China's Exports

China is now the world's fourth largest exporter. Its exports account for 30 percent of its GDP. The value of China's merchandise exports grew in

27. A few analysts continue to argue that greater flexibility in China's currency regime would bring deflation with it. E.g., McKinnon and Schnabl (2003) have argued that if China were either to revalue or to float the RMB, it would soon be caught in a dangerous liquidity trap with the risk of prolonged deflation (à la Japan's recent experience). Central to their argument is the proposition that any appreciation of the RMB would generate expectations of further appreciation. Assuming that open interest rate parity needs to hold between dollar and RMB assets and that China has no influence on US interest rates, they arrive at the conclusion that interest rates in China will be driven (lower) into a liquidity trap to offset the expected appreciation of the RMB. I find their argument unpersuasive on at least two counts. First, it is no appreciation or small appreciation of the RMB that will drive expectations of further appreciation—not a 15 to 25 percent appreciation that would remove the existing disequilibrium in China's balance of payments. Second, it is going too far to suggest that international integration of capital markets has proceeded sufficiently that Chinese monetary policy is driven exclusively by arbitrage and exchange rate considerations; it has been monetary policy developments in China that have had a major influence on China's inflation rate—not exchange rate expectations (e.g., in 1994).

2003 by 35 percent, providing a substantial impetus to growth and employment. It thus makes perfect sense for the Chinese authorities to be concerned about prospects for China's exports.

Many critics of an RMB revaluation have focused on the expected contractionary effect of an exchange rate change on China's trade balance, output, and employment. Implicitly, they are assuming that, without a revaluation, China could continue for the indefinite future to record rapid export growth and to accumulate ever larger stockpiles of international reserves. I think such a view underestimates the protectionist threat to China's exports associated with continuation of the current regime. Imagine complaints about the lack of a level playing field against a backdrop in which the US bilateral trade deficit with China continues to be large, the RMB continues to depreciate in real effective terms alongside the dollar, and China and Japan continue as part of their large reserve accumulation to increase their share of US Treasury securities held abroad. Is this the kind of environment in which protectionist pressures in China's major export markets can confidently be forecast to be held at bay? Is this the kind of environment in which China's own trade liberalization can move ahead, with sufficient domestic popular support? I doubt it.

Half of China's total exports go to the United States, Euroland, and Japan. Reformers in China fought long and hard domestically to convince skeptics that China's accession to the WTO and full participation in the international trading system would be to China's advantage. The question that the Chinese authorities need to ask themselves is whether it pays to put in jeopardy the gains linked to market access for China's exports and to continued liberalization of China's import regime—for the sake of trying to maintain for a little longer an undervalued real exchange rate that may well be unsustainable anyway for other reasons. I know what my answer would be.

A High and Sustainable Rate of Economic Growth

Perhaps the single most popular argument against RMB revaluation is that it would be inconsistent with China's overriding need for rapid economic growth to employ its growing labor force and to ensure social stability (e.g., see Mundell 2004). In my view, this argument is flawed on three principal grounds.

First, a key threat to high and sustainable growth in China comes from an unsustainable credit boom in China itself and from a protectionist backlash against China's exports. If the credit boom is not brought under control soon, the chances increase that the monetary authorities will have to implement large increases in domestic interest rates and in reserve requirements. Such a monetary policy "crunch" would initiate a hard landing for the Chinese economy and depress growth significantly. The undervalued RMB, via its effect on speculative capital inflows and the pace of reserve accumulation, increases the risk that the monetary authorities will get so far behind the curve that they will have to act more aggressively.

Second, the experience of the 1990s does *not* suggest that real appreciation of the RMB will cause China's growth performance to fall unduly. Between 1994 and early 2002, the real trade-weighted exchange rate of the RMB rose by 29 percent; see figure 9.14. Yet the average growth rate of the Chinese economy from 1985 through 2001 was 8½ percent, and in no single year did the growth rate fall below 7½ percent.

Third, a revaluation of the RMB would put more focus within China on the *domestic* sources of economic growth and on what policy changes would be needed to strengthen domestic demand.[28] Chief among those policy changes would be an improvement in the system of financial intermediation and particularly a strengthening of the domestic banking system.

Conclusions on China's Interest in an RMB Revaluation

Whatever its earlier virtues, China's exchange rate policy has become increasingly problematic in the period 2002–04. The significantly undervalued RMB has been working against efforts to rein in an excessive growth of bank lending. It has been handicapping efforts to bring an end to overheating of the economy and to keep inflation from rising too much. And it could interrupt the market access that China now enjoys for its exports and weaken popular support within the country for further trade liberalization. The proposition that an RMB revaluation would be antigrowth and antiemployment is based on a fallacious assumption: that China's growth can be maintained at very high rates indefinitely without substantial changes in either the exchange rate or interest rates. This is most unlikely. A revaluation of the RMB would actually improve China's prospects for healthy, *sustainable*, noninflationary economic growth.[29]

---

28. Fernandez (2004) argues that a consistently undervalued currency also impedes industrial restructuring.

29. The same fallacious line of argument applies to the view that an RMB revaluation should be avoided because it will lead to a sizable decline in the RMB value of China's international reserves. The longer the RMB remains undervalued, the greater the likelihood that the subsequent revaluation will be even larger; meanwhile the undervaluation increases reserve accumulation, so that any subsequent revaluation would apply to a larger base. Unlike many other emerging economies, China has a net foreign asset position and thus does not have to worry that any future devaluations would generate large-scale insolvencies; see Goldstein and Turner (2004) on the measurement and control of currency mismatches.

Figure 9.14   Renminbi real trade-weighted exchange rate, 1994–2004 (index: 2000 = 100, monthly averages)

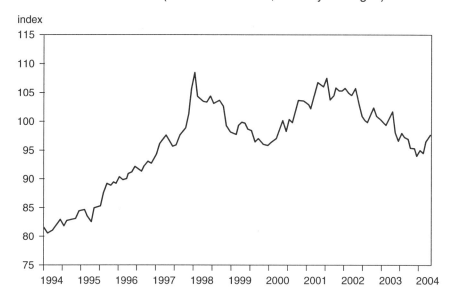

Note: Tick marks are for January and July of years indicated.
Source: JPMorgan data.

What Would Be in the Interest of the Rest of the World?

An RMB revaluation would also be in the strong interest of the rest of the world. If a lack of exchange rate action were to prompt a hard landing for the Chinese economy, China's imports would be expected to fall markedly. This would have an adverse impact on both partner countries' exports to China and on global commodity prices.

Eswar Prasad and Thomas Rumbaugh (2004), for example, report that (using purchasing power parity–based GDP) China accounted for about one-quarter of world economic growth during the 2001–03 period. Stephen Roach (2004) estimates that in 2003 China accounted for 32 percent of Japan's total export growth, 21 percent for the United States, 28 percent for Germany, 36 percent for South Korea, 68 percent for Taiwan, and about 30 percent (on average) for the countries that belong to the Association of Southeast Asian Nations.

To illustrate China's impact on primary commodity prices, the IMF (2004) estimates that China's net imports now account for 20 percent of world trade in soybeans, 15 percent in copper, and just under 5 percent in oil. Equally relevant, in 2003 China accounted for 121 percent of the increase in global copper demand; respectively, the corresponding percentages for steel, iron ore, aluminum, and primary nickel were 90, 66, 51, and 44 (Simpfendorfer 2004). Clearly, the "harder" the landing for Chinese growth, the more negative would be the growth implications for China's trading partners. Economies where exports to China account for a relatively high share of GDP (e.g., Hong Kong, Taiwan, Malaysia, Singapore, South Korea, Thailand, the Philippines, Russia, Indonesia, and Japan) would be the most affected.[30]

As was suggested above, the absence of an RMB revaluation would also make it more difficult to reduce global payments imbalances, especially the correction of the US current account deficit. To reduce the US external deficit in a more controlled manner, the US dollar needs to depreciate further and US spending needs to decline relative to US output. Since the peak in early 2002, the dollar has fallen on a real, trade-weighted basis by about 15 percent. But that first round of dollar depreciation has taken place against a relatively limited group of currencies—principally the euro, the Canadian dollar, the Australian dollar, the New Zealand kiwi, the Chilean peso, and, only slightly, the Japanese yen. Notably, the currencies of most Asian emerging economies have generally depreciated in real terms against the dollar since early 2002, even though most of them have balance of payments surpluses.

If the burden of adjustment is not more "balanced" across countries and regions during the necessary second round of dollar depreciation, the consequences would be adverse; either the overall dollar depreciation would be too small to correct the US deficit or the concentration of currency appreciation in regions (e.g., Euroland) with relatively slow growth and earlier significant appreciation would slow regional and global growth unduly. Economic policy cooperation, both among the Group of Seven (G-7) coun-

---

30. See Anderson (2004c). Along similar lines, Hueck (2004) concludes that a hard landing of the Chinese economy would most adversely affect Thailand, Singapore, Malaysia, and Indonesia. Effects on Latin America and the transition economies of Eastern Europe would be more subdued. Among the industrialized countries, Hueck finds that the negative consequences would be larger for Japan than for either the United States or the euro zone. He estimates that a decline of Chinese growth by 6 percentage points would yield a slowdown of global growth by 0.2 percent this year and 0.4 percent in 2005. Eichengreen (2004) argues that the countries that will benefit most from an RMB revaluation are Cambodia, Vietnam, Bangladesh, Sri Lanka, and Pakistan. These are the countries whose exports, broken down by industry, have the highest-rank correlation with Chinese exports, according to Shafaeddin (2003). These countries are argued to benefit because an RMB revaluation will increase China's relative unit labor costs and because it will induce China to shift into more technologically advanced, higher-value-added product lines. He argues that the next tier of Asian countries, like Thailand, will benefit less because China's move up the technology ladder will increase competition with them. Finally, he argues that the region's most advanced economies will feel mainly negative effects of an RMB revaluation.

tries and between the G-7 countries and Asia, might also suffer if global rebalancing via currency realignments did not take place in 2004; this, in turn, could damage confidence, especially if there were more serious conflicts over currency and trade policies.

Because Asian emerging economies plus Japan account for almost a 40 percent weight in the trade-weighted value of the dollar, because most of these economies have current account surpluses and strengthening domestic demand, and because their currencies did not participate in the first round of dollar depreciation, it is time for them to play a leading role in the second round of exchange rate adjustment.

China's role in this adjustment of Asian currencies is crucial. For if China does not permit the value of the RMB to rise significantly, other Asian economies—fearful of losing competitiveness to China if they acted alone—will be reluctant to allow their currencies to appreciate. In contrast, if the currencies of these Asian economies appreciate simultaneously (although by a somewhat smaller amount than China), each will gain competitiveness vis-à-vis China while limiting the decline in their overall competitive position. The global adjustment process will then be shared across a broader base.

Conclusions on the Rest of the World's Interest in Renminbi Revaluation

If an RMB revaluation is good for China in terms of promoting sustainable growth, it will also be good for the rest of the world; conversely, an exchange rate policy that would push China into a hard landing (because of its unhelpful contribution to rising domestic financial pressures within the country) would likely have adverse spillover effects on the rest of the world's exports to China. In addition, a rebalancing of global payments imbalances—and the avoidance of a hard landing stemming from a disorderly correction of the excessively large current account deficit in the United States—will be more difficult to achieve without the appreciation of Asian emerging economies. And China's own exchange rate appreciation is the linchpin for wider Asian currency adjustment.

What Kind of Currency Regime Would Best Facilitate an Appreciation of the Renminbi?

Once it is agreed that an appreciation of the RMB would be both in China's interest and in the global interest, the next operational issue is how that appreciation should be implemented. There are at least four alternative approaches: go slow in making changes to the currency regime, open capital markets and float the currency, float the currency but maintain controls on capital outflows, or implement two-stage currency reform.

The Go-Slow Approach

Under the go-slow approach, China would make only minor changes to the status quo. Specifically, a series of trade, capital account, and tax measures would substitute for a medium-sized revaluation. The exchange rate substitutes would be measures like a further reduction in the value-added-tax export rebate, promotion of tourist expenditures abroad, allowing banks to issue more dollar-denominated bonds, easing further surrender requirements on foreign exchange earnings, treating more favorably requests for outward foreign direct investment, and permitting mainland residents and certain financial institutions to purchase agreed-on amounts of foreign securities. The authorities might also consider a very small (2 to 3 percent) revaluation or small widening of the exchange rate band, perhaps in conjunction with a shift to a currency basket.

The appeal of the go-slow approach to the Chinese authorities is presumably that it will have only a minor negative effect on China's exports, on its incoming foreign direct investment, and on its near-term growth prospects. But as was suggested above, if the undervaluation of the RMB is substantial—say, 15 to 25 percent—then the go-slow approach is likely to be inadequate for removing the disequilibrium. This in turn means that the go-slow approach will not stop the huge capital inflow and the associated very large reserve accumulation.

Indeed, the go-slow approach may actually *increase* incoming capital flows, because speculators will assume that these small policy adjustments are only a precursor to a larger exchange rate appreciation. Put in other words, the go-slow approach may well create a "one-way bet" for speculators and thereby increase speculation on an RMB appreciation.

Opening Capital Markets and Floating the Currency

Another suggested prescription is for China to move rapidly to open its capital markets and to freely float its currency. This approach was proposed by US Treasury secretary John Snow during his visit to Beijing last fall. It is a good idea for the long run but not for now.

What makes the Snow proposal inappropriate for China's present circumstances is the still-fragile state of the Chinese banking system.[31] If China's restrictions on capital outflows were lifted, the risk is that there could be large-scale capital flight and sharp currency depreciation in response to bad news about the banking system or the economy. Given the unhappy experience of many of its neighbors during the Asian financial

---

31. Anderson (2004b) also argues that China cannot lift restrictions on capital flows now because Chinese interest rates are not sufficiently flexible to adjust to prevent speculative arbitrage.

crisis, China is understandably reluctant to risk repeating that outcome. Instead, it would rather phase in the liberalization of its capital account according to the progress made in strengthening the banking system. In addition, the foreign exchange market in China is still dominated by the government; getting a proper price signal will thereby require widening the number of participants in the market, as well as making a series of technical improvements.[32]

Floating the Currency but Maintaining Controls on Capital Outflows

A third approach would retain controls on capital outflows but would introduce a managed float right away. In so doing, it would (appropriately) delink the capital account regime decision from the currency regime decision. Because I am a longtime supporter of managed floating for emerging economies that have heavy involvement with private capital markets, this is the regime I would ordinarily prefer.[33] But not in this case. The reason is that I fear that a managed floating regime in China will in practice have plenty of "management" and very little "floating." If the managed float is heavily managed, the movement in the exchange rate may well be very little different from that in the go-slow approach. In that event, it too would not remove most of the existing disequilibrium, with adverse effects on the quest for financial stability and sustainable growth.

Implementing Two-Stage Currency Reform

It was because of the disadvantages of the three alternative approaches outlined above that Lardy and I (Goldstein and Lardy 2003b) proposed that China implement "two-stage currency reform." The first stage, to be undertaken immediately, would entail three elements: the switch from a unitary peg to the dollar to a currency basket, a medium-sized (15 to 25 percent) revaluation of the RMB, and a widening of the currency band (to between 5 to 7 percent, from less than 1 percent). Also, the substantive restrictions on capital outflows would be retained. Stage two, to be implemented after China strengthened its banking system enough to permit a significant liberalization of capital outflows, should be adoption of a managed float.

---

32. The four state-owned commercial banks now account for 95 percent of interbank market trading in foreign exchange. Risk-hedging products in the market are very limited relative to enterprises' demand for them. Financial trading (vs. trading for commercial purposes) in the foreign exchange market is low in China relative to that in the international foreign exchange market.

33. E.g., see the case for a "managed floating plus" regime in Goldstein (2002).

This two-stage approach does not ask the rest of the world to live with a seriously undervalued RMB until China is ready to lift the restrictions on its capital outflows; nor does it ask China to put its domestic financial stability at risk by undertaking premature liberalization of its capital account. And by implementing immediately a sizable revaluation of the RMB, the two-stage approach removes the incentives for further large capital inflows and reserve accumulation; the external component of the monetary base would therefore no longer be working at cross-purposes with the domestic component. Exchange rate policy would thus become the ally—not the enemy—of bank reform and of anti-inflationary monetary policy.

Because there would no longer be a need for large-scale, prolonged exchange market intervention in one direction, allegations of currency manipulation would cease. Moreover, because a significant down payment would have been made on currency flexibility in stage one, there would be less risk that a Chinese announcement of a move to "greater currency flexibility" would be more press release than de facto exchange rate flexibility. Finally, by implementing a revaluation of the RMB and improving the incentive for other Asian economies to follow its lead, China would (once again, as during the Asian financial crisis) become part of the solution to global payments imbalances—not part of the problem.

By moving to a currency basket, the stability of China's overall effective exchange rate would be enhanced. Contrary to what is often asserted, the present currency regime does not deliver exchange rate stability to China, as evidenced by the significant volatility that one observes in China's overall, real, trade-weighted exchange rate during the past decade (see figure 9.14). Also, the currency basket would permit a further depreciation of the dollar with respect to the RMB without the need for a series of further parity changes. If China retains its current unitary peg to the dollar, this will not be possible. By widening the currency band, China could gain valuable experience with managing greater currency flexibility and at the same time improve the institutional structure and depth of the foreign exchange market.

By adopting a managed float in stage two, China would acquire the monetary policy independence it increasingly needs. As the events of 2003 demonstrated, the domestic requirements for monetary policy in China can at times be quite different from the domestic requirements in the anchor country (i.e., in the United States).[34] Also, it is not necessary for China to have a fixed exchange rate to produce good inflation performance in the future. Instead, it can do what an increasing number of other emerging

---

34. Because of the increased openness of the Chinese economy, it will also become more and more difficult for China to control capital flows; this too argues for increased exchange rate flexibility down the road.

economies are doing, namely, adopt a monetary policy framework of inflation targeting (along with a managed float).[35]

Most studies conclude that countries adopting inflation targeting have been relatively successful in meeting their announced inflation targets, that the track record in meeting inflation targets has been much better than that in meeting announced monetary growth targets, that countries adopting inflation targeting still allow monetary policy to respond to falls in output, and that inflation targeting has rarely been associated with a subsequent loss of fiscal prudence.[36] In short, two-stage currency reform will permit China to solve its exchange rate policy dilemma.

Conclusions

China should not change its exchange rate policies simply because other countries are urging it to do so. But, by the same token, the fact that many are recommending a revaluation of the RMB is not sufficient reason for rejecting that policy option if it is the best one available.

The main reason for revaluing the RMB by an appropriate amount is that it increases the odds that China will be able to achieve the economic objectives it has long pursued, namely, domestic financial reform, domestic macroeconomic stability, open market access for its exports, and a healthy, sustainable rate of economic growth. Exchange rate action differs from other policy measures in one crucial respect: It addresses simultaneously internal balance (overheating) and external balance (the surplus in the balance of payments). The cost of a hard landing is too high to rely on half measures.

China's decisions on its future currency regime should pay primary attention to China's own circumstances—not to one-size-fits-all prescriptions. Given the still-fragile state of China's banking system, the capital account decision should be delinked from the currency regime decision. All things considered, two-stage currency reform is better than the alter-

---

35. Following Mishkin (2000) and Truman (2003), inflation targeting is a framework for monetary policy that constrains discretion in at least four key elements: (1) There is an institutional commitment to low inflation as a primary objective of monetary policy; (2) there is public announcement of a numerical target (or sequence of targets) for inflation, with a specified time horizon for meeting that target; (3) the central bank is given enough independence from political pressures and/or government directives that it can set the instruments of monetary policy as it sees fit in pursuit of its mandate; and (4) the conduct of monetary policy is subject to transparency and accountability guidelines, so that the public is informed about both the reasons for monetary policy decisions and the extent to which the objectives of monetary policy have been attained. Jenkins (2004) also suggests that China should move to an inflation-targeting regime for monetary policy, along with a flexible exchange rate. Mundell (2004) takes the opposite view that a fixed exchange rate would be better.

36. See Truman (2003), and see Mishkin and Schmidt-Hebbel (2001) for a review of these studies.

natives because it reduces China's current internal and external imbalances, it promotes the right sequencing of internal reforms, it contributes to the timely correction of payments imbalances abroad, and it moves monetary policy independence and capital account liberalization in the desired direction in the long term.

Addendum

This paper was written relying on data through the first quarter of 2004. Data for the second quarter of 2004 have since then become available. In brief, the second-quarter data show evidence of a slowing of growth for real fixed investment, industrial value added, broad monetary aggregates, and bank lending. On the other hand, growth of private consumption increased, inflation rates are still rising, the trade balance began showing monthly surpluses in May, and international reserves increased by $30 billion. Also, investment is still rising faster than GDP, pushing the investment share up yet further. Second-quarter growth of real GDP was 9.6 percent—just a bit below the figure for the first quarter and somewhat higher than the figure for 2003 as a whole. Enough to say that I think it premature to conclude at this stage that China has achieved its desired "soft landing."[37]

References

Anderson, Jonathan. 2003. The Complete RMB Handbook. Asian Economic Perspectives, UBS Investment Research, Hong Kong. Photocopy (October).

Anderson, Jonathan. 2004a. The Asian Liquidity Primer. UBS Investment Research, Hong Kong. Photocopy (March).

Anderson, Jonathan. 2004b. Can China Manage a Full Float? Paper presented at an IMF seminar on China's foreign exchange system, Dalian, China, May 26–27.

Anderson, Jonathan. 2004c. China Exposures Chartbook. UBS Investment Research, Hong Kong. Photocopy (May).

Anderson, Jonathan. 2004d. What Does the PBC Do Now? UBS Investment Research, Hong Kong. Photocopy (May).

Baily, Martin. 2004. The US Economic Outlook. Presentation at the Institute for International Economics, Washington, April 1.

Bergsten, C. Fred. 2003. The Correction of the Dollar and Foreign Intervention in the Currency Markets. Testimony before the Committee on Small Business, US House of Representatives, June 25.

Boughton, James. 2001. *Silent Revolution: The International Monetary Fund, 1979–1989.* Washington: International Monetary Fund.

---

37. See Goldstein and Lardy (2004) for an explanation of why the unwinding of China's investment boom was barely begun and of why administrative controls are not likely to prove effective over the medium term.

Dooley, Michael, David Folkerts-Landau, and Peter Garber. 2003. *An Essay on the Revived Bretton Woods System*. NBER Working Paper 9971. Cambridge, MA: National Bureau of Economic Research.

Dooley, Michael, David Folkerts-Landau, and Peter Garber. 2004. *The Revived Bretton Woods System: The Effects of Periphery Intervention and Reserve Management on Interest Rates and Exchange Rates in Center Countries*. NBER Working Paper 10332. Cambridge, MA: National Bureau of Economic Research.

Eichengreen, Barry. 2004. Chinese Currency Controversies. Paper prepared for Asian Economic Panel, Hong Kong, April.

Fernandez, David. 2004. *An Asian Intervention Reader*. Singapore: JPMorgan. (March).

Frankel, Jeffrey. 2004, On the Yuan: The Choice Between Adjustment Under a Fixed Exchange Rate and Adjustment Under a Flexible Rate. Paper presented at an IMF seminar on China's foreign exchange system, Dalian, China, May 26–27.

Gavin, Michael, and Ricardo Hausmann. 1996. The Roots of Banking Crises: The Macroeconomic Context. In *Banking Crises in Latin America*, ed. Ricardo Hausmann and Liliana Rojas-Suarez. Washington: Inter-American Development Bank.

Goldstein, Morris. 1997. *The Case for an International Banking Standard*. POLICY ANALYSES IN INTERNATIONAL ECONOMICS 47. Washington: Institute for International Economics.

Goldstein, Morris. 1998. *The Asian Financial Crisis*. POLICY ANALYSES IN INTERNATIONAL ECONOMICS 55. Washington: Institute for International Economics.

Goldstein, Morris. 2002. *Managed Floating Plus*. POLICY ANALYSES IN INTERNATIONAL ECONOMICS 66. Washington: Institute for International Economics.

Goldstein, Morris. 2003. China's Exchange Rate Regime. Testimony before the Subcommittee on Domestic and International Monetary Policy, Trade, and Technology, Committee on Financial Services, US House of Representatives, Washington, October 1.

Goldstein, Morris. 2004. *Adjusting China's Exchange Rate Policies*. Working Paper WP04-1. Washington: Institute for International Economics. (Revised version of the paper presented at the International Monetary Fund's seminar on China's foreign exchange system, Dalian, China, May 26–27, 2004.)

Goldstein, Morris, and Mohsin Khan. 1985. Income and Price Effects in Foreign Trade. In *Handbook of International Economics*, vol. 2, ed. Ronald Jones and Peter Kenen. Amsterdam: North-Holland.

Goldstein, Morris, and Nicholas Lardy. 2003a. A Modest Proposal for China's Renminbi. *Financial Times*, August 26.

Goldstein, Morris, and Nicholas Lardy. 2003b. Two-Stage Currency Reform for China. *Asian Wall Street Journal*, September 12.

Goldstein, Morris, and Nicholas Lardy. 2004. Don't Hail China's Soft Landing Too Soon. *Financial Times* (October 6).

Goldstein, Morris, and Nicholas Lardy. N.d. *The Future of China's Exchange Rate Regime*. Washington: Institute for International Economics (forthcoming).

Goldstein, Morris, and Philip Turner. 2004. *Controlling Currency Mismatches in Emerging Markets*. Washington: Institute for International Economics.

Hueck, Thomas. 2004. A Hard Landing in China: How Much Growth Would It Cost? HVB Group, Munich, May 5.

IMF (International Monetary Fund). 2004. *World Economic Outlook*. Washington: International Monetary Fund, April.

Jenkins, Paul. 2004. Asia and the Global Economy. Remarks delivered at the University of British Columbia, Vancouver, March 30.

Kim, Sun-Bae, Hong Liang, and Enoch Fung. 2004. Introducing the Goldman Sachs China Financial Conditions Index. Goldman Sachs Global Economics Paper 11. Goldman Sachs, Hong Kong. Photocopy (May 19).

Lardy, Nicholas. 1998. *China's Unfinished Economic Revolution*. Washington: Brookings Institution Press.

Li, Rougu. 2004. Latest Developments and Experience of China's Financial System Reform. Presentation at a Group of Twenty workshop on developing strong domestic financial markets, Ottawa, April 26–27.

Mann, Catherine. 2003. How Long the Strong Dollar? In *Dollar Overvaluation and the World Economy*, ed. C. Fred Bergsten and John Williamson. Washington: Institute for International Economics.

McKinnon, Ronald, and Gunther Schnabl. 2003. China: A Stabilizing or Deflationary Influence in East Asia? The Problem of Conflicted Virtue. Stanford University, Stanford, CA. Photocopy (November).

Meade, James. 1951. *The Balance of Payments*. London: Oxford University Press.

Mishkin, Frederic. 2000. Inflation Targeting in Emerging Market Countries. *American Economic Review* (May).

Mishkin, Frederic, and Klaus Schmidt-Hebbel. 2001. *One Decade of Inflation Targeting in the World: What Do We Know and What Do We Need to Know?* NBER Working Paper 8397. Cambridge, MA: National Bureau of Economic Research.

Mundell, Robert. 2004. China's Exchange Rate: The Case for the Status Quo. Paper presented at an IMF seminar on China's foreign exchange system, Dalian, China, May 26–27.

Noland, Marcus. 1998. US-China Economic Relations. In *After the Cold War: Domestic Factors in US-China Relations*, ed. Robert S. Ross. Armonk, NY: M. E. Sharpe.

PBC (Peoples Bank of China). 2004. *Monetary Policy Report for 2003*. Beijing: People's Bank of China.

Prasad, Eswar, and Thomas Rumbaugh. 2004. Overview. In *China's Growth and Integration into the World Economy: Prospects and Challenges*, ed. Eswar Prasad. IMF Occasional Paper 232. Washington: International Monetary Fund.

Roach, Stephen. 2004. Global Rebalancing and the China Play. *Economic Trends* (March). Morgan Stanley.

Shafaeddin, S. M. 2003. *The Impact of China's Access to WTO on the Exports of Developing Countries*. UNCTAD Discussion Paper 160, June.

Simpfendorfer, Ben. 2004. *China and the World Economy*. Hong Kong: JPMorgan (April).

Truman, Edwin. 2003. *Inflation Targeting in the World Economy*. Washington: Institute for International Economics.

Truman, Edwin. 2004. Budget and External Deficits: Same Family But Not Twins. Paper presented at a conference on the macroeconomics of fiscal policy, Federal Reserve Bank of Boston, Boston, June 14–16.

Wang, Tao. 2004. Exchange Rate Dynamics. In *China's Growth and Integration into the World Economy: Prospects and Challenges*, ed. Eswar Prasad. IMF Occasional Paper 232. Washington: International Monetary Fund.

Comment

PETER GARBER

First, I address the issue of global imbalances. The number that comes up throughout part III of this book seems to be 25 percent. The US dollar should depreciate overall by 25 percent; China should appreciate 25 percent. This seems to be the magic number based on fundamental exchange rate calculations. In other words, instead of costing a buck to assemble a DVD player in China and package it for export, now it will cost $1.25. And Wal-Mart will now sell it at $39.75 instead of at $39.50.

From the point of view of the United States, such a change is not going to do a lot. The result might be a shifting of assembly plants in Asia from China, perhaps to Vietnam. At least from the data that we can see, China does not have an overall trade surplus anymore, but it does have a huge bilateral surplus with the United States. This is simply a pass-through of the surplus of much of Asia's value added to the United States, which gets placed on China's bilateral books. If we just disintermediate China from the assembly process and disaggregate the surplus to the rest of Asia, the US deficit is still going to be quite similar. Of course, there may be a multi-country Asian game where, after a coordinated appreciation led by China, everyone else can appreciate their currencies as well; and that might have some impact in the United States. But the direct impact of a revaluation by China would not be consequential.

The telling image that I want to use as background is the one that Jim O'Neill presents on what the world economy will look like in 2050 (see figure II.1 in his comment on part II of this volume), when US GDP is projected

Peter Garber is a global strategist in Global Markets Research at Deutsche Bank and a research associate of the National Bureau of Economic Research.

to be three times larger than it is now in real terms. China's GDP will be larger than the US GDP and India's will be almost as large. These two countries are at the heart of the current and future imbalances because they have more than 2 billion, mostly underemployed people.

It is clear where the US growth will come from: a rise in the labor force from natural increase and immigration, productivity growth, and perhaps capital deepening. China already has four times the population of the United States, as does India. So for either country approximately to equal the United States in 2050 must mean that its productivity and capital intensity 40 years from now will have to be equivalent to the productivity and capital that the United States has right now. To construct these forecasts, we must multiply the projected labor force by the projected productivity to get the projected GDP. To get these numbers in the case of China, the 200 million people who are now unemployed, or underemployed, plus the natural population increase, will have to move into employment. Similarly, this must also be done in India, which is even more profoundly underemployed than is China.

The question is how do we get from here to there, and that is the crux of the issue of global imbalances. The analysis in part III on what should be the equilibrium exchange rates uses concepts from and is done in the context of relatively fully employed economies. But China has unemployment that in any industrial economy would be regarded as at depression levels. It has a profound internal imbalance that makes irrelevant all of the analyses that look exclusively at external balance.

One of the principles that seems to be in general use is that the capital account should finance the current account. That is, a country with a capital account surplus should be running a current account deficit; in that sense, there is balance. This is a first-best analysis, of the sort that generated recommendations that produced the Latin American development results. Of course, Asian countries have studied this history, which emanated from this prescription, and they have observed a financial and economic disaster. So they have opted for the Japanese and the South Korean method of growth. True, Japan's growth strategy led ultimately to 10 years of stagnation, but after 40 years of really rapid growth. Yet looking at Japan's performance from the perspective of a country at the early stages of development, even these past 10 years in Japan, with high real income and wealth, must look like paradise. So 40 years down the road, a country would be willing to pay with a 10-year stagnation and a major loss in its financial system in return for supergrowth in the meantime. It does not look like a real problem when discounted to the present over 40 years.

Two issues under discussion in this part of the book confuse me. One is the currency manipulation argument. In particular, it is well known—as Morris Goldstein mentions early in chapter 9—that a global monetary system is simply a reflection and a solution of the fundamental global economic problems that have to be resolved at any given time.

In particular, the Bretton Woods system itself was such a solution, although an imperfect one. It was the result of the deal between the United States and the United Kingdom during World War II, made after several bilateral meetings. The multilateral meeting in Bretton Woods itself was simply a ratification of what the United Kingdom and the United States presented. The only items at issue in New Hampshire were what fixed exchange rates and what quotas would be set—it was a tidying-up exercise.

The basic Bretton Woods system actually had been established months before in Washington. The US perspective was that of a postwar creditor with a trade surplus. The United States was worried about discrimination against its goods as experienced in the middle of the 1930s, through controls and multiple exchange rate regimes. It also wanted to avoid beggar-thy-neighbor devaluation policies, so it wanted a stable exchange rate system. Conversely, the United Kingdom, whose delegation was led by John Maynard Keynes, was a major debtor. Expecting a depression after the war in the usual Keynesian way, it was focused fundamentally on having a flexible enough exchange rate to establish internal balance. In other words, it wanted to manipulate its currency to insulate it against disturbances in external accounts. Ultimately, the compromise was to establish a system with fixed but changeable exchange rates. Later on, although the "currency manipulation" clause was added, the International Monetary Fund in its entire history hardly ever invoked it—and rightly so, because the concept was so ill defined.

There is also a comment that "currency manipulation" is an academically narrow concept. I would agree with that. It is so narrow that it is zero-dimensional. There is no academic discussion of this concept at all because it has no scientific content. If it wants, a country can manipulate its currency to advantage its goods without intervening in the exchange markets at all. At its core, the currency manipulation concept is simply a contrivance of political rhetoric in the protectionist tool kit. It is invoked when it is convenient, just like child labor or prison labor or environmental degradation or whatever it is that suits the purpose in implementing a protectionist regime.

The second confusing issue is the metric that quantifies the size and nature of the fundamental imbalance: Add the current account surplus to the surplus of foreign direct investment (FDI). This looks suspiciously like double counting to me. The key impact on the rest of the world is encapsulated in the current account surplus alone. That is what policy is aimed at implementing, and that is what affects the rest of the world's labor markets, especially if policy has a mercantilist intent. If a country uses exchange market intervention, and it happens to be associated also with an FDI inflow into the country, well, that is simply a balance sheet manipulation. It determines that foreigners will intermediate between domestic savers and investors. If a country intervenes by buying foreign exchange and the funds return as FDI, it is just indirectly financing the foreign direct investor. It could just as well have intermediated domestic savings through its domestic financial system, which might then have lent to the foreign investor. By going through foreign balance sheets, the FDI entrepreneur has to get funds at his own cost of capital, not at some arbitrary one established in the inefficient domestic financial system.

Aside from China, there have been similar complaints about the Bank of Japan's recent huge interventions that far exceeded not only Japan's own current account surplus but also the US current account deficit at annual rates. But, as Takatoshi Ito points out in chapter 8, most of this again is financing equity investment from the United States into Japan. Imagine that a US resident or a global investor wants to buy Japanese equity. She sells a Treasury bill in the United States. The US resident then sells dollars for yen and buys equity in Japan. To keep this inflow from appreciating the exchange rate, the Japanese Ministry of Finance buys the Treasury bill and thereby accumulates foreign exchange. To finance its part of this circle of transactions, the ministry sells financing bills on the market; so the ministry is indirectly financing the foreign purchase of Japanese equity. Finally, to close the circle, the seller of equity in Japan buys the ministry's issue of financing bills.

In this circle, the intervention of the Japanese Ministry of Finance is good for the sellers of equity because indirectly it supports yen equity prices. Although it may be a subsidy for equity sellers, at the end of the day this effect of the intervention does not change the flow of goods and services across countries. It is the current account surplus that you have to watch; adding capital account components to the current account tells us little. I am not sure what politics are behind proposing that sort of metric. If you are worried about the subsidization of local industries implicit in a current account surplus, just look at the current account surplus.

Let us get to the fundamental forces underlying this ascendant monetary system: In a nutshell, there are 200 million underemployed people in China who have to be employed at a gross rate of 20-plus million a year, a net rate of 10 million a year. There is a huge, exhaustible supply of labor that is socially and politically problematic. If it is not employed, it may cause real political trouble. It is desirable to employ it as fast as possible. The development strategy that the Chinese have selected, having seen what happened to Latin America, is export driven. The friction, though, is that the faster they employ the labor, the more pressure they get from their trading partners, whose labor markets they are disrupting.

So they have to think of a way to offset this. Straight beggar-thy-neighbor policies launched in the fundamentally depressed economies of the 1930s were shown not to work. Depreciating the exchange rate so that goods could be exported at fire sale prices might have increased employment, but trading partners soon intervened with counterdepreciations or commercial policy to undo the result. The political clout of consumers in the partner country could never overcome that of the combination of labor and capital in the affected industries.

The solution is to align the interest of foreign capital with the strategy by allowing it access to the labor pool via FDI. More than 50 percent of China's exporting is done via FDI firms. The excess profit to foreign capital is the present value of the real wage differential between the United States, or the rest of the world, and Chinese wages, discounted from the time when this system finally ends and Chinese wages converge.

This export system is financed with Chinese savings, although intermediated through the US financial system by the purchase of official foreign exchange reserves. China employs a repressed financial system to force large savings, to employ its unemployed labor at a maximum rate. China provides the savings that normally would go directly to capital in China through a domestic financial system. I am surprised that Michael Mussa states in chapter 5 that it might be four years before this policy ends; I thought it was a principle of the Institute for International Economics that it should have happened two years ago. But I would say that this can go on for twice that long.

What is the effect of all this on Europe? Because the euro floats against the dollar with no intervention from the official sector, Europe's current account is determined by the decisions of its investors, by private capital flows. If there is cheap, subsidized capital flowing into the United States via the Asian official sector, that will push private European capital out because it expects a better return for the increasing risks than the subsidized capital is getting. The other side of the coin is that the European current account has to shrink, via an exchange rate appreciation. This will cause European goods to be pushed out of both the United States and Asia, with rising European imports from these areas. This is problematic for Europe; it finds it difficult to expand its own domestic demand so this will lead to more unemployment and stagnant growth. One way around this problem is to use monetary policy to keep the exchange rate from appreciating, that is, to join the party.

I feel compelled to say a bit about outsourcing, or offshoring, given Martin Baily and Robert Lawrence's discussion of it in chapter 6, because I have just returned from India after an outsourcing mission. The organization with which I am affiliated has been exploring whether it can outsource various parts of research—not call center or back office operations, but some of the research itself. Some equity research has already been outsourced by some firms, in part to India.

The answer to this question is problematic, even though the economics of the decision is superficially straightforward. Just to put some hypothetical numbers on it, the outsourcing firm that one might contract to manage this activity can buy a unit of labor at 15 and sell it to us at 30; we would have to pay 90 for it here, a two-thirds cost saving for us, just on the face of it. In addition, this staff can be terminated quickly in a downturn in accord with contractual arrangements. Now you might think investment banks are pretty ruthless in that situation anyway, but it is not that easy. In general, it is painful.

The idea is that these are not necessarily substitutes but complements to existing research staff because it would free up our personnel in the United States and in the other main financial centers for higher-value activities. The kinds of activities to outsource might start with simple things like the publication of economic calendars or dailies, and perhaps the construction of reports and charts. All of this would, by virtue of regulation, have to be approved by supervisory analysts back in the United States. Moving up to a higher-level activity, which would be regarded as serious research—like derivatives research or relative value calculations—presents a much more serious management problem.

One problem that might materialize is that the supply curve of such staff might be upward sloping, so that current pricing is deceptive, but we have become convinced that the supply curve is flat for recruits, even from the very top institutes of engineering and management. Also, a large stock of previous graduates have been forced over time to sit around in government planning agencies.

On the downside, a lack of recruitment here at entry levels means that we are eating our seed corn. It is from the new staff that people develop into more senior managers of research, and quickly in our industry. So we have to worry that we may be trading a short-term gain for a larger medium-term loss. As another issue, some of the information technology activities of our index group are already being done in India, but we have found that it takes two people in India to match one in the United States. This is not because of intelligence or training differentials, but just because of management difficulties and lack of access. The time zone differences are a problem, although staff in India are willing to work New York hours. But that leads to social problems anyway, and it is one of the factors that produces a 40 percent turnover in much of business process outsourcing. Constantly having to train new staff thus has to be factored in.

One major drawback is whether you can keep control of intellectual property. In particular, after training people to a level where their research output is similar to what is being done in New York but paying them a third as much, they can be poached. In the United States, poaching is made difficult because people are already being paid more or less the going market wage, and they are building up unvested equity claims, so it gets more and more costly to pry them away. In India, you spend the effort to train someone up to a level where they can actually do front-line research, then competitive firms immediately jump in to buy, not at one-third the New York cost but at something much higher, so it is very difficult to hold on to the apparent rent.

One question we ask is why not outsource instead to a US Midwestern university town where the wage would be in proportion to the cost-of-living differential with New York. The training is good; people speak English; so why go to India? That brings us to ask just what it is that the outsourcing firms provide and what value added they have developed in India. Over the course of time, they have developed intense expertise in breaking down business processes into mechanical units that actually can be outsourced and intellectually protected. Their expertise might be such that we could just as well recruit one of these firms from Bangalore to outsource a center somewhere in the United States. So it is not clear whether outsourcing is actually going to move jobs to India, rather than move Indian management expertise to the United States.

IV

THE USE OF INTERVENTION TO ACHIEVE DESIRED CURRENCY VALUES

10

Intervention When Exchange Rate Misalignments Are Large

CHRISTOPHER KUBELEC

Recent developments in the foreign exchange markets have once again put the issue of exchange rate stability at the center of the policy arena. The continued fall of the dollar since February 2002 has potentially serious consequences for growth and recovery in Europe and Japan. In addition, the record levels of intervention in the foreign exchange markets by the Japanese authorities in 2003 have once again raised the issue of the controversial effects of foreign exchange intervention.

In particular, the issue of the effectiveness of sterilized intervention tends to polarize both policymakers and researchers into one of two distinct camps: those who believe that such interventions in the foreign exchange market are, to all intents and purposes, ineffective in influencing exchange rate movement; and those who take the view that they can play a substantial role in exchange rate management. Indeed, this division of views regarding intervention's effectiveness is reflected in the frequency of its use by the Group of Three (G-3) monetary authorities. Whereas the Japanese Ministry of Finance has intervened both massively and frequently in the foreign exchange markets during the past decade, intervention by the US and European authorities has been relatively rare since the later half of the 1990s.

This chapter makes the case that sterilized intervention can be an effective tool for managing exchange rates, but with some qualifications. In particular, it proposes that sterilized intervention is most effective when used to limit exchange rate misalignments, when the intervention is strong, and when it is conducted to address large misalignments of the exchange rate.

Christopher Kubelec is an economist at the Bank of England. This chapter is based on his doctoral thesis for the University of Warwick.

The first section reviews the causes and episodes of exchange rate misalignment, with a focus on the role of "chartist" or technical trading strategies by market participants who extrapolate exchange rate trends. The second section briefly examines the evidence regarding the effects of sterilized intervention, and it discusses the various channels by which it may have an effect. A particular focus is the idea that intervention may affect market participants' expectations of the future path of the exchange rate. The third section lays out the analytical framework used to make these ideas more concrete. A key feature is the theory that traders select between destabilizing and stabilizing strategies on the basis of the relative profitability of chartist techniques.

The chapter's fourth section describes the role intervention can play in coordinating traders to become a force for the stabilization of exchange rates. Essentially, this can be achieved because sterilized intervention directly affects the profitability of competing strategies. Furthermore, it is shown how the processes by which long swings in exchange rates emerge imply that intervention is most effective when misalignments are large. Evidence on the importance of this effect is presented for the yen-dollar exchange rate in the 1990s. The fifth section discusses the implications for exchange rate policy, with a focus on the potential benefits of regimes based on exchange rate bands. The sixth section draws conclusions.

Market Participants and Exchange Rate Misalignments

The key justification for undertaking any sort of intervention in the foreign exchange markets lies in the observation that exchange rates do not always reflect underlying economic conditions. More precisely, it is the tendency for floating exchange rates to suffer from prolonged misalignments, which can have serious economic consequences. The proximate cause of misalignments is the tendency of asset market participants to herd: to buy overvalued assets or sell undervalued ones.

This kind of behavior is particularly prevalent at short forecasting horizons. There is growing evidence from foreign exchange markets the world over that, at least for horizons shorter than one month, exchange rate forecasts are not dominated by underlying economic conditions.[1] Rather, at short horizons, traders place more weight on "chartist" or technical trading strategies that effectively extrapolate recent trends. In addition to simple charts of past exchange rate behavior, a technical analyst may use a variety of trading rules based on statistical and mathematical techniques. Popular examples

---

1. See, inter alia, Allen and Taylor (1990) and Taylor and Allen (1992) for studies of the London markets; Menkhoff (1997, 1998) for the German markets; Lui and Mole (1998) for the Hong Kong markets; Cheung and Wong (1999, 2000) for the Hong Kong, Tokyo, and Singapore markets; and Cheung and Chinn (1999) for the US markets.

include the "head and shoulders" reversal pattern, and a variety of moving-average rules for predicting turning points. However, a common feature of all the rules is that their use adds a positive feedback into the exchange rate, tending to accentuate deviations from the equilibrium level implied by economic fundamentals. Because most trading in the foreign exchange market involves taking and unwinding positions at hourly horizons rather than months or years, these findings have potentially serious implications.

There are a number of well-documented periods in recent years when severe exchange rate misalignments have developed. Perhaps the best known is that of the dollar bubble of the mid-1980s. In a series of papers, Jeffrey Frankel and Kenneth Froot (1986a, 1986b, 1987) showed how the behavior of the dollar in this period could be understood as a bubble caused by the actions of portfolio managers basing their forecasts on technical analysis rather than macroeconomic fundamentals.

This was not an isolated event, however. The long swings observed in the value of the yen in the 1990s are striking. In particular, the appreciation of the yen-dollar rate to 80 in April 1995 was widely thought of as inconsistent with economic fundamentals. Takatoshi Ito (2002) suggests that possible causes of this were technical forces, such as the use of knockout options and delta hedge strategies, as well as trade conflicts over the United States–Japan automobile dispute. In addition, the initial undervaluation of the euro was only loosely connected to underlying economic factors.

Can Sterilized Intervention Influence Exchange Rates?

While monetary policy clearly can be used to moderate any destabilizing market behavior, a country may be understandably unwilling to sacrifice its use for domestic objectives. As a result, monetary authorities typically sterilize intervention so that there is no net effect on the domestic money supply.[2] Such intervention can produce an effect if domestic and foreign assets are imperfect substitutes—in which case the change in the relative supply of domestic and foreign assets leads to a change in the risk premium on foreign assets demanded by investors.

Though direct evidence for this "portfolio balance channel" of intervention is somewhat mixed,[3] there is increasing evidence that intervention

---

2. The two standard views of the channels by which sterilized intervention can influence the exchange rate are the portfolio balance channel and the signaling channel. The portfolio balance channel refers to the theory that sterilized intervention can influence the exchange rate by changing the relative outside supplies of domestic and foreign assets (normally government bonds), and hence the risk premium.

3. While Dominguez and Frankel (1993) provide evidence in support of a portfolio balance effect, both Jurgenson (1983) and Edison (1993) conclude sterilized intervention did not have much effect on exchange rates.

can substantially affect the exchange rate, at least in the short run. In particular, Kathryn Dominguez and Jeffrey Frankel (1993) found strong evidence that sterilized interventions in the G-3 currencies were successful in the 1980s, while further evidence that intervention in the 1990s was effective is provided by Dominguez (2003). A recent study by Ito (2002) found evidence that the characteristically large interventions conducted by the Japanese authorities in the latter half of the 1990s were largely successful in achieving their aims. Further evidence on the effectiveness of Japanese interventions is given by Ramaswamy and Hossein (2000) and Fatum and Hutchinson (2003), among others.

A common finding is that intervention can be particularly effective when conducted in concert by the authorities on both sides of the market. Examples include the interventions following the Plaza Accord and the Louvre Accord in the mid-1980s, and concerted interventions by the US and Japanese authorities in 1995. For example, Ito (2002) finds that during the second half of the 1990s, joint US-Japanese interventions were much more effective than unilateral interventions by the Japanese authorities. He estimates that while unilateral interventions by the Japanese authorities of ¥100 billion moved the yen-dollar rate by 0.1 percent, cooperative interventions of approximately the same size moved the yen by 5 percent.

A number of studies, most notably Dominguez and Frankel (1993), have concluded that this increase in potency is even more pronounced when interventions are announced. That the announcement of intervention plays an important role in eliciting a response from the market suggests that the impact of intervention on expectations is important in maximizing their efficiency. In addition to the portfolio balance view, there are two ways by which intervention may affect exchange rates through market expectations. First, intervention may act as a signal of the future course of monetary policy, in which case it clearly cannot be used as an independent policy tool. Second, it may directly affect the importance investors give to technical analysis in forecasting exchange rate movements. Indeed, if the proximate cause of misalignments is the use of such rules by market participants, then an analysis of the effects of intervention on the choice of forecasting technique can demonstrate how the efficiency of intervention can be improved.

The Analytical Framework

The traditional portfolio balance view of the effects of sterilized intervention implicitly assumes intervention attempts to influence the *equilibrium* level of the exchange rate. However, the authorities typically intervene when they view the exchange rate to be undervalued or overvalued. Thus interventions are carried out with the intent of reducing current *misalignments,* or indeed excessive volatility.

The view that intervention is most potent when aimed at influencing market expectations is best seen in the light of the use of technical analysis by traders discussed in the previous section. In practice, policymakers seem to be well aware of this. Sushil Wadhwani (2000) notes that "under some circumstances, intervention can give the fundamentals-based traders greater confidence to initiate positions during overshoots. Alternatively, in an overextended market, intervention can sometimes directly affect the behavior of the momentum-based traders." Similarly, the descriptions given by Eisuke Sakakibara (2000) of his experiences directing intervention operations at the Japanese Ministry of Finance frequently refer to the goal of changing market sentiment.

Although many studies find that the effects of intervention are typically short-lived, this is not necessarily problematic when the goal is a shift in expectations. The analogy employed by Dominguez and Frankel (1993) for intervention emphasizes this nicely. They liken the role of intervention to the role of herd dogs among cattle. Clearly, a small number of dogs cannot always sustain control of the steers. So when a stampede gets under way because each panicked steer is following its neighbors, the herd can wander off quite far from its initially desired direction. However, the dogs can be helpful in a stampede because, by turning a few steers around, they might induce the herd to follow.

To pin down how exactly intervention can exert this kind of influence over markets, it is important to be clear about the processes underlying market participants' selection of forecasting strategy. If intervention is undertaken with the specific aim of inducing traders to switch from destabilizing technical rules to forecasts based on fundamentals, a theoretical underpinning is paramount. Recent work by De Grauwe and Grimaldi (2004) has highlighted how the foreign exchange market is well characterized by "behavioral finance models," drawing particularly on the work of Brock and Hommes (1997).

The implications of this kind of model for the functioning of sterilized intervention are examined in Kubelec (2004). In that paper, traders are modeled as either paying a fixed cost to purchase a rule based on macroeconomic fundamentals,[4] or simply extrapolating recent trends in the exchange rate by using a "chartist" or "technical" rule. As described in box 10.1, at each point in time, traders choose whether to put their money on the exchange rate moving further from fundamentals (i.e., using the "chartist rule"), or moving back toward fundamentals (i.e., using the "fun-

---

4. This cost represents the information gathering cost necessary to correctly forecast the level of the equilibrium exchange rate, and may by no means be insignificant. E.g., De Grauwe and Embrechts (1994) note that in a world where authorities are bound by few commitments the number of possible future paths of debt and money is increased. This is due both to the move toward floating exchange rates and also to the dramatic increase in international capital mobility allowing for a much wider range of debt financing options than before. The net effect is that correct forecasting of the equilibrium exchange rate is more difficult, and hence more costly.

Box 10.1 A model of traders' strategy choice

This box summarizes the model of traders' strategy choice detailed in Kubelec (2004). In each period, given the level of the last period's exchange rate s_{t-1}, traders are assumed to select between a generic "chartist" forecasting rule:

$$f_{chart,t} = g s_{t-1} \quad g > 1 \tag{10.1}$$

and a generic "fundamentalist" forecasting rule:

$$f_{fund,t} = v s_{t-1} \quad 0 < v < 1 \tag{10.2}$$

The model of strategy choice extends work by Brock and Hommes (1997), so that traders select their strategy on the basis of an evolutionary "fitness measure"—a weighted function of past realized profits and expected profits for each strategy. For example, the fitness of the fundamentalist strategy is given by

$$U_{fund,t} = (1 - \delta)\, \rho_t\, z_{fund,t-1} + \delta\, E_{fund,t}\, [\rho_{t+1}\, z_{fund,t}] - C_h \tag{10.3}$$

where ρ_t is the excess return on, and $z_{fund,t}$ the demand for, foreign bonds; and δ is an exogenous parameter, giving the weight traders place on the expected component of the fitness function. The term C_h represents the cost of purchasing each strategy, and for the chartist strategy is assumed to be zero, so that $C_{chart} = 0$, and $C_{fund} = c$. The utility gained from employing the fundamentalist strategy is given by its fitness, plus a double exponentially distributed error term that captures random shifts in preferences:

$$U_{fund,t} = U_{fund,t} + \varepsilon_t \tag{10.4}$$

As the number of traders in the market tends to infinity, the probability that traders choose the fundamentalist strategy is given by the discrete choice model:

$$\omega_{fund,t} = \{1 + \exp\,[\beta(U_{chart,t-1} - U_{fund,t-1})]\}^{-1} \tag{10.5}$$

The parameter β measures how sensitive traders are to differences in the profitability of each strategy. Using the fact that the excess return from holding foreign bonds at time t is given by

$$\rho_t = (i^*_{t-1} - i_{t-1}) + (s_t - s_{t-1}) \tag{10.6}$$

The relative fitness of the chartist strategy may be expressed in terms of deviations from the fundamental level of the exchange rate, x_t, as

$$U_{chart,t-1} - U_{fund,t-1} = \left[(1 - \delta)x_{t-1} - \frac{(1 + \delta)(1 + \alpha)}{\alpha} x_{t-2} + \delta(g + v)x_{t-3} - \theta \right]$$
$$\frac{q}{a\sigma^2} x_{t-3} + c \tag{10.7}$$

where α is the interest elasticity of money demand; $q = g - v$; a and σ^2 capture investors' degree of risk aversion and the variance of asset returns, respectively; and θ is a function of the relative private holdings of domestic over foreign bonds. Equations 10.5 and 10.7 provide the theoretical underpinning for the estimated transition function, equation 10.9 in box 10.2.

damentalist rule") by considering both the past realized profits and the expected profits from each market view.

This kind of strategy choice can explain the long swings in exchange rates so commonly observed in the data. When close to fundamentals, the cost of accurate forecasting of the future path of macroeconomic variables that influence the exchange rate leads the bulk of traders to rely on chartist, or extrapolative, techniques. Following a small shock to the exchange rate, trend chasing by traders leads the exchange rate to move further and further from equilibrium. However, as the size of the misalignment increases, the *expected* profit from adopting a view of exchange rate correction to levels in line with fundamentals also increases. The upshot is that, as the degree of misalignment grows, an increasing proportion of the market begins to sell overvalued currencies. Eventually, the proportion of the market selling the currency becomes large enough to reverse its rise. Once this occurs, the remaining traders who buy into the view of the currency as continuing to appreciate start to lose money, causing them to begin to sell, which rapidly returns the currency to levels in keeping with fundamentals.

A key feature of this story is the view that whether traders are stabilizing or destabilizing depends primarily on the relative profitability of alternative strategies. It is this that allows the monetary authorities to use sterilized intervention to coordinate traders to stabilize the exchange rate. For example, consider the scenario of the Japanese authorities conducting sterilized sales of yen because they view the yen as overvalued relative to the dollar. If identical classes of Japanese and US assets are imperfect substitutes, a dollar-supporting sterilized intervention results in traders requiring an increase in the excess return on yen-denominated bonds in order to willingly hold the increased supply. In this case, the effect of the increase in excess return on yen bonds will be to hit the profits of those traders who had been betting that the overvaluation of the yen would extend still further.

In other words, because sterilized intervention changes the excess return on foreign bonds, it also affects the realized profits from investing in them. In this way, it can be used by the authorities to reduce the profitability of destabilizing forecasting strategies.

Evidence consistent with this effect is provided by Neely (2002). He examines the temporal pattern of trading rule returns and interventions for Australian, German, Swiss, and US intervention series. His study demonstrates that, particularly in the German, Swiss, and US cases, high trading rule returns precede intervention. He concludes that intervention and trading rule returns are correlated because intervention responds to the exchange rate trends from which the trading rules profit.

The key message is this: When traders choose between trend chasing and stabilizing forecasting rules on the basis of the profitability of competing strategies, the authorities can use sterilized intervention to coordinate traders to stabilize the exchange rate.

Intervention When Misalignments Are Large

The interplay between the stabilizing and destabilizing behavior of traders has strong implications for the efficiency of intervention when misalignments are large. As was described above, as the size of the misalignment grows, the increase in expected profits from selling the overvalued currency leads fewer and fewer traders to forecast that the misalignment of the exchange rate will persist. A direct result of this is that, when misalignments are large, the authorities need to turn fewer traders to the fundamentalist strategy to facilitate the exchange rate's return to equilibrium.

Alternatively, *interventions become more effective the greater the size of misalignment.* Intuitively, if the long swings in exchange rates are "endogenous," in the sense that they are a direct result of the behavior of market participants, then policies aimed at encouraging stabilizing speculation must become more effective further from equilibrium because they are reinforced by the markets' own tendency to correct extreme misalignments.

To provide empirical evidence on the importance of this effect, in Kubelec (2004) I estimate a reduced form of the model of the foreign exchange market described in the previous section. Monthly data on the yen-dollar exchange rate from 1991 to 2003 are used, and the deviations from an equilibrium exchange rate based on monetary fundamentals are estimated.[5]

Although this measure of the equilibrium rate is not particularly sophisticated, it does give plausible figures—ranging from ¥111.2 in November 1992 to ¥119.4 in December 2002. The percentage deviations from this equilibrium are used to estimate the model.[6] The results indicate that, though intervention can play an important role in correcting misalignments, it has a negligible effect on the equilibrium rate (see box 10.2). Intuitively, given the enormous outstanding stock of US and Japanese assets, interventions are not large enough to have a sufficient effect on the equilibrium rate to be economically significant. However, this is not true of exchange rate misalignments.

This apparent paradox can be rationalized because market participants are highly sensitive to differences in profitability between alternative

---

5. Specifically, monetary fundamentals are calculated as relative monetary velocity, using monthly data for M1 from the United States and Japan, and industrial production indices as proxies for aggregate demand.

6. It is worth pointing out that the model provides a market-based rationale for the application of Smooth Transition Regression (STR) models suggested by Granger and Terasvirta (1993), which have recently become popular in modelling nonlinearities in exchange rates. The function $\Phi(\cdot)$ may be recognized as an (albeit complicated) form of logistic transition function used in LSTAR models.

Box 10.2 Model estimation results

The estimated model had the following specification:

$$x_t = \varphi_0 Int_t + \varphi_1 X_{t-1} - \varphi_2 X_{t-1} \; \Phi(\cdot) + \epsilon_\tau \qquad (10.8)$$

where x_t gives the deviation from equilibrium in the exchange rate, Int_t the size of intervention at time t, and $\epsilon_t \sim iid(0,\sigma^2)$. The transition function, $\Phi(\cdot)$, is a reduced form of equation 10.5 and takes values from 0 to 1 (because the path of the exchange rate is explosive when a large enough proportion of traders employ the chartist strategy, standard t-statistics are invalid; reported bootstrapped confidence intervals are based on 1,000 replications of the model).

Equation 10.8 captures the estimated proportion of market participants using the fundamentalist forecasting rule. It may be written in reduced form as:

$$\Phi(\cdot) = \{1 + \exp[-(\beta_1 x_{t-1} - \beta_2 x_{t-2} - \beta_3 x_{t-3} + - \beta_4 Int_t)x_{t-3} - c]\}^{-1} \qquad (10.9)$$

The final parameter estimates, together with bootstrapped confidence intervals, are given as follows:

Parameter	Estimate	95 percent confidence interval
φ_0	2.62×10^{-8}	$(-1.24 \times 10^{-5}, 1.08 \times 10^{-5})$
φ_1	1.1968	(1.1241, 1.2613)
φ_2	0.4650	(0.3821, 0.5577)
β_1	−8,474.2600	(−22 725.388, −7 299.812)
β_2	−10,767.3000	(−32 033.44, −10 043.96)
β_3	1,712.4700	(−1274.055, 3461.349)
β_4	−3.5227	(−7.7765, −1.8285)
c	−97.5961	(−256.49, −70.838)

The first term in equation 10.8 captures the effect of intervention on the equilibrium exchange rate. The confidence interval for the estimate of parameter φ_0 indicates that intervention has no detectable effect on the equilibrium rate. If the parameters φ_1 and φ_2 take the values of 1 and 0 respectively, this would imply that the exchange rate follows a random walk. However, with the estimate of φ_1 being 1.1968, when all traders employ a chartist strategy, that is, $\Phi(\cdot) = 0$, the exchange rate follows an explosive path moving away from equilibrium at a rate of 19.68 percent a month. When all traders employ the fundamentalist rule, so that $\Phi(\cdot) = 1$, the estimates of φ_1, and φ_2 imply that the exchange rate moves toward equilibrium at a rate of 26.82 percent a month.

The large estimated values of β_1, β_2, β_3, and β_4 in equation 10.9 indicate that traders are highly sensitive to differences in the relative profitability between strategies. The implication is that the behavior of the exchange rate can be approximated by a stochastic process that jumps between two limit cycles, one above and one below the equilibrium rate. The confidence interval of the parameter β_4 indicates that intervention has a significant effect on traders' strategy choice, while that for parameter c indicates there are significant costs to traders for pursuing the fundamentalist strategy.

Figure 10.1 Probability of an intervention effectively inducing a turning point

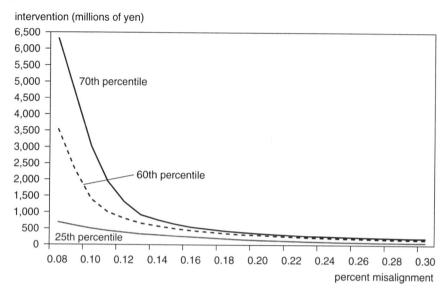

intervention (millions of yen)

Note: The distributions illustrated in figure 10.1 may be used to calculate the ex ante probability that actual interventions by the Japanese authorities would result in a reversal of trend in the exchange rate. (However, many of the interventions by the Japanese during this period were not necessarily intended to reverse the trend in the exchange rate. Other possible goals include aiming only to slow the rise of the overvalued currency—smoothing intervention—and reinforcing movements toward equilibrium—"leaning with the wind" intervention. See Ito (2002) for details. Clearly, these types of interventions could be considerably smaller and yet still achieve their intended effects.) These probabilities are shown in figure 10.2, together with actual interventions and the estimated degree of misalignment when the intervention took place.
Source: Kubelec (2004).

strategies. Under the right circumstances, only a small change in the excess return on foreign assets is required to prompt traders to buy into a "fundamentalist" market view. Because such a change amounts to traders buying assets that they had been selling, this can lead to large changes in the exchange rate. On the basis of the estimated models, simulations are used to calculate the probability that intervention of a given size will reverse a destabilizing trend in the exchange rate at various sizes of misalignment.

The distributions illustrated in figure 10.1 may be used to calculate the ex ante probability that actual intervention operations by the Japanese authorities would result in a reversal of trend in the exchange rate.[7] These probabilities are illustrated in figure 10.2, together with actual interven-

---

7. In keeping with previous studies, instrumental variables estimation is used to avoid problems caused by simultaneous determination of intervention and the exchange rate, although nonlinear instrumental variables are used due to the cyclical dynamics predicted by the model.

Figure 10.2   Probability of an actual intervention inducing a turning point, 1991–2003

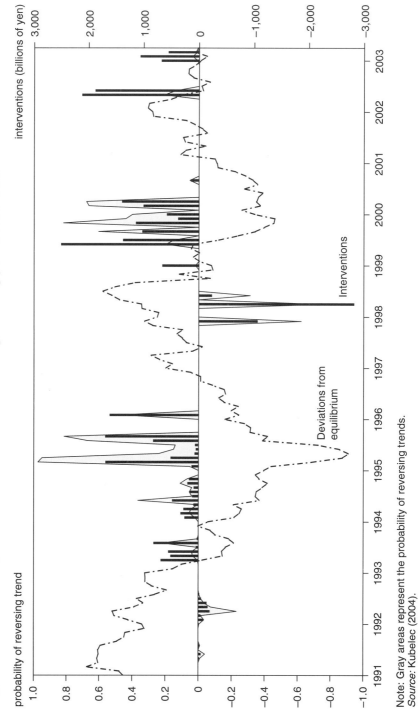

Note: Gray areas represent the probability of reversing trends.
Source: Kubelec (2004).

251

tion operations and the estimated degree of misalignment when the intervention took place.

Figure 10.1 shows the size of intervention in millions of yen necessary to have a 25 percent, 60 percent, and 70 percent chance of success as the percentage misalignment grows. For example, to have a 70 percent chance of moving the exchange rate toward fundamentals when the size of the misalignment is 13 percent, interventions of approximately ¥1 trillion per month are required. To achieve the same probability of mean reversion at a deviation from equilibrium of 9 percent requires interventions of about ¥5 trillion per month. However, within the sample there were only 13 months in which total interventions exceeded ¥1 trillion, and the largest total intervention in a single month was of the order of ¥2.8 trillion.

One may conclude from figure 10.1 that the degree of misalignment is of great importance to the likely efficiency of intervention. To have any reasonable chance of success, "leaning into the wind"–type intervention must be both determined and conducted only when the misalignment is substantial. In fact, the magnitude of intervention necessary to achieve a reasonable probability of success when closer to equilibrium than, say, 12 percent is so large as to be infeasible.

Figure 10.2 highlights how the efficiency of interventions by the Japanese monetary authorities has varied with the period in which they occurred. It further clarifies the importance of the degree of misalignment in determining interventions' success. For example, the Japanese authorities intervened with yen sales totaling approximately ¥1.4 trillion ($14 billion, at ¥100/$1) in both July 1999 and April 2000. However, the former intervention was conducted at a misalignment of approximately 4 percent, whereas for the latter the degree of misalignment was closer to 12 percent. As a result, though the probability of successfully engineering a yen depreciation was only 15 percent in July 1999, the intervention in April 2000 had a 70 percent chance of success.

These results also lend support to the findings of Ito (2002), who shows that interventions conducted when Eisuke Sakakibara was director general of the International Finance Bureau at the Japanese Ministry of Finance were particularly effective. Referring to his book (Sakakibara 2000), Ito details how Sakakibara's intervention policy was distinctively different from that of his predecessor. Specifically, interventions became much less frequent, and they were considerably larger than before. Ito's results indicate that, in contrast to his predecessor, intervention under Sakakibara was successful in producing the authorities' desired effects on the yen. Figure 10.2 illustrates a sharp contrast in the probability of intervention being effective between the period when Sakakibara was in office at the Ministry of Finance, from 1995 to 1999, and the periods before he took up his position and after he had left.

Up to this point, the discussion has focused on the efficiency of intervention aimed at reversing destabilizing market trends. However, intervention can also be effective in preventing the development of severe misalignments, even when it fails to completely correct them. This is because even if the intervention fails to prompt enough traders to switch to strategies to bring about a market correction, it will nevertheless result in a reduction in the proportion of market participants using chartist techniques, thereby reducing the force of the trend away from equilibrium. Furthermore, even if the intervention fails to result in the exchange rate bubble bursting immediately, it may still prove effective in prompting a medium-run collapse of the bubble at significantly smaller misalignments of the exchange rate than would have been the case had the authorities not intervened.

To see why this is the case, recall that in the medium run the proportion of traders employing the chartist strategy inevitably falls as the exchange rate moves further from equilibrium. An intervention operation by the authorities has the effect of reducing still further the proportion of traders using the chartist rule. This will have two key consequences. First, the rate at which the exchange rate is moving away from equilibrium may be substantially reduced. Second, if the reduction in the mass of traders on the chartist strategy persists (i.e., traders who switched to the fundamentalist strategy following the intervention do not switch back to the chartist strategy once the authorities stop intervening), then, as the bubble grows larger, a relatively smaller proportion of traders is required to endogenously switch to the fundamentalist strategy for the bubble to burst. This implies that even if the intervention fails to reduce the misalignment in the short run, it may well prove effective in the medium run at substantially smaller deviations from fundamentals than would have been the case had the authorities failed to intervene.

This delayed effect of intervention may be clarified, and a fuller picture of the actual effect of intervention operations gained, by using the estimated model to calculate the counterfactual exchange rate that would have prevailed if the exchange rate had been allowed to float freely. The simulated path of the exchange rate in the absence of intervention is compared with the actual path in figure 10.3.

Figure 10.3 clearly illustrates how intervention by the Japanese authorities has been successful in reducing medium-run volatility in the exchange rate. Though many interventions apparently failed to precipitate a movement toward equilibrium, the figure illustrates how they were effective in *reducing the strength* of the trend. Intervention by the authorities thus seems to have been highly successful in limiting erratic and persistent movements in the exchange rate created by herding behavior among market participants.

Policy Implications

The growing evidence that sterilized intervention can indeed be effective, together with the finding that intervention is much more successful when

Figure 10.3 Simulated path of the exchange rate in the absence of intervention, 1991–2003

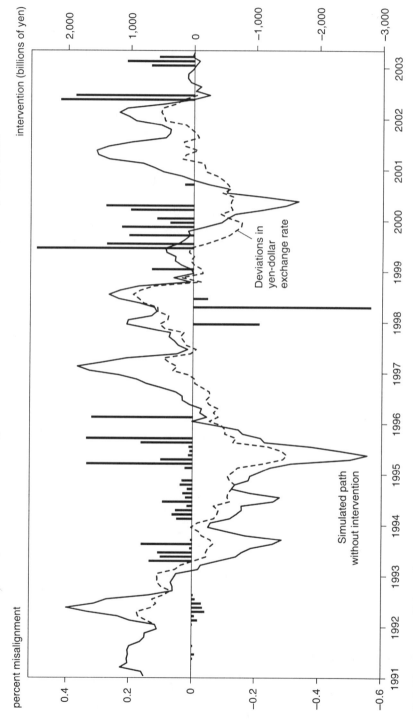

Note: Bars represent interventions.

Source: Kubelec (2004).

254

misalignments are large, has at least two strong implications for exchange rate management regimes based on sterilized intervention in a world with free movement of capital. First, the finding that sterilized intervention can have strong effects on misalignments, but negligible effects on the equilibrium rate, is in keeping with the received wisdom that a country cannot maintain an exchange rate policy wholly independent of other policy choices. Instead, the role of intervention is likely limited to maintaining exchange rates at levels broadly in keeping with underlying economic conditions.

Second, the considerable gains in efficiency of intervention when misalignments are large provides further ammunition for basing intermediate exchange rate regimes on exchange rate bands. Clearly, the quantity of intervention required to keep the exchange rate within a band falls rapidly as the width of the band increases. More important, perhaps, the size of the intervention necessary to significantly influence the exchange rate when it is close to equilibrium is so large as to make such a policy unworkable in practice.

A key feature of much of the discussion surrounding the likely success of a target zone is the focus on the credibility of the authorities' commitment. For example, Paul Krugman and Marcus Miller (1993) argue that traders' speculation shifts from being destabilizing to stabilizing as long as they are assured that the target zone will be maintained. Their argument focuses on the role of stop-loss traders, who cover their exposure to large losses by selling their assets when prices fall below a certain level. If a target zone commands sufficient credibility to assure such traders that their stop-loss orders will not be triggered, it removes the fuel for destabilizing speculation. A similar case is put forward by Olivier Jeanne and Andrew Rose (2002), who suggest that a sufficiently credible commitment to keep the volatility of the exchange rate within a preannounced range can prevent destabilizing speculators from entering the market. This effect is achieved by lowering the risk premium on foreign bonds, which removes the high excess returns on foreign assets that lure destabilizing speculators in the first place.

Note, however, that the results discussed here suggest that an exchange rate band could still prove effective even when lacking full credibility. Though an even partially credible announcement to intervene does improve the effectiveness of intervention in the model presented here, it is not necessary to reduce the attractiveness of chartist strategies.[8] This is because, by its very nature, chartist behavior is backward looking. Intervention that reduces the profitability of technical rules in one period therefore affects the strategy choice the next.

---

8. An announcement by the authorities to intervene improves an intervention's effectiveness when market participants condition their choice of forecasting strategy on the likelihood of intervention. They do so because they are aware that intervention will reduce the profitability of chartist strategies.

What kind of exchange rate band would be most appropriate given these results? A key implication of the use of *sterilized* intervention is that even massive interventions may not be immediately successful in reversing destabilizing trends. Given this observation—and the well-documented susceptibility to speculative attack of target zones where the authorities are committed to defending the edges of the band—the most appropriate arrangement would seem to be the "monitoring exchange rate band" proposed by the Tarapore committee and discussed by John Williamson (1998). In a monitoring band, the authorities announce their intention to maintain the exchange rate within a band, but they are not committed to intervene when the edge of the band is reached. This allows for flexibility in the face of overwhelming market pressure, and it removes the threat of speculative attack.

This kind of regime would take full advantage of the increased efficiency of intervention at large misalignments. There is also no requirement for the announced band to be fully credible. Prolonged misalignments are generated when traders find forecasts based on past movements in the exchange rate more profitable than forecasts based on underlying economic conditions. Intervention can be successful because it reverses this situation. Indeed, this is exemplified by the experience of the Japanese authorities in the second half of the 1990s, when intervention proved quite successful despite the absence of an announced band for the exchange rate.

Conclusion

This chapter has put forward the case for sterilized intervention in foreign exchange markets when misalignments are large. The arguments used have been based on both a theoretical underpinning and empirical evidence from the yen-dollar exchange rate from 1991 to 2003. Work on the use of backward-looking, "technical" trading strategies in the foreign exchange market suggests that the large and persistent swings evident in G-3 exchange rates have little relation to movements in economic fundamentals. To limit the negative effects of these misalignments on competitiveness, inflation, and financial stability, foreign exchange intervention has successfully been used to reduce the severity of such swings. The central hypothesis of this chapter is that such interventions can succeed by reducing the profitability of destabilizing trading strategies, thereby inducing market participants to base their forecasts on economic fundamentals. It has been shown that even sporadic interventions can significantly alter the path of the exchange rate in the medium term, effectively controlling the development of exchange rate misalignments.

Drawing on 12 years of data on Japanese interventions, there is significant empirical support for this view. Even when intervention by the Japanese authorities has apparently failed to correct misalignments in the short run, simulations of the model suggest that interventions have often led to a return to equilibrium somewhat earlier than would have otherwise been the case. Furthermore, estimates of the ex ante probability that interventions of a given size will be effective have been provided. For these results to constitute an operational guide to the authorities on the necessary size of an intervention clearly requires modeling at daily or higher frequencies. However, the results do provide an indication of the likely efficiency of interventions in the medium term. The key message of the results is that intervening when the exchange rate is close to fundamentals is unlikely to be effective, or at least that to be effective is likely to be prohibitively expensive.

More broadly, these results argue for the use of de facto monitoring bands to limit misalignments in G-3 exchange rates. Sterilized intervention would be sufficient to operate such a regime, allowing monetary policy to focus on domestic objectives.

References

Allen, H., and M. P. Taylor. 1990. Charts, Noise, and Fundamentals in the London foreign exchange market. *Economic Journal* 100: 49–59.

Brock, W., and C. Hommes. 1997. A Rational Route to Randomness. *Econometrica* 65: 1059–95.

Cheung, Y., and M. Chinn. 1999. *How Do UK-Based Foreign Exchange Dealers Think Their Market Operates?* CEPR Discussion Paper 2230. London: Centre for Economic Policy Research.

Cheung, Y., and C. Wong. 1999. Foreign Exchange Traders in Hong Kong, Tokyo and Singapore: A Survey Study. *Advances in Pacific Basin Financial Markets* 5, no. 1: 111–34.

Cheung, Y., and C. Wong. 2000. A Survey of Market Practitioners' Views on Exchange Rate Dynamics. *Journal of International Economics* 51, no. 2: 401–19.

De Grauwe, P., and M. Embrechts. 1994. *Exchange Rate Theory.* London: Blackwell.

De Grauwe, P., and M. Grimaldi. 2004. *Bubbles and Crashes in a Behavioural Finance Model.* University of Leuven Working Paper. Leuven: University of Leuven.

Dominguez, K. 2003. Foreign Exchange Intervention: Did It Work in the 1990s? In *Dollar Overvaluation and the World Economy,* ed John Williamson and C. Fred Bergsten. Washington: Institute for International Economics.

Dominguez, K., and J. A. Frankel. 1993. *Does Foreign Exchange Intervention Work?* Washington: Institute for International Economics.

Edison, H. J. 1993. The Effectiveness of Central-Bank Intervention: A Survey of the Literature after 1982. *Special Papers in International Economics* 18, Princeton University.

Fatum, R., and M. Hutchinson. 2003. Is Sterilized Foreign Exchange Market Intervention Effective After All? An Event Study Approach. *Economic Journal* 113, no. 487: 390–411.

Frankel, J., and K. Froot. 1986a. *The Dollar as a Speculative Bubble: A Tale of Fundamentalists and Chartists.* NBER Working Paper 1854. Cambridge, MA: National Bureau of Economic Research.

Frankel, J., and K. Froot. 1986b. Understanding the US Dollar in the Eighties: The Expectations of Fundamentalists and Chartists. *Economic Record* (December): 24–38.

Frankel, J., and K. Froot. 1987. Short-Term and Long-Term Expectations of the Yen/Dollar Exchange Rate: Evidence from Survey Data. *Journal of the Japanese and International Economies* 1: 24–38.

Granger, C., and T. Terasvirta. 1993. *Modelling Nonlinear Economic Relationships*. Oxford: Oxford University Press.

Ito, T. 2002. *Is Foreign Exchange Intervention Effective? The Japanese Experience in the 1990s*. NBER Working Paper 8914. Cambridge, MA: National Bureau of Economic Research.

Jeanne, O., and A. Rose. 2002. Noise Trading and Exchange Rate Regimes. *Quarterly Journal of Economics* 117, no. 2: 537–70.

Jurgenson, P. 1983. *Report of the Working Group on Exchange Market Intervention*. Washington: US Department of the Treasury.

Krugman, P., and M. Miller. 1993. Why Have a Target Zone? *Carnegie-Rochester Series on Public Policy* 38: 279–314.

Kubelec, Christopher J. 2004. FOREX Trading Strategies and the Efficiency of Sterilized Intervention. Ph.D. thesis, University of Warwick.

Lui, Y., and D. Mole. 1998. The Use of Fundamental and Technical Analysis by Foreign Exchange Dealers: Hong Kong Evidence. *Journal of International Money and Finance* 17, no. 3: 535–45.

Menkhoff, L. 1997. Examining the Use of Technical Currency Analysis. *International Journal of Finance and Economics* 2, no. 4: 307–18.

Menkhoff, L. 1998. The Noise Trading Approach: Questionnaire Evidence from Foreign Exchange. *Journal of International Money and Finance* 17, no. 3: 547–64.

Neely, C. 2002. The Temporal Pattern of Trading Rule Returns and Exchange Intervention: Intervention Does Not Generate Trading Rule Profits. *Journal of International Economics* 58: 211–32.

Ramaswamy, R., and S. Hossein. 2000. *The Yen-Dollar Rate: Have Interventions Mattered?* IMF Working Paper WP/00/95. Washington: International Monetary Fund.

Sakakibara, E. 2000. *The Day Japan and the World Shuddered: The Establishment of Cyber-Capitalism*. Tokyo: Chuo-Koron Shinsha.

Taylor, M. P., and H. Allen. 1992. The Use of Technical Analysis in the Foreign-Exchange Market. *Journal of International Money and Finance* 11: 304–14.

Wadhwani, S. 2000. The Exchange Rate and the MPC: What Can We Do? *Bank of England Quarterly Bulletin* 40, no. 3: 304–28.

Williamson, John. 1998. Crawling Bands or Monitoring Bands? How to Manage Exchange Rates in a World of Capital Mobility. *International Finance* 1, no. 1: 59–79.

11

Exchange Rate Policy Strategies and Foreign Exchange Interventions in the Group of Three Economies

MARCEL FRATZSCHER

The literature on the pattern and effectiveness of official interventions in foreign exchange markets has continued to grow significantly in recent years. Much of the literature has focused on the Group of Three (G-3) economies, for which data on actual foreign exchange intervention have become available recently (for comprehensive surveys, see Sarno and Taylor 2001, Edison 1993). The growth in this literature is nevertheless somewhat puzzling because US and euro area authorities, including their predecessors, basically abandoned actual interventions in foreign exchange markets almost a decade ago. Between 1990 and 1995, the United States and Germany bought or sold foreign exchange on 83 days and 82 days, respectively. Since mid-1995, however, the US Federal Reserve has intervened only twice—both times in coordination with other countries' central banks—and the European Central Bank has also acted merely twice in foreign exchange markets. Only Japan continues to conduct regular foreign exchange interventions, which increased both in frequency and in magnitude in 2003.

A key point that has not received much attention in the literature so far is that monetary authorities have not one but *two* policy instruments to directly influence exchange rates: actual interventions as well as oral interventions—that is, public statements about the desired level or direction of

Marcel Fratzscher is an adviser at the European Central Bank. He thanks Terhi Jokipii for excellent research assistance. He is also grateful to Martin Evans, Philipp Hartmann, John Williamson, participants in the Institute for International Economics conference on which this book is based, and the seminar participants at the European Central Bank for comments and suggestions. The views expressed in this chapter are those of the author and do not necessarily reflect those of the European Central Bank.

the exchange rate. In this chapter, I argue that G-3 exchange rate policies underwent a fundamental regime change in the 1990s as oral interventions essentially replaced actual interventions as the primary policy tool for affecting exchange rates in both the United States and the euro area.

The objective of this chapter is to identify and characterize the *strategies* and *pattern* of exchange rate policy among the G-3 policymakers during the past 15 years. The chapter is a companion paper to an article I wrote (Fratzscher 2004) focusing solely on the *effectiveness* of actual and oral intervention policies. The analyses of the two papers are based on the same data set of oral interventions (derived from reports from news wire services) and of actual interventions (as provided by G-3 central banks).

The chapter analyzes the questions of what induces policymakers in the G-3 economies to intervene and conduct actual interventions, and whether one can identify a motivation and pattern behind oral intervention policies. The literature for actual interventions has argued that such interventions are systematically related to (1) monetary policy conditions, (2) past and/or future monetary policy changes, (3) the past exchange rate trend and the deviation from sustainable exchange rate, (4) the degree of market uncertainty, and (5) the extent to which actual interventions are coordinated.

The particular questions this chapter therefore asks are: Do G-3 actual interventions indeed follow a pattern related to these factors? And do oral interventions show a similar pattern? The chapter uses a binomial logit model to answer these questions for G-3 actual and oral interventions since 1990. The chapter has two key findings. First, both actual interventions and oral interventions indeed follow a well-defined pattern. Second, an important result is that the two types of interventions are quite distinct in that, overall, actual interventions seem to follow a more well-defined pattern than oral interventions.

Moreover, actual and oral interventions tend to (1) follow a "leaning against the wind" pattern against the exchange rate trend; (2) be more frequent when exchange rate deviations and volatility are high; (3) be mostly consistent with and supportive of monetary policy changes, both before and after these changes occur; and (4) be coordinated domestically and internationally. There are also some distinct differences in exchange rate policy strategies across the G-3 countries.

The remainder of the chapter is organized as follows. The second section outlines the data on actual and oral interventions and presents several stylized facts of the exchange rate strategies since the 1990s. The third section sheds light on the question of what may explain the regime change in G-3 foreign exchange policies over the past decade, and it compares the evidence on the effectiveness found in the literature about actual interventions relative to oral interventions. The fourth section outlines the empirical methodology and results for identifying the pattern of actual and oral intervention policies, based on a binomial logit model and the derived odds ratio. The fifth section offers conclusions.

Table 11.1   Group of Three actual foreign exchange (FX) interventions, 1990–2003

Period	US Federal Reserve			Bundesbank / ECB			Bank of Japan		
	All	Buy FX	Sell FX	All	Buy FX	Sell FX	All	Buy FX	Sell FX
Number of intervention days									
1990–2003	84	27	57	87	43	44	278	251	27
1990–94	74	25	49	79	39	40	131	104	27
1995–98	9	1	8	4	4	0	59	59	0
1999–2003	1	1	0	4	0	4	88	88	0
Magnitude of interventions (average, millions of dollars)									
1990–2003	284	202	323	1,591	2,589	617	1,554	1,697	223
1990–94	203	125	242	1,709	2,811	634	385	427	223
1995–98	821	833	819	419	419	—	1,706	1,706	—
1999–2003	1,500	1,500	—	n.a.	—	n.a.	3,192	3,192	—

— = no actual interventions of this type took place in the subperiod.
n.a. = not available
ECB = European Central Bank

Sources: US Federal Reserve, Bundesbank, European Central Bank, Bank of Japan.

The Regime Shift in Exchange Rate Policy

Publicly available data on actual interventions show that the authorities in the United States and in the euro area intervened frequently before 1995 but have basically abandoned such interventions, intervening only during two episodes since 1995 (table 11.1). By contrast, Japanese authorities have increased their actual interventions in recent years, both in frequency and in magnitude. For the United States and the euro area, it is therefore somewhat puzzling why there is still a large and continuously growing literature on the effects and effectiveness of actual foreign exchange interventions, when in fact such interventions have all but stopped in these economies.

Looking at the behavior of monetary authorities shows that increased communication on exchange rates, or what I call oral interventions, have replaced actual intervention policies in the United States and in the euro area. To measure oral interventions, I employ the methodology used in Fratzscher (2004) to extract all statements about exchange rates by the relevant policymakers in the G-3 economies since 1990 from a commonly used wire service, Reuters News. These statements are then transformed into an indicator function, IO_t, with $IO_t = 1$ if the statement supports a stronger domestic currency, $IO_t = -1$ if it promotes a weaker currency, and $IO_t = 0$ if there is no statement on any given day during the sample period 1990–2003.

The search criteria are based on (1) the name or title of the relevant policymaker and (2) the word "exchange rate" or the name of the domestic currency. Exchange rate policy in the United States and Japan lies in the realm of the finance ministries, so that the statements extracted are therefore those of the secretary and his deputy in each country. By contrast, exchange rate policy is the domain of the central banks in the euro area, and the policymakers whose statements are extracted are the members of the Bundesbank Zentralbankrat before 1999 and the European Central Bank's Governing Council after 1999.[1] A more detailed analysis and explanation of the database is available in Fratzscher (2004).

Table 11.2 shows that there has been a clear shift toward a "strong-dollar policy" in the United States with the beginning of Bill Clinton's administration in 1993, which has continued also in recent years despite a rather strong US dollar exchange rate. Policymakers in the euro area have similarly pursued a "strong-euro policy," although they were less adamant about this policy in some periods, including the first months after the introduction of the euro in 1999. By contrast, Japan altered its communication policy about the yen several times in the 1990s and 2000s, promoting a strong yen in the early 1990s and briefly in 1998, while otherwise arguing for a weaker yen during the past 14 years.

Explaining the Regime Change: The Effectiveness of Interventions

Why have the United States and the euro area effectively stopped conducting actual interventions in foreign exchange markets, and why have they used primarily oral interventions instead? The answer to this question does not seem to lie in the behavior of exchange rates, for the major world currencies have experienced significant changes and misalignments in recent years. Even the sharp drop of the dollar-euro exchange rate to close to 0.82 in late 2000 and in mid-2001 triggered only two episodes of interventions between September and November 2000. Moreover, a significant change in the monetary policy strategy in the two economies has also not taken place. In fact, the rise in openness of both during the past two decades has made them more rather than less exposed to exchange rate developments.

Two findings that emerge from the literature on foreign exchange interventions go a long way toward explaining the observed regime shift in instruments from actual to oral interventions: the uncertain effectiveness and the time-consistency problem of actual interventions. Concerning uncertain effectiveness, the seminal work by Kathryn Dominguez and Jeffrey Frankel (1993) finds evidence that some intervention episodes in the 1980s may indeed have been partly successful. However, the recent literature

---

1. There were relatively fewer additional statements on exchange rates by central bank officials in the United States and Japan, and by finance ministry officials in the euro area. Adding such statements, however, does not significantly alter the empirical results presented below.

Table 11.2 Group of three oral foreign exchange interventions, 1990–2003

Period	United States		Euro area		Japan	
	Strengthen	Weaken	Strengthen	Weaken	Strengthen	Weaken
Number of intervention days						
1990–2003	125	30	77	37	66	71
1990–1994	18	15	13	4	34	16
1995–1998	31	5	3	15	16	4
1999–2003	76	10	61	18	16	51

Sources: Reuters News, author's categorization.

using data for interventions in the 1980s and 1990s reveals much less compelling evidence that actual interventions have had a significant effect on the level of exchange rates and also shows that actual market interventions by central banks are frequently counterproductive in that they merely raise market uncertainty and volatility (e.g., Baillie and Osterberg 1997; Beine, Bénassy-Quéré, and Lecourt 2002).

Concerning the time-consistency problem, a key finding in the literature is that actual interventions tend to be more successful if they are publicly announced and if they are coordinated. However, the time-consistency problem states that publicly announced interventions may trigger speculative behavior by investors, which in turn may make the actual intervention costly and possibly counterproductive (Flood and Marion 2000). This time-consistency problem may partly explain why most actual interventions are in fact conducted in secret (Sarno and Taylor 2001).

In more recent work, researchers (e.g., Ito 2002) find that actual foreign exchange interventions may indeed be effective in the G-3 economies, but that the *magnitude* of the interventions needs to be relatively large to have a significant effect on the level of the exchange rate. For instance, Ito's (2002) results indicate that a $17 billion purchase in exchange for yen of the Bank of Japan is needed to depreciate the yen by 1 percent against the dollar.

Fratzscher (2004) compares the effectiveness of actual interventions with that of oral intervention policies by the G-3. The paper analyzes the impact of actual and oral interventions by the G-3 economies in the period 1990–2003. Using daily intervention data, the empirical findings of the paper show that both types of intervention have a significant effect on exchange rates on intervention days. An oral intervention by monetary authorities in the United States, Japan, and the euro area is shown to move exchange rates in the desired direction by, on average, about 0.20 percent on the intervention day. The results for the effectiveness of actual interventions differs across the G-3 economies. For the United States and Germany, which intervened almost exclusively before 1996, the effect of a given intervention amount on exchange rates is significantly larger than that for Japan, which has intervened heavily, in particular since 2002. This finding suggests that in an environment of more closely integrated global financial markets and rapidly rising trade volumes, an ever larger intervention amount is required to move the exchange rate by the desired magnitude.

Another key result of Fratzscher (2004) is that there are strong asymmetries in the effects of oral and actual interventions. A particularly striking result is that an oral intervention that goes *against* the prevalent policy mantra—that is, a statement by US and euro area policymakers that attempts to weaken the dollar or the euro—is substantially more effective in influencing exchange rates than are statements that confirm the existing policy mantra. For instance, statements by US officials to weaken the dollar have tended to depreciate the dollar by as much as 1 percent, on average, on the day of the statement, whereas statements to strengthen the dollar had a much smaller influence. There are similar results for the euro area and Japan, and also for the effectiveness of actual interventions.

However, there are several key differences between oral and actual interventions. Most important, actual interventions tend to be effective only under very specific market conditions. For instance, actual interventions tend to be effective only when they move in the same direction as the previous exchange rate trend (again, leaning-with-the-wind interventions), if they are consistent with the monetary policy trend and monetary policy decisions, and frequently only if they are coordinated internationally.

By contrast, oral intervention policies tend to be quite different, in the sense that they are effective in moving the level of the exchange rate in the desired direction quite independently of market conditions and circumstances. Although oral interventions are also more effective if they are coordinated and are consistent with monetary policy decisions and the previous direction of the exchange rate, this type of intervention can be effective even if these conditions are not present.

A further key difference is that oral interventions tend to *lower* exchange rate volatility, whereas actual interventions almost always *raise* it. This is an important difference, because foreign exchange policy may often have the objective of stabilizing the movements of exchange rates and foreign exchange markets, as for instance expressed by the Group of Seven in the 1987 Louvre Accord; that is, they focus on the volatility of exchange rates rather than their levels. This distinction also underlines the fundamental difference between these two types of interventions: Oral interventions provide a public and transparent signal to the markets about policymakers' views and intentions, thereby reducing uncertainty. By contrast, actual interventions are frequently conducted in secret and therefore do not provide public information, thus raising market uncertainty and volatility. The important result of Fratzscher (2004) is not only that there are key differences between actual and oral intervention policies but also that oral interventions constitute a relatively autonomous tool for policymakers in the G-3 economies.

Patterns and Strategies of Oral and Actual Interventions

Foreign exchange interventions by monetary authorities tend to have an objective. The focus of this chapter is therefore: What is this objective? The literature has focused on three broad characteristics of foreign exchange interventions: exchange rate developments, monetary policy, and the coordination of interventions. First, interventions have been shown to focus on achieving a particular level, reducing deviations from what authorities believe are sustainable levels or lowering volatility. In particular, actual interventions often attempt to lean against the wind, in that they try to reverse a particular trend (Edison 1993, Sarno and Taylor 2001).

Second, several studies have argued that there may be a close relation between foreign exchange interventions and monetary policy. Through the signaling channel, foreign exchange interventions may be used by authorities to signal to the markets the timing and direction of future monetary policy changes. On the contrary, there is also some evidence that central banks in the 1980s intervened *after* a monetary policy change and in the opposite direction to reverse some of the undesired exchange rate effects of monetary policy changes (Lewis 1995; Kaminsky and Lewis 1996; Bonser-Neal, Roley, and Sellon 1998).

Third, monetary authorities in the past have frequently coordinated their interventions across countries to raise the effectiveness of the signal on exchange rates (Bonser-Neal and Tanner 1996; Beine, Bénassy-Quéré, and Lecourt 2002). But coordination may occur not only across countries. Because I analyze in this chapter not only actual interventions but also particularly oral interventions, the coordination may also imply that interventions are coordinated domestically, in that several actual or oral interventions occur in a short period of time. In addition, authorities may use both actual and oral interventions together to increase their effect on the exchange rate.

I conduct a logit analysis to identify whether there is a systematic pattern of oral and actual interventions. In this analysis, the dependent variable is the intervention itself, where $Y_t = 1$ for those days when an intervention occurred and $Y_t = 0$ when no intervention occurred. The explanatory variables X_t are those related to exchange rate developments, monetary policy conditions, and coordination. The multivariate logit model, with the vector of independent variables X_j, is defined as

$$\Pr(Y = 1) = F(X_j\beta) = \frac{e^{X_j\beta}}{1 + e^{X_j\beta}} \tag{11.1}$$

From the logit model, I derive odds ratios for each of the independent variables that indicate whether an intervention is more likely to occur under condition X_1 than under X_0:

Table 11.3 Pattern of odds ratio related to exchange rate developments

| | | (1) Past exchange rate trend[a] | | (2) Deviation from PPP[b] | | (3) Exchange rate volatility[c] | |
| | | X₁: Depreciation X₀: Appreciation | | X₁: Large deviation X₀: Small deviation | | X₁: High X₀: Low | |
		Odds ratio	SE	Odds ratio	SE	Odds ratio	SE
Oral interventions							
United States, IO^{US}	All	1.406**	0.234	0.862	0.143	1.205	0.210
	Strengthen	1.481**	0.275	0.800	0.148	0.995	0.198
	Weaken	1.115	0.410	1.171	0.429	2.386**	0.876
Germany/euro area, $IO^{GE/EA}$	All	0.975	0.185	2.001***	0.392	1.174	0.237
	Strengthen	0.901	0.208	2.989***	0.761	1.008	0.254
	Weaken	1.144	0.374	0.946	0.310	1.551	0.518
Japan, IO^{JA}	All	0.654**	0.116	1.035	0.180	1.680***	0.301
	Strengthen	1.355	0.342	0.463***	0.125	2.578***	0.642
	Weaken	0.310***	0.085	2.146***	0.543	1.063	0.279
Actual interventions							
United States, IA^{US}	All	1.616**	0.391	1.051	0.247	2.162***	0.510
	Strengthen	4.832***	1.882	1.588	0.472	1.768*	0.526
	Weaken	0.884	0.149	0.490*	0.207	2.987***	1.162
Germany/euro area, $IA^{GE/EA}$	All	0.930	0.296	1.590	0.511	9.728***	3.862
	Strengthen	2.328**	0.992	0.857	0.341	10.120***	5.049
	Weaken	0.079**	0.082	7.060**	5.397	8.759***	5.714
Japan, IA^{JA}	All	0.256***	0.038	5.322***	0.846	1.509***	0.197
	Strengthen	1.155	0.379	0.091***	0.055	1.169	0.410
	Weaken	0.187***	0.032	17.024***	4.446	1.558***	0.217

SE = standard error; in italics
***, **, and * indicate significance at 99, 95, and 90% respectively.
PPP = purchasing power parity
a. "Depreciation" and "appreciation" mean that oral interventions (*IO*) or actual interventions (*IA*) occur when exchange rate has been depreciating or appreciating over past two weeks.
b. "Large deviation" means that *IO* or *IA* occur when level of exchange rate deviates more than its period median from the PPP exchange rate; "small deviation" implies the opposite.
c. "High" means that *IO* or *IA* occur in periods when exchange rate volatility is high, i.e., above its median value, in the past two weeks, and "low" when the intervention happens during periods of low volatility.

$$\frac{\Pr(Y = 1|X_1)}{\Pr(Y = 1|X_0)} = e^{(X_1 - X_0)\beta} \qquad\qquad (11.2)$$

If this odds ratio is larger than 1, then an intervention is more likely to occur when conditions X_1 are present compared with X_0. When the odds ratio is smaller than 1, then this is accordingly less likely. In the case of a dummy variable, such that X_1: $X = 1$ and X_0: $X = 0$, the odds ratio simplifies to e^β.

Tables 11.3, 11.4, and 11.5 show the odds ratios e^β for the various hypotheses related to exchange rates, monetary policy, and coordination that have been discussed above. Note that the null hypothesis for each of

Table 11.4   Pattern of odds ratio related to monetary policy

Intervention		(4) Direction of monetary policy[a] X₁: Tightening X₀: Easing		(5) Change in next monetary policy meeting[b] X₁: Same direction X₀: Not same direction		(6) Change in last monetary policy meeting[c] X₁: Same direction X₀: Not same direction	
		Odds ratio	*SE*	Odds ratio	*SE*	Odds ratio	*SE*
Oral interventions							
United States, IO^{US}	All	1.441**	*0.242*	1.512*	*0.341*	1.720**	*0.380*
	Strengthen	1.885***	*0.345*	1.466	*0.384*	1.798**	*0.476*
	Weaken	0.325**	*0.175*	1.623	*0.712*	1.531	*0.605*
Germany/euro area, $IO^{GE/EA}$	All	0.881	*0.186*	1.971**	*0.550*	1.910**	*0.544*
	Strengthen	1.245	*0.301*	2.218**	*0.864*	2.612**	*1.047*
	Weaken	0.345**	*0.166*	1.731	*0.685*	1.413	*0.577*
Japan, IO^{JA}	All	0.941	*0.270*	0.629	*0.325*	0.411	*0.243*
	Strengthen	2.278***	*0.697*	17.279***	*15.809*	0.877	*0.912*
	Weaken	0.589	*0.388*	0.160*	*0.162*	0.326	*0.235*
Actual interventions							
United States, IA^{US}	All	0.405***	*0.129*	0.412**	*0.174*	1.189	*0.412*
	Strengthen	0.571	*0.204*	1.188	*0.768*	1.784	*1.130*
	Weaken	0.169**	*0.124*	0.221**	*0.135*	1.002	*0.419*
Germany/euro area, $IA^{GE/EA}$	All	4.380***	*1.944*	0.977	*0.443*	0.813	*0.398*
	Strengthen	5.554***	*2.116*	0.199	*0.203*	0.572	*0.352*
	Weaken	3.073**	*1.663*	4.425**	*2.805*	2.203	*1.910*
Japan, IA^{JA}	All	0.284***	*0.089*	1.371***	*0.303*	0.528**	*0.166*
	Strengthen	0.708	*0.428*	1.889***	*0.303*	0.505**	*0.158*
	Weaken	0.128***	*0.046*	0.956	*0.772*	0.535**	*0.169*

SE = standard error; in italics
***, **, and * indicate significance at 99, 95, and 90% respectively.
a. "Tightening" and "easing" mean that oral interventions (*IO*) or actual interventions (*IA*) occur during a period when monetary policy rates are being raised and lowered, respectively.
b. "Same direction" means that *IO* or *IA* occur in the same direction of the change in the next monetary policy meeting, i.e., an intervention to strengthen the domestic currency when the central bank will raise interest rates in the next meeting or an intervention to weaken it when the central bank will lower interest rates.
c. "Same direction" means that *IO* or *IA* occur in the same direction of the change in the last monetary policy meeting, i.e., an intervention to strengthen the domestic currency when the central bank has raised interest rates in the last meeting or an intervention to weaken it when the central bank has lowered interest rates.

the tests is $e^{\beta} = 1$. It should also be noted that the model shown for the bivariate case in equations 11.1 and 11.2 above is estimated in a multivariate setting, with X being a vector of the dummy variables capturing the different conditioning variables relating to the exchange rate, monetary policy, and coordination, as shown in tables 11.3 through 11.5. Estimating this multivariate model thus allows controlling, as much as possible, for

Table 11.5 Pattern of odds ratios related to coordination

Interventions		(7) Coordination with past IO/IA[a] X₁: Coordination X₀: No coordination		(8) Coordination with domestic IO/IA[b] X₁: Coordination X₀: No coordination		(9) Coordination with foreign IO/IA[c] X₁: Coordination X₀: No coordination	
		Odds ratio	SE	Odds ratio	SE	Odds ratio	SE
Oral interventions							
United States, IO^{US}	All	3.033***	0.502	1.090	0.287	1.723***	0.301
	Strengthen	3.814***	0.709	0.846	0.271	1.850***	0.354
	Weaken	1.068	0.427	2.225*	1.023	1.211	0.502
Germany/euro area, $IO^{GE/EA}$	All	3.559***	0.679	0.608	0.213	1.755***	0.339
	Strengthen	4.376***	1.020	0.498	0.232	1.519*	0.362
	Weaken	2.189**	0.732	0.852	0.452	2.263**	0.740
Japan, IO^{JA}	All	2.853***	0.500	2.102***	0.385	2.061***	0.363
	Strengthen	3.199***	0.798	1.273	0.362	1.743**	0.441
	Weaken	2.448***	0.590	3.081***	0.746	2.332***	0.561
Actual interventions							
United States, IA^{US}	All	12.675***	3.132	0.728	0.203	5.486***	1.572
	Strengthen	34.337***	10.874	0.939	0.308	1.604	0.847
	Weaken	1.325	0.866	0.425	0.231	16.928***	6.643
Germany/euro area, $IA^{GE/EA}$	All	12.315***	4.083	0.992	0.353	8.737***	2.963
	Strengthen	29.678***	12.172	0.783	0.366	1.228	0.897
	Weaken	1.299	0.953	1.455	0.814	15.334***	5.691
Japan, IA^{JA}	All	1.630**	0.393	1.500***	0.195	5.461***	0.910
	Strengthen	26.271***	8.829	2.388***	0.780	1.817	0.969
	Weaken	0.799	0.556	1.367**	0.192	5.967***	1.028

SE = standard error; in italics

***, **, and * indicate significance at 99, 95, and 90% respectively.

a. Coordinated intervention means that, in case of oral interventions (IO), IO is preceded by at least one other domestic IO in same direction in previous two weeks. In case of actual interventions (IA), it implies that IA is preceded by at least one other domestic IA in same direction in previous two weeks.

b. Coordinated intervention means that, in case of IO, IO is preceded by at least one IA in same direction in previous two weeks. In case of IA, it implies that IA is preceded by at least one IO in same direction in previous two weeks.

c. Coordinated intervention means that, in case of IO, IO is preceded by at least one IO in same exchange rate direction by foreign authority in previous two weeks; and analogously in case of IA.

omitted variables. However, this potential problem proved to be of minor importance because the different independent variables mostly exhibit a low degree of correlation.

Past Exchange Rate Developments

With regard to exchange rates, G-3 monetary authorities seem to have been conducting leaning-against-the-wind actual interventions (model 1; see table 11.3). The US Federal Reserve has been intervening to strengthen the dollar 4.8 times more often when the dollar was depreciating compared with when it was appreciating. By contrast, the Bank of Japan also frequently conducted leaning-against-the-wind actual interventions, but it took the opposite direction: A Bank of Japan actual intervention to weaken the yen was about five times more likely when the yen had been appreciating (with an odds ratio of 0.187 in model 1). The most systematic leaning-against-the-wind actual intervention behavior is found for Germany, where the Bundesbank has been intervening against the exchange rate trend both when the deutsche mark was depreciating and when it was appreciating.

For actual interventions, there is also evidence that all of the G-3 central banks intervened more frequently when the deviation of the domestic currency was large from its average purchasing power parity level over the sample[2] (model 2) and in periods of high exchange rate volatility (model 3).

An important finding is that for oral interventions, there is much less evidence that authorities have been using public statements in a systematic manner to the same extent that actual interventions have been used. Most important, there is no empirical evidence that euro area authorities' oral interventions were leaning either against the wind or with the wind. For the United States and Japan, there is some evidence for the leaning-against-the-wind hypothesis, though the strength of this behavior is substantially smaller for oral intervention policy than for actual interventions. Finally, there is also less evidence that G-3 oral interventions reacted to large currency deviations and to high market volatility to the same extent as actual interventions have done.

Monetary Policy Trends and Changes

With regard to monetary policy, the overall finding is that both oral interventions and actual interventions have been consistent with the monetary policy cycle and changes in the G-3 economies. In most cases, interventions to strengthen the domestic currency have occurred in periods of rising interest rates, and those to weaken the currencies in times of falling interest rates (model 4; see table 11.4).

There is also evidence for the signaling hypothesis in that actual and oral interventions have tended to occur more frequently before monetary policy changes, and that these interventions were consistent with monetary policy decisions (model 5).

Finally, I do not detect evidence for the leaning-against-the-wind hypothesis of monetary policy, found in Lewis (1995) and Kaminsky and

---

2. Purchasing power parity deviations are measured as deviations from the average real exchange rate against the US dollar for Japan and the Germany / euro area, and a trade-weighted real exchange rate against the yen and the euro for the United States.

Lewis (1996) for the 1980s. In other words, monetary policy changes do not lead to more frequent interventions in the opposite direction—for example, an attempt to strengthen the exchange rate after lowering interest rates, if interest rates have been changed at the last monetary policy meeting (model 6).

Coordination of Actual and Oral Interventions

There is ample proof that interventions tend to be coordinated, both domestically and across countries. There is particularly strong evidence that oral interventions and actual interventions have been clustered in time; that is, many of them occur within a few days or weeks of other such domestic interventions (model 7; see table 11.5). Both actual and oral interventions are also frequently coordinated across the G-3 economies (model 9). Moreover, oral interventions are frequently followed within days by actual interventions, and vice versa, in Japan (model 8). By contrast, oral interventions do not seem to be much coordinated with actual interventions in the United States and in Germany / the euro area. This is likely to reflect the fact that the United States and Germany / the euro area basically stopped conducting actual foreign exchange interventions in 1995.

Conclusions

The objective of this chapter has been to analyze the strategy that G-3 policymakers have pursued with their oral and actual interventions. Overall, both oral and actual interventions indeed follow a particular pattern related to exchange rate developments, monetary policy, and coordination. However, a key finding is that actual intervention policies seem to be systematic to a sometimes substantially larger extent than oral ones. More generally, actual and oral interventions tend to (1) follow a leaning-against-the-wind pattern against the exchange rate trend; (2) be more frequent when exchange rate deviations and volatility are high; (3) be mostly consistent with and supportive of monetary policy changes, both before and after these changes occur; and (4) be coordinated domestically and internationally. Moreover, clear differences exist in intervention policies across countries: US and German / euro area authorities have tended to intervene to strengthen their domestic currencies and react more strongly when these are weak, whereas Japan has mostly pursued the opposite strategy.

References

Baillie, Richard T., and William P. Osterberg. 1997. Central Bank Intervention and Risk in the Forward Market. *Journal of International Economics* 43, no. 3–4, 483–97.

Beine, Michel, Agnès Bénassy-Quéré, and Christelle Lecourt. 2002. Central Bank Intervention and Foreign Exchange Rates: New Evidence from FIGARCH Estimations. *Journal of International Money and Finance* 21, 115–44.

Bonser-Neal, Catherine, V. Vance Roley, and Gordon H. Sellon. 1998. Monetary Policy Actions, Intervention, and Exchange Rates: A Reexamination of the Empirical Relationships Using Federal Funds Rate Target Data. *Journal of Business* 71, no. 2: 147–77.

Bonser-Neal, Catherine, and Glenn Tanner. 1996. Central Bank Intervention and the Volatility of Foreign Exchange Rates: Evidence from the Options Market. *Journal of International Money and Finance* 15, no. 6: 853–78.

Dominguez, Kathryn M., and Jeffrey A. Frankel. 1993. Does Foreign Exchange Intervention Matter? The Portfolio Effect. *American Economic Review* 83, no. 5, 1356–69.

Edison, Hali J. 1993. *The Effectiveness of Central-Bank Intervention: A Survey of the Literature After 1982.* Special Papers in International Economics 18. Princeton, NJ: Department of Economics, Princeton University.

Flood, Robert P., and Nancy P. Marion. 2000. Self-Fulfilling Risk Predictions: An Application to Speculative Attacks. *Journal of International Economics* 50, no. 1: 245–68.

Fratzscher, Marcel. 2004. *Communication and Exchange Rate Policy.* ECB Working Paper 363. Frankfurt: European Central Bank.

Ito, Takatoshi. 2002. *Is Foreign Exchange Intervention Effective? The Japanese Experience in the 1990s.* NBER Working Paper 8914. Cambridge, MA: National Bureau of Economic Research.

Kaminsky, Graciela L., and Karen K. Lewis. 1996. Does Foreign Exchange Intervention Signal Future Monetary Policy? *Journal of Monetary Economics* 37, no. 2: 285–312.

Lewis, Karen K. 1995. Are Foreign Exchange Intervention and Monetary Policy Related and Does It Really Matter? *Journal of Business* 68, no. 2: 185–214.

Sarno, Lucio, and Mark Taylor. 2001. Official Intervention in the Foreign Exchange Market: Is It Effective and, If So, How Does It Work? *Journal of Economic Literature* 39: 839–68.

Comment

MARTIN EVANS

It is a pleasure to comment on chapters 10 and 11 by Christopher Kubelec and Marcel Fratzscher, respectively. Each chapter brings some new perspective to the long-standing question of whether sterilized intervention can be used to move exchange rates. To assess their contributions, I divide my discussion into three sections. First, I briefly summarize the textbook view of how intervention could potentially affect the exchange rate. Second, I extend this view to incorporate recent research on the role played by market makers and traders in the determination of exchange rates. This research has had notable success in accounting for the high frequency dynamics of exchange rates and so is clearly relevant in any discussion of intervention. Moreover, adding a role for market makers and traders also opens up some new channels for intervention to be effective. In the third section, I discuss how the empirical evidence presented by Fratzscher and Kubelec informs us about the efficacy of intervention via these channels.

A Textbook View of Intervention

A familiar textbook model of exchange rate determination starts with the difference equation $s_t = f_t + \lambda E_t[s_{t+1} - s_t]$ with $\lambda > 0$, where s_t is the log spot exchange rate (dollars/foreign exchange, or \$/FX), E_t is the conditional

Martin Evans is a professor of economics at Georgetown University and a research economist with the National Bureau of Economic Research.

expectations operator, and f_t denotes macroeconomic fundamentals. Solving this equation forward (ruling out bubbles) gives

$$S_t = (1 - \theta)\sum_{i=0}^{\infty} \theta^i E_t[f_{t+i}],\qquad\qquad\text{(IV.1)}$$

where $\theta = \lambda/(1 + \lambda)$. This present-value equation for spot rates is consistent with a wide range of macroeconomic models, depending on how fundamentals are defined. In the well-known monetary model, for example, f_t is a linear combination of US and foreign log income and money supplies. In other models, the definition of fundamentals may include the real exchange rate, the risk premium of foreign exchange, and the international distribution of wealth. Aside from differences in the definition of fundamentals, macroeconomic models typically assume that all agents have access to the same information. Expectations of fundamentals, denoted by E_t, are therefore conditioned on common information known at time t.

To see how intervention may potentially affect spot rates within this setting, it is useful to consider the dynamic implications of equation IV.1. Let ψ_t denote the foreign exchange risk premium, defined as the expected excess return on holding foreign bonds for one period; $E_t[\Delta s_{t+1} + i_t^* - i_t]$ where i_t and i_t^* are the US and foreign one-period interest rates. With this definition, we may write the rate of depreciation as $\Delta s_{t+1} \equiv i_t - i_t^* + \psi_t + \Delta s_{t+1} - E_t\Delta s_{t+1}$. Combining this expression with equation IV.1, we obtain

$$\Delta s_{t+1} = (i_t - i_t^* + \psi_t) + (1-\theta)\sum_{i=0}^{\infty} \theta^i \{E_{t+1}[f_{t+1+i}] - E_t[f_{t+1+i}]\}.\qquad\text{(IV.2)}$$

The first term on the right-hand side identifies the expected rate of depreciation at time t. The second term identifies the unexpected component of depreciation, $\Delta s_{t+1} - E_t\Delta s_{t+1}$, as a function of changing expectations concerning future fundamentals.

How can equation IV.2 help us think about the possible channels through which intervention can operate? Let us consider an unexpected sterilized intervention undertaken after the period t spot rate has been determined. If the intervention is to have any impact on s_{t+1}, it must operate through the second term in equation IV.2. (Recall that the first term identifies $E_t\Delta s_{t+1}$ and so cannot be influenced by an unexpected intervention after time t.) Thus, according to this textbook model, an intervention can be effective only if it leads to a revision in the expected path of future fundamentals.

Two transmission channels have been considered in the intervention literature: the signaling and portfolio balance channels. Intervention operates via the signaling channel by changing expectations concerning fundamentals directly. The act of intervening signals to all agents in the economy that they should revise their fundamentals' forecasts. This seems most plausible in the case of the money stock component of fundamentals because it is controlled by the central bank.

However, the signaling channel could also operate if the central bank is believed to have superior information about the future path of any fundamentals component. The portfolio balance channel of influence operates directly on one component of fundamentals, the risk premium. Sterilized intervention between t and $t + 1$ changes the currency composition of publicly held government debt. This, in turn, must lead to a change in the equilibrium risk premium, provided debt in different denominations is not a perfect substitute in agents' portfolios. As a result, the path of fundamentals may be altered from $t + 1$ onward, a fact that is recognized by agents leading to a revision in expectations.

The empirical evidence on the efficacy of intervention operating via either the signaling or portfolio balance channel has not been compelling (for a recent survey, see Sarno and Taylor 2001). For example, examining the signaling channel, Graciela Kaminsky and Karen Lewis (1996) found that intervention was informative about the course of future monetary policy. However, they also found that the reaction of the exchange rate was inconsistent with the implied signal about future policy. It has also proved difficult to establish that interventions significantly affect the risk premium in the manner necessary for the portfolio balance channel to operate.

These results are symptomatic of a larger empirical problem: Macro models do a very poor job of accounting for exchange rate dynamics over horizons of one year or less. However broadly we interpret the definition of fundamentals, empirical specifications derived from equation IV.2 explain almost nothing of the day-to-day, week-to-week, or month-to-month changes in spot rates. It would be remarkable indeed if we could find robust evidence supporting the efficacy of intervention through either the signaling or portfolio balance channels when macroeconomic models of exchange rate determination have performed so poorly.

A Microeconomic-Based View of Intervention

Macroeconomic exchange rate models pay little attention to the details of how trading in the foreign exchange market actually takes place. The implicit assumption is that the details of trading (e.g., who quotes prices and how trade takes place) are unimportant for the behavior of exchange rates over months, over quarters, or longer. This view, though still widely held, is being questioned by a new class of exchange rate models that explicitly study the behavior of market participants.[1]

These microeconomic-based models start from the premise that information about the current (and future) state of the economy is dispersed

---

1. E.g., see Evans and Lyons (2002b, 2004b). A comprehensive list of recent research papers in micro-based exchange rate modeling can be found at http://www.georgetown.edu/faculty/evansm1.htm.

across agents. They then examine how dispersed information about the state of the economy becomes embedded into the exchange rate via trading in the foreign exchange. Specifically, microeconomic-based models examine how agents trade in foreign currency (and other assets) based on their private information and the spot rate quotes made by market makers. They also study how market makers revise their spot rate quotes in response to both public information (i.e., from macroeconomic announcements) and private information gleaned from the trades initiated by other agents. Because market-maker quotes determine the prices at which foreign currency is traded, the quote-revision process governs the dynamics of spot exchange rates.

The need to model the behavior of traders and market makers makes microeconomic-based models rather mathematically complex. Nevertheless, we can illustrate the essential principle at work with a slight modification of equation IV.2:

$$\Delta s_{t+1} = (i_t - i_t^* + \psi_t) + (1 - \theta)\sum_{i=0}^{\infty} \theta^i \{E_{t+1}^m[f_{t+1+i}] - E_t^m[f_{t+1+i}]\} \quad \text{(IV.3)}$$

where E_t^m denotes the expectations of a representative market maker at the start of period t. Equation IV.3 represents how the market maker would change her quote for the spot exchange rate between the start of periods t and $t + 1$.[2] Although this equation looks strikingly similar to equation IV.2, its potential for explaining exchange rate dynamics is quite different. To see why, suppose that market makers have a too pessimistic view about fundamentals at the start of period t with the result that the dollar price for FX they quote is too low. On seeing this, traders will initiate purchases of FX at s_t because they have a less pessimistic view of fundamentals.

This positive order flow for FX will not go unnoticed by market makers. Recognizing that traders have private information about the state of fundamentals, they will revise their forecasts of fundamentals upward so that their next dollar price for FX (i.e., s_{t+1}) will be higher. Thus, spot rate dynamics are driven by changing expectations, as in macro models. However, the key difference is that the revision in expectations is induced by order flow, which is itself induced by the presence of heterogeneous information. This prediction concerning the link between exchange rate dynamics and order flows is strongly supported in the data. For example, Evans and Lyons (2002a) find that order flows can account for up to 80 percent of the variance in daily spot rate changes.

Equation IV.3 helps us think about how intervention could be effective in a micro-based model. As above, any effect must take place via a revision in the expected path of fundamentals. Here, however, it is market-maker

---

2. Equation IV.3 does not distinguish between bid and ask quotes for the sake of clarity. To see how equation IV.3 can be derived from an optimizing model of market makers and traders, see Evans and Lyons (2004a).

expectations that are the focus of attention. As in the macro model, interventions could affect market-maker expectations directly via the portfolio balance channel insofar as they induce changes in the risk-premium component of fundamentals.

Interventions could also affect expectations indirectly via trading. Notice that sterilized intervention in support of the dollar takes the form of negative order flow for FX initiated by the central bank. In cases where the intervention is secret, it should have the same effect on the spot rate as negative order flow from private traders of the same size. Evans and Lyons (forthcoming) estimate that a $1 billion intervention of this type would have moved the dollar-mark spot rate by approximately 0.44 percent.

In practice, interventions are rarely secret. In these cases, their effectiveness will depend on two interrelated factors. First, the inferences that market makers draw from the order flow initiated by a central bank will generally differ from those based on order flows from private traders: The central bank is presumably a more credible source of superior information concerning future fundamentals. (This is a variation on the signaling channel described above.)

Second, nonsecret intervention trades may lead other traders to reassess their desired portfolio positions. As a result, the order flow initiated by the central bank may trigger a much larger order flow from other traders. If the order flow implications of the central bank's intervention are magnified in this manner, their impact on market-maker expectations, and hence the spot rate, could be significant.

Fratzscher's and Kubelec's Results

The empirical evidence presented by Marcel Fratzscher and Christopher Kubelec is most readily interpreted in terms of microeconomic-based models. Indeed, it is hard to see how the results they present could be consistent with macroeconomic exchange rate models.

Chapter 11, by Fratzscher, starts from the observation that during the 1990s actual interventions by the US and euro/German monetary authorities were largely replaced by "oral interventions"—statements by government officials advocating either a strengthening or weakening of the currency. The author constructs a novel data set based on wire service news releases that categorizes these statements by US Treasury secretaries, Japanese finance ministers, and central bank officials and the members of the Bundesbank Zentralbankrat (1990–98) and the European Central Bank's Governing Council (after 1998). He then examines how the incidence of oral interventions relates to (1) exchange rate developments, (2) monetary policy, and (3) the history of recent interventions.

Understanding when and why oral interventions take place is interesting only if they are effective. If they are ineffective, oral interventions appear to be nothing more than a form of market commentary. In a companion paper, Fratzscher argues that this is not the case in the dollar/deutsche mark–euro and yen/dollar markets (Fratzscher 2004). In particular, he claims that (1) oral interventions are at least as effective as actual interventions, (2) oral interventions are equally effective across different monetary policy regimes, and (3) oral interventions reduce spot rate volatility.

How should we interpret these results? From the perspective of the macroeconomic model (i.e., equation IV.2), oral interventions should have no impact on spot rates unless the official making the statement was disclosing news about the future course of fundamentals (hitherto unknown to the public). This seems particularly hard to believe in the US case, given the independence of the Federal Reserve. Could statements about the strength of the dollar really lead everyone to change their forecasts for future US monetary policy?

The microeconomic-based model provides a different perspective. Suppose traders' opinions about the future path of fundamentals diverge widely but market makers quote a spot rate based on expectations equal to the average among traders. In this world, oral interventions may be interpreted by traders as changing the risk or expected return associated with holding their particular portfolio. And, as a result, the statement may induce an order flow that is interpreted by market makers as signaling new information about fundamentals.

Notice that under these circumstances oral interventions can move spot rates if they change the balance of opinion among traders. This is a much weaker condition than required in the macroeconomic exchange model. Even if the US Treasury secretary has no private information about future monetary policy, statements about the strength of the dollar could still lead rational traders to reassess the desirability of their portfolio positions and so trigger the order flow necessary to move spot rates.

Unfortunately, it is difficult to assess whether such microeconomic-based mechanisms lie behind the results in Fratzscher (2004) because they only tell us how spot rates changed (on average) on days when positive or negative statements about the currency were made. Moreover, although oral interventions appear to have a statistically significant effect on the daily change in spot rates, their economic significance is much less clear.

This is particularly apparent if we plot the incidence of oral interventions on a graph of each spot rate (see figures 1 through 6 in Fratzscher 2004). If oral interventions had an economically significant impact, we should see a series of statements in support of a strong dollar followed by a persistent fall in the dollar/deutsche mark–euro rate. This happened during some periods (e.g., in 1999) but not in others (e.g., around the start of 1998 and 2002).

In fact, I think a reasonably unbiased eye would conclude from this visual evidence that oral interventions had only a 50-50 chance of being followed by a sizable spot rate move in the "right" direction. Similarly, if the incidence of interventions is linked to recent exchange rate developments, as the statistical results in table 11.3 indicate, this should also be evident from the plots. Again, I think any reasonably unbiased eye would find the evidence far from compelling. This contrast between the statistical and visual evidence points to a potentially important flaw. The results in tables 11.3, 11.4, and 11.5 are derived from a logit model that includes a set of explanatory variables that are meant to proxy for the conditions before an oral intervention. Because none of the estimates come from a model that contains all the (possible) explanatory variables, the estimates reported in the three tables are almost surely subject to omitted-variable bias. Furthermore, all the explanatory variables are constructed as dummies. This seems reasonable when describing the history of recent interventions, but much less so when summarizing past monetary or exchange rate conditions. Imposing an artificial classification scheme on the history of monetary policy and spot rates so that all the explanatory variables take the form of dummies most likely introduces a significant specification error into the results.

Chapter 10, by Kubelec, is also cast within the class of microeconomic-based models in that it focuses on how the choice of trading strategy affects the dynamics of spot rates. The basic idea is that traders choose between a "chartist" and "fundamentalist" forecasting rule for spot rates depending upon their past and expected future profitability. On the basis of this decision, they then make trading decisions, which in aggregate determine the spot exchange rate. Intervention plays a role in this model via its effect on the forecasting choice made by traders. In particular, Kubelec argues that intervention will be most effective in states of the world where the current spot rate is viewed as being far from some long-run level. Essentially, intervention can more easily persuade traders following "destabilizing" strategies to change their plans in these states than when the spot rate is close to its long-run level.

Clearly, this line of argument is very much in the spirit of the microeconomic-based channels for intervention discussed above. What is much less clear from Kubelec's chapter is how changes in the strategies followed by traders affect spot rates. This is an important omission. Even if intervention changes the behavior of other traders in the market, this need not change spot rates in the "right" direction unless market makers have an incentive to do so.

Kubelec's empirical evidence comes from a nonlinear regression model estimated in monthly data using the yen-dollar exchange rate:

$$s_t - s_t^m = \varphi_0 Int_t + G(Int_{t-d}, s_{t-i} - s_{t-i}^m)(s_{t-1} - s_{t-1}^m) + \varepsilon_t \qquad (IV.4)$$

where $s_t - s_t^m$ is the deviation of the current spot rate s_t from the long-run level s_t^m implied by a monetary model, and Int_t denotes the size of the intervention in month t. The $G(.)$ function governs the rate of mean reversion in $s_t - s_t^m$ and depends on three lags of $s_t - s_t^m$ and a lagged value of Int_t.

Kubelec's contention is that intervention is more successful in changing trading behavior when $s_t - s_t^m$ is large and that this change will be manifest in a higher level of mean reversion. In other words, intervention should push the value of $G(.)$ closer to zero when the lagged values of $s_t - s_t^m$ are large. Kubelec's estimates support this hypothesis. His figure 10.3 provides an elegant comparison, based on the model estimates, of how the absence of intervention would have resulted in much less mean reversion in $s_t - s_t^m$ over the sample period.

Of course, the evidence in figure 10.3 is only as convincing as the specification of the nonlinear regression. Although the specification appears generally consistent with Kubelec's theoretical argument, equation IV.4 above does not represent a structural model. And, as such, estimates of the model are open to alternative interpretations. Moreover, the model estimates provide no direct evidence that interventions affect trading behavior. Another concern centers on the form of the $G(.)$ function. Ideally, we would like the data to determine the most appropriate form of this function. In practice, however, Kubelec's specification imposes the restriction that interventions affect $G(.)$ only when $s_{t-3} - s_{t-3}^m \neq 0$. This means that intervention can affect the rate of mean reversion only in the manner Kubelec hypothesized. The evidence in figure 10.3 would have been more convincing if the model specification had allowed intervention to affect the rate of mean reversion even when the spot rate was close to its long-run level.

Endogeneity is also a potential problem. Because interventions are undoubtedly related to the strength of the currency before they are undertaken, it can be difficult to disentangle the impact of intervention per se from the exchange rate conditions that prompted the action. In particular, the fact that interventions appear most effective when $s_t - s_t^m$ is large could be attributed to the fact that the size of $s_t - s_t^m$ governs the rate of mean reversion. Although Kubelec attempts to control for this by including the lagged value of $s_t - s_t^m$ in $G(.)$, we have no way to judge whether these controls are adequate.[3] In the end, interventions may appear to have been effective in this sample simply because they were timed to coincide with market pressures turning the spot rate back to its long-run level.

In summary, Fratzscher and Kubelec have presented some interesting results on the connections between intervention and spot rate dynamics. I think it is fair to say that their findings provide suggestive evidence supporting the idea that intervention is effective, at least under some circumstances. Unfortunately, in common with much of the literature, both

---

3. Similarly, there is no way to assess whether the instrumental variable procedure (mentioned only in a footnote) adequately addresses the endogeneity problem.

chapters lack evidence on the channel through which intervention could operate. Addressing this aspect of intervention should, in my view, be a high priority for future research.

References

Evans, M., and R. Lyons. 2002a. Informational Integration and FX Trading. *Journal of International Money and Finance* 21: 807–31.

Evans, M., and R. Lyons. 2002b. Order Flow and Exchange Rate Dynamics. *Journal of Political Economy* 110: 170–80.

Evans, M., and R. Lyons. 2004a. Do Transaction Flows Forecast Fundamentals? Georgetown University, Washington. Photocopy.

Evans, M., and R. Lyons. 2004b. *A New Micro Model of Exchange Rate Dynamics.* NBER Working Paper 10379. Cambridge, MA: National Bureau of Economic Research.

Evans, M., and R. Lyons. Forthcoming. Are Different-Currency Assets Imperfect Substitutes? In *Exchange Rate Economics,* ed. Paul De Grauwe. Cambridge, MA: MIT Press.

Fratzscher, M. 2004. *Communication and Exchange Rate Policy.* ECB Working Paper 363. Frankfurt: European Central Bank.

Kaminsky, G., and K. Lewis. 1996. Does Foreign Exchange Intervention Signal Future Monetary Policy? *Journal of Monetary Economics* 37: 285–312.

Sarno, L., and M. Taylor. 2001. Official Intervention in the Foreign Exchange Market: Is It Effective and, If So, How Does It Work? *Journal of Economic Literature* 39: 839–68.

About the Contributors

Martin Neil Baily, senior fellow at the Institute for International Economics since 2001, was chairman of the Council of Economic Advisers under President Clinton (1999–2001) and a member of President Clinton's cabinet. He is a senior adviser to the McKinsey Global Institute. He was a senior fellow at the Brookings Institution (1979–89) and a professor of economics at the University of Maryland (1989–96). He is coauthor of *Transforming the European Economy* (2004).

Agnès Bénassy-Quéré is a professor at the University of Paris X-Nanterre and an associate professor at Ecole Polytechnique. She is deputy director of the Centre d'etudes Prospectives et d'Informations Internationales (CEPII), where she was a scientific adviser until 2003. She is a member of the THEMA research unit at the University of Paris X-Nanterre, the Economic Commission of the Nation, and the Circle of Economists. As part of her research at CEPII on economic policy and the international monetary system, she heads the international money and finance research program.

C. Fred Bergsten has been the director of the Institute for International Economics since its creation in 1981. He is also chairman of the "Shadow G-8," which advises the G-8 countries on their annual summit meetings. He was chairman of the Competitiveness Policy Council, which was created by Congress, throughout its existence from 1991 to 1995, and chairman of the APEC Eminent Persons Group throughout its existence from 1993 to 1995. He was assistant secretary for international affairs of the US Treasury (1977–81); assistant for international economic affairs to Dr. Henry Kissinger at the National Security Council (1969–71); and a senior fellow at the Brookings Institution (1972–76), the Carnegie Endowment for International Peace (1981), and the Council on Foreign Relations (1967–68). He is the author, coauthor, or editor of 34 books on a wide range of international economic issues, including *United States and the World Economy: Foreign Economic Policy for the Next Decade* (2004), *Dollar Overvaluation and the World Economy* (2003), *No More Bashing: Building a New Japan-United States Economic Relationship* (2001), *Global Economic Leadership and the Group of Seven* (1996), and *The Dilemmas of the Dollar* (2d ed, 1996).

Pascale Duran-Vigneron is a PhD student at the University of Paris X-Nanterre. Her research focuses on the analysis of exchange rates dynamics.

Martin Evans is a professor of economics at Georgetown University and a research economist at the National Bureau of Economic Research. Before joining Georgetown in 1996, he held faculty positions at New York University's Stern School of Business, the London School of Economics, and the University of Michigan. He was also a senior research fellow at the Bank of England (1995–96), and a research fellow in international economics at Princeton University in 2003–04. His current research focuses on the microeconomic foundations of exchange rate dynamics—a field called new Micro exchange rate economics.

Marcel Fratzscher is an adviser at the European Central Bank in Frankfurt. His main responsibilities lie in helping formulate the institution's positions on international economic policy and in conducting and coordinating research on international financial and monetary issues. His current research focuses on international financial market linkages, on central bank communication and exchange rate policy, on monetary policy and asset prices, on financial crises and contagion, and on capital flows and sustainable current account positions. Before joining the bank in 2001, he was a visiting fellow at the Institute for International Economics (2000–01) and worked on macroeconomic and monetary policy issues at the Ministry of Finance of the Republic of Indonesia, Jakarta, for the Harvard Institute for International Development before and during the Asian crisis. Before moving to Indonesia, he worked at the World Bank and briefly at the Asian Development Bank in Manila.

Peter Garber is a global strategist in Global Markets Research at Deutsche Bank. He was a professor of economics at Brown University (1985–2000), the University of Rochester (1980–85), and the University of Virginia (1976–80). He was a visiting scholar at the Board of Governors of the Federal Reserve, the Bank of Japan, and the IMF. He has published numerous articles and books on the economics of speculative attacks, speculative bubbles, financial crisis, financial history, and financial and banking structure. He is the author of *Famous First Bubbles: The Fundamentals of Early Manias* (MIT Press, 2000), *Bubbles, Speculative Attacks, and Regime Switching* (MIT Press, 1994), *The Mexico-US Free Trade Agreement* (MIT Press, 1993), and *The Economics of Banking, Liquidity, and Money* (DC Heath, 1992).

Morris Goldstein, Dennis Weatherstone Senior Fellow at the Institute for International Economics since 1994, has held several senior staff positions at the International Monetary Fund (1970–94), including Deputy Director of its Research Department (1987–94). He has written extensively on international economic policy and on international capital markets. He is the author, coauthor, or coeditor of *Controlling Currency Mismatches in Emerging Markets* (2004), *Assessing Financial Vulnerability: An Early Warning System for Emerging Markets* (2000), *The Asian Financial Crisis: Causes, Cures, and Systemic Implications* (1998), *The Case for an International Banking Standard* (1997), and *Private Capital Flows to Emerging Markets after the Mexican Crisis* (1996). He was the project director of *Safeguarding Prosperity in a Global Financial System: The Future International Financial Architecture* (1999) for the Council on Foreign Relations Task Force on the International Financial Architecture.

Ellen Hughes-Cromwick directs the corporate economics group at Ford Motor Company. She joined the company in 1996. She is responsible for the company's global economic and automotive industry forecasts used to support business strategy, finance, and planning. Before joining Ford, she was a senior economist at Mellon Bank from 1990 to 1996 and assistant professor of economics at Trinity College in Hartford, Connecticut, during the late 1980s. She also served for two years as a staff economist on the Council of Economic Advisers during the Reagan administration.

Takatoshi Ito, former deputy vice minister for international affairs at the Ministry of Finance, Japan, is a professor at the Faculty of Economics and Research Center for Advanced Science and Technology, University of Tokyo. He was an assistant and tenured associate professor at the University of Minnesota (1979–88), associate and full professor at Hitotsubashi University (1988–99 and 2001–02), and visiting professor at Harvard University (1992–94). He is the president of the Japanese Economic Association and a research associate at the National Bureau of Economic Research. He was a senior adviser in the research department of the International Monetary Fund (1994–97). During and in the aftermath of the Asian currency crisis (1997–99), he advised a team of the Japan Export-Import Bank to Thailand and the Foreign Exchange Council at the Ministry of Finance, Japan. He also served as a special personal adviser to Finance Minister Tarrin Nimmanahaeminda of Thailand (1998–99). He is author or coauthor of *No More Bashing: Building a New Japan-United States Economic Relationship* (2001).

Christopher Kubelec is an economist in the financial stability area of the Bank of England. He was a research fellow in applied international finance at Warwick Business School, University of Warwick. His main focus is on the economics of international capital markets and their interaction with the macroeconomy.

Amina Lahrèche-Révil is an economist at the Centre d'Etudes Prospectives et d'Informations Internationales and a lecturer at the University of Amiens, France. Her research interests include exchange rates issues and economic policy.

Robert Z. Lawrence, senior fellow at the Institute for International Economics, is also the Albert L. Williams Professor of Trade and Investment at the John F. Kennedy School of Government at Harvard University. He served as a member of President Clinton's Council of Economic Advisers from 1999 to 2000. He held the New Century Chair as a nonresident senior fellow at the Brookings Institution between 1997 and 1998 and founded and edited the Brookings Trade Forum in 1998. He was a senior fellow in the Economic Studies Program at Brookings (1983–91), a professorial lecturer at the Johns Hopkins School of Advanced International Studies (1978–81), and an instructor at Yale University (1975). He is the author of *Crimes and Punishments? Retaliation under the WTO* (2003) and *Globaphobia: Confronting Fears about Open Trade* (Brookings Institution Press, 1998), among others.

Paul Masson is adjunct professor and research fellow at the Rotman School of Management of the University of Toronto. He is a nonresident senior fellow at the Brookings Institution and research fellow at the C.D. Howe Institute, Toronto. He was the deputy chief of the Bank of Canada and a senior adviser with the International Monetary Fund. He is coauthor of *Economic Cooperation in an Uncertain World* (Basic Blackwell, 1994).

Valérie Mignon is a full professor at the University of Paris X-Nanterre. She is a member of the THEMA research group and a scientific adviser to the Centre d'Etudes Prospectives et d'Informations Internationales. She specializes in time series analysis applied to finance and macroeconomics.

Michael Mussa, senior fellow at the Institute for International Economics since 2002, served as economic counselor and director of the Department of Research at the International Monetary Fund from 1991 to 2001. By appointment of President Ronald Reagan, he served as a member of the US Council of Economic Advisers from August 1986 to September 1988. He was a member of the faculty of the Graduate School of Business of the University of Chicago (1976–91) and was on the faculty of the Department of Economics at the University of Rochester (1971–76). During this period he also served as a visiting faculty member at the Graduate Center of the City University of New York, the London School of Economics, and the Graduate Institute of International Studies in Geneva. He is the author of *Argentina and the Fund: From Triumph to Tragedy* (2002).

Jim O'Neill has been managing director and head of global economic research at Goldman Sachs since September 2001. He joined Goldman Sachs in October 1995 as a partner and chief currency economist. He is the editor of Goldman Sachs' global economics weekly and its foreign exchange monthly. After a brief spell with Bank of America in 1982–83, he joined International Treasury Management, a division of HSBC, and spent over six years with the group as a foreign exchange economist initially in London and then in New York. In 1988, he joined SBC to start off a fixed income research group in London, and in 1991, he became head of global research.

John Williamson, senior fellow at the Institute for International Economics since 1981, was a professor of economics at Pontifícia Universidade Católica do Rio de Janeiro (1978–81), University of Warwick (1970–77), Massachusetts Institute of Technology (1967, 1980), University of York (1963–68), and Princeton University (1962–63). He also served as adviser to the International Monetary Fund (1972–74); economic consultant to the UK Treasury (1968–70); and senior economist for the South Asia Region of the World Bank (1996–99) while on leave from the Institute. He is author, coauthor, or editor of numerous studies on international monetary and development issues, including *After the Washington Consensus: Restarting Growth and Reform in Latin America* (2003), *Dollar Overvaluation and the World Economy* (2003), *Delivering on Debt Relief: From IMF Gold to a New Aid Architecture* (2002), *Exchange Rate Regimes for Emerging Markets: Reviving the Intermediate Option* (2000), *The Crawling Band as an Exchange Rate Regime: Lessons from Chile, Colombia, and Israel* (1996), *What Role for Currency Boards?* (1995), *Estimating Equilibrium Exchange Rates* (1994), and *The Political Economy of Policy Reform* (1994).

Simon Wren-Lewis has been a professor at Exeter University since 1995. He began his career as an economist in the UK Treasury. In 1981 he moved to the National Institute of Economic and Social Research, where as a senior research fellow he constructed the first versions of the world model NIGEM and as head of macroeconomic research he supervised development of this and the Institute's domestic model. In 1990 he took up a chair at Strathclyde University and built the UK econometric model COMPACT. He has published papers on macroeconomics in a wide range of academic journals including the *Economic Journal, European Economic Review,* and *American Economic Review.* His current research focuses on interactions between monetary and fiscal policy, and equilibrium exchange rates. He also wrote one of the background papers for the UK Treasury's 2003 assessment of its five economic tests for joining EMU, and has recent advised the Bank of England on the development of its new macroeconomic forecasting model.

Index

China—*continued*
  base money growth, 214*f*
  capital accounts, 199*f*
  capital outflow liberalization and misalignment
    calculations, 205, 205*n*
  China Bank Regulatory Commission, 211*n*
  current account, 32–33, 200*f*
    alternative sustainable current accounts, 49*t*
  exchange rate policies, 197–98, 220–23, 227*n*
    floating currency and controls on capital
      outflows, 225
    go-slow approach to reforming, 224
    open capital markets and floating currency,
      224–25
    two-stage reform of, 225–27
  exchange rates
    adjustment of global payments balances,
      201–04
    currency regime and, 197
    real effective (REER), 200–01
    stability of, 226
    trade-weighted, 202–04, 221*f*
    underlying balance approach, 198–201
  export markets, 218–19, 234-35
  foreign direct investment, 234–35
  foreign exchange reserves, 207*f*, 208*f*
  International Monetary Fund (IMF) and,
    206–08
  lending
    banking reform and, 209–11
    exchange rate and, 212–13
    foreign exchange reserves and loans out-
      standing, 213*f*
    increase in the stock of outstanding loans,
      210*t*
    nonperforming loan (NPL) problem, 210,
      214–15
    real rates of, 216*f*
    State Council lending policies, 211*n*
    volume, 210–11, 211*n*, 212*f*
  M2 growth, 211*f*, 215*f*
  People's Bank of China (PBC)
    corporate goods price index, changes in, 217*f*
    intervention in foreign exchange markets, 217*f*
    price stability and inflation, 215–18, 217*f*, 218*f*,
      218*n*
  renminbi
    appreciation approaches, 223–27
    manipulation, 206–09
    misalignment, 205
    policies, 197, 224–27
    real trade-weighted exchange with index,
      221*t*
    reevaluation, costs versus benefits, 219–20,
      220*n*, 221–23, 222*n*, 227–28
    valuation, 10, 14–15, 23, 96–97, 197, 201*n*, 209
  US exchange rate adjustments and, 128
Clinton administration, fiscal and monetary
    policies of, 169, 262
cointegration vector, 74*t*

consumer price index, US, 105*f*
Cooper, Richard N., 114
currency manipulation, definition, 232–33
current account
  adjustment targets, 30
    advanced economies, 32
    Africa, 32
    Asia, developing countries, 33
    China, 32–33
    Euroland, 31
    Japan, 31
    Middle East (including Turkey), 33
    new industrial economies, 32
    Western Hemisphere, 33–34
  balances, 29*t*
  deficits, 23, 28*n*
    Australia, 46–47, 69
    Canada, 13, 155–57
    China, 47–48, 48*n*
    Hong Kong, 69, 129
    Russia, 69, 109*n*
    Saudi Arabia, 69
    Taiwan, 69, 221
    US, 43, 44*n*, 69, 113–14
  feasibility of adjustment, 34–35
  principal economies and regions, 29*t*
  reporting errors, 119–21
  sustainability of, 37, 37*n*, 43–49
    alternative equilibrium exchange rates under
      different assumptions for, 44*f*, 45*t*

DEERs. *See* exchange rates: dynamic equilibrium
    exchange rates (DEERs)
developing countries, economic policy challenges,
    115, 135–37
dollar. *See under specific countries (Australia,
    Canada, New Zealand, United States)*
domestic demand versus domestic output, 114–15

equilibrium exchange rates. *See* exchange rates:
    equilibrium
Euroland (eurozone), 10
  adjustment imbalances, Euroland and emerging
    Asia, 203*t*, 204
  currency valuation, 12–13, 124–25
  current account balances
    adjustment targets, 31
    private capital flows and, 235
    underlying surplus, 41–42
  current account surplus, 104
  dollar/euro Goldman Sachs dynamic equilib-
    rium exchange rate (GSDEER), 107*f*
  equilibrium exchange rates, 41
  exchange rate adjustments, 135
Europe
  currency policies, 5
  exchange rate adjustments, 134–35
European Central Bank, 21
  intervention in foreign exchange markets, 259,
    262

Other Publications from the Institute for International Economics

* = out of print

US Taxation of Internaitonal Income: Blueprint for Reform*   Gary Clyde Hufbauer, assisted by Joanna M. van Rooij
October 1992   ISBN 0-88132-134-6

Who's Bashing Whom? Trade Conflict in High-Technology Industries   Laura D'Andrea Tyson
November 1992   ISBN 0-88132-106-0

Korea in the World Economy*   Il SaKong
January 1993   ISBN 0-88132-183-4

Pacific Dynamism and the International Economic System*
C. Fred Bergsten and Marcus Noland, editors
May 1993   ISBN 0-88132-196-6

Economic Consequences of Soviet Disintegration*
John Williamson, editor
May 1993   ISBN 0-88132-190-7

Reconcilable Differences? United States-Japan Economic Conflict*
C. Fred Bergsten and Marcus Noland
June 1993   ISBN 0-88132-129-X

Does Foreign Exchange Intervention Work?
Kathryn M. Dominguez and Jeffrey A. Frankel
September 1993   ISBN 0-88132-104-4

Sizing Up U.S. Export Disincentives*
J. David Richardson
September 1993   ISBN 0-88132-107-9

NAFTA: An Assessment
Gary Clyde Hufbauer and Jeffrey J. Schott/*rev. ed.*
October 1993   ISBN 0-88132-199-0

Adjusting to Volatile Energy Prices
Philip K. Verleger, Jr.
November 1993   ISBN 0-88132-069-2

The Political Economy of Policy Reform
John Williamson, editor
January 1994   ISBN 0-88132-195-8

Measuring the Costs of Protection in the United States
Gary Clyde Hufbauer and Kimberly Ann Elliott
January 1994   ISBN 0-88132-108-7

The Dynamics of Korean Economic Development*
Cho Soon
March 1994   ISBN 0-88132-162-1

Reviving the European Union*
C. Randall Henning, Eduard Hochreiter, and Gary Clyde Hufbauer, editors
April 1994   ISBN 0-88132-208-3

China in the World Economy   Nicholas R. Lardy
April 1994   ISBN 0-88132-200-8

Greening the GATT: Trade, Environment, and the Future   Daniel C. Esty
July 1994   ISBN 0-88132-205-9

Western Hemisphere Economic Integration*
Gary Clyde Hufbauer and Jeffrey J. Schott
July 1994   ISBN 0-88132-159-1

Currencies and Politics in the United States, Germany, and Japan
C. Randall Henning
September 1994   ISBN 0-88132-127-3

Estimating Equilibrium Exchange Rates
John Williamson, editor
September 1994   ISBN 0-88132-076-5

Managing the World Economy: Fifty Years After Bretton Woods   Peter B. Kenen, editor
September 1994   ISBN 0-88132-212-1

Reciprocity and Retaliation in U.S. Trade Policy
Thomas O. Bayard and Kimberly Ann Elliott
September 1994   ISBN 0-88132-084-3

The Uruguay Round: An Assessment*
Jeffrey J. Schott, assisted by Johanna W. Buurman
November 1994   ISBN 0-88132-206-7

Measuring the Costs of Protection in Japan*
Yoko Sazanami, Shujiro Urata, and Hiroki Kawai
January 1995   ISBN 0-88132-211-3

Foreign Direct Investment in the United States, 3d ed., Edward M. Graham and Paul R. Krugman
January 1995   ISBN 0-88132-204-0

The Political Economy of Korea-United States Cooperation*
C. Fred Bergsten and Il SaKong, editors
February 1995   ISBN 0-88132-213-X

International Debt Reexamined*   William R. Cline
February 1995   ISBN 0-88132-083-8

American Trade Politics, 3d ed., I.M. Destler
April 1995   ISBN 0-88132-215-6

Managing Official Export Credits: The Quest for a Global Regime*   John E. Ray
July 1995   ISBN 0-88132-207-5

Asia Pacific Fusion: Japan's Role in APEC*
Yoichi Funabashi
October 1995   ISBN 0-88132-224-5

Korea-United States Cooperation in the New World Order*
C. Fred Bergsten and Il SaKong, editors
February 1996   ISBN 0-88132-226-1

Why Exports Really Matter!*   ISBN 0-88132-221-0
Why Exports Matter More!*   ISBN 0-88132-229-6
J. David Richardson and Karin Rindal
July 1995; February 1996

Global Corporations and National Governments
Edward M. Graham
May 1996   ISBN 0-88132-111-7

Global Economic Leadership and the Group of Seven   C. Fred Bergsten and C. Randall Henning
May 1996   ISBN 0-88132-218-0

The Trading System After the Uruguay Round*
John Whalley and Colleen Hamilton
July 1996   ISBN 0-88132-131-1

Private Capital Flows to Emerging Markets After the Mexican Crisis*   Guillermo A. Calvo, Morris Goldstein, and Eduard Hochreiter
September 1996   ISBN 0-88132-232-6

The Crawling Band as an Exchange Rate Regime: Lessons from Chile, Colombia, and Israel
John Williamson
September 1996   ISBN 0-88132-231-8

DISTRIBUTORS OUTSIDE THE UNITED STATES

**Australia, New Zealand,
and Papua New Guinea**
D.A. Information Services
648 Whitehorse Road
Mitcham, Victoria 3132, Australia
tel: 61-3-9210-7777
fax: 61-3-9210-7788
email: service@adadirect.com.au
www.dadirect.com.au

United Kingdom and Europe
(including Russia and Turkey)
The Eurospan Group
3 Henrietta Street, Covent Garden
London WC2E 8LU England
tel: 44-20-7240-0856
fax: 44-20-7379-0609
www.eurospan.co.uk

Japan and the Republic of Korea
United Publishers Services Ltd.
1-32-5, Higashi-shinagawa,
Shinagawa-ku, Tokyo 140-0002 JAPAN
tel: 81-3-5479-7251
fax: 81-3-5479-7307
info@ups.co.jp
**For trade accounts only.
Individuals will find IIE books in
leading Tokyo bookstores.**

Thailand
Asia Books
5 Sukhumvit Rd. Soi 61
Bangkok 10110 Thailand
tel: 662-714-07402 Ext: 221, 222, 223
fax: 662-391-2277
email: purchase@asiabooks.co.th
www.asiabooksonline.com

Canada
Renouf Bookstore
5369 Canotek Road, Unit 1
Ottawa, Ontario KIJ 9J3, Canada
tel: 613-745-2665
fax: 613-745-7660
www.renoufbooks.com

India, Bangladesh, Nepal, and Sri Lanka
Viva Books Pvt.
Mr. Vinod Vasishtha
4325/3, Ansari Rd.
Daryaganj, New Delhi-110002
India
tel: 91-11-327-9280
fax: 91-11-326-7224
email: vinod.viva@gndel.globalnet. ems.vsnl.
net.in

Southeast Asia (Brunei, Cambodia,
China, Malaysia, Hong Kong, Indonesia,
Laos, Myanmar, the Philippines, Singapore,
Taiwan, and Vietnam)
Hemisphere Publication Services
1 Kallang Pudding Rd. #0403
Golden Wheel Building
Singapore 349316
tel: 65-741-5166
fax: 65-742-9356

> **Visit our Web site at:
> www.iie.com
> E-mail orders to:
> orders@iie.com**